Management for Professionals

The Springer series Management for Professionals comprises high-level business and management books for executives, MBA students, and practice-oriented business researchers. The topics span all themes of relevance for businesses and the business ecosystem. The authors are experienced business professionals and renowned professors who combine scientific backgrounds, best practices, and entrepreneurial vision to provide powerful insights into how to achieve business excellence.

Uli Schneider • Jürgen Hoika
Editors

Digital Marketing in the Automotive Electronics Industry

Redefining Customer Experience through Digital Customer Engagement

Springer

Editors
Uli Schneider
Infineon Technologies AG
Unterhaching, Germany

Jürgen Hoika
Infineon Technologies AG
Vagen, Germany

ISSN 2192-8096 ISSN 2192-810X (electronic)
Management for Professionals
ISBN 978-3-031-30719-5 ISBN 978-3-031-30720-1 (eBook)
https://doi.org/10.1007/978-3-031-30720-1

This Springer imprint is published by the registered company Springer Nature Switzerland AG
The registered company address is: Gewerbestrasse 11, 6330 Cham, Switzerland

Preface and Acknowledgment

Digital marketing has transformed the interaction between companies and their customers, and the transformation does not spare the automotive semiconductor industry either. The shift of sales and marketing through digital channels has been crucial in facilitating digital customer and prospect engagement in this industry.

This book aims to providing insights into various aspects of digital customer engagement in the automotive semiconductor industry, including organizational design, strategy, operation, and campaign optimization, to mention a few. Therefore, the chapters cover a wide range of topics, from the opportunities and necessities of digital transformation to the key role of disruptive digital marketing approaches, and from creating meaningful marketing content to enhancing the customer journey with digital self-services.

The contributing authors of this book are leading experts in their respective fields in the industry, and their diverse perspectives and practical experience provide a valuable and unique perspective on digital marketing in the automotive industry.

We extend our gratitude to all the authors who contributed to this book, namely Lukas Trautner, Theo Göpfert, Kati Zieger, Lore Darcos, Robin Schneider, Eric Siegel, Alexander Schwertlein, Anup Shukla, Julia Remmele, Gudmund Semb, Dr. Marian Wenking, Christoph Tienken, Professor Dr. Thomas Friedli, and Jonathan Rösler, for their significant contributions to the book.

We would also like to thank our management for providing us with the necessary support to share our successful practices with a wider audience. Once again, thank you all for your hard work and dedication to this project. It has been a pleasure working with such a talented and knowledgeable team.

We hope this book serves as a guide for those seeking to navigate the complex landscape of digital transformation of sales and marketing and leverage its benefits to engage their customers effectively. We believe that the insights provided in this book will help readers develop innovative and effective digital marketing strategies and ultimately transform their organizations.

Unterhaching, Germany — Uli Schneider
Vagen, Germany — Jürgen Hoika

Contents

Contributors

Lore Darcos Infineon Technologies AG, Neubiberg, Germany

Thomas Friedli University of St. Gallen, St. Gallen, Switzerland

Theo Göpfert Infineon Technologies AG, Neubiberg, Germany

Jürgen Hoika Infineon Technologies AG, Neubiberg, Germany

Julia Remmele Mann+Hummel Group, Ludwigsburg, Germany

Jonathan Rösler University of St. Gallen, St. Gallen, Switzerland

Robin Schneider Rheinzabern, Germany

Uli Schneider Infineon Technologies AG, Neubiberg, Germany

Alexander Schwertlein Infineon Technologies AG, Neubiberg, Germany

Gudmund Semb Mann+Hummel Group, Ludwigsburg, Germany

Anup Shukla Infineon Technologies AG, Neubiberg, Germany

Eric Siegel Infineon Technologies AG, San Jose, USA

Christoph Tienken University of St. Gallen, St. Gallen, Switzerland

Lukas Trautner Infineon Technologies AG, Neubiberg, Germany

Marian Wenking Mann+Hummel Group, Ludwigsburg, Germany

Kati Zieger Infineon Technologies AG, Neubiberg, Germany

Part I

Understanding Digital Marketing in the Automotive Semiconductor Industry

Opportunities of and Necessities for a Digital Transformation in Sales and Marketing in a Leading Electronics Company

Uli Schneider and Jürgen Hoika

1 It Looks Like We Are at a Crossroads. It Is Time to Change Our Future, Now

During the COP21 conference in Paris, world leaders set a goal of limiting the global temperature increase to 1.5 °C (Rhodes, 2016). To reach this ambitious target, it is up to all of us to enable the transition to a low-carbon economy and make it a reality. So why is this target so important to us? Because climate change is a global phenomenon that has a significant impact on many parts of the world and on current and future generations. There are many current and dramatic examples of climate change, such as the wildfires that occurred in the United States and Canada in 2021 which were intensified by hot and dry conditions that are associated with climate change (Tymstra et al., 2021). Another example is Hurricane Eta, which caused severe damage in Central America and the United States in November 2021. The storm was fueled by warm ocean temperatures, which are a result of climate change (Sheehan, 2021; Shultz et al., 2021). Drought conditions have also been experienced in parts of the United States and Canada over the past year, particularly in the western United States. These droughts have become worse through climate change, which is causing temperatures to rise and increasing the likelihood of dry conditions (Singh et al., 2022). Heatwaves have also increased in Europe and North America over the past year with record-breaking temperatures being recorded in many locations. These heatwaves are likely the result of climate change, as rising temperatures make heatwaves more likely (Van Oldenborgh et al., 2022). Flooding has also increased in many parts of Europe and North America over the past year including in the United Kingdom, France, and the United States. Climate change is making flooding more likely by increasing the frequency and intensity of extreme

U. Schneider (✉) · J. Hoika
Infineon Technologies AG, Neubiberg, Germany
e-mail: Uli.Schneider@infineon.com; Juergen.Hoika@infineon.com

U. Schneider, J. Hoika (eds.), *Digital Marketing in the Automotive Electronics Industry*, Management for Professionals,
https://doi.org/10.1007/978-3-031-30720-1_1

weather events. In 2021, there were several floods across Europe (Faranda et al., 2022). The floods damaged roads and buildings, disrupted transportation, and forced the evacuation of several communities. In July 2021, heavy rains caused flooding in parts of Bavaria and Baden-Württemberg, with some areas experiencing their worst floods in 100 years (Thieken et al., 2022). The flooding had serious implications for the people affected, including damage to homes and businesses, disruption of transportation and other infrastructure, and the risk of injury or loss of life. Flooding can also cause food and water shortages, as well as health problems due to contaminated water or increased exposure to disease. In the aftermath of a flood, people may also face financial challenges, as they may need to repair or rebuild their homes and businesses, and may be unable to work due to the damage caused by the flooding.

So, with wildfires, hurricanes, droughts, heatwaves, floodings on the rise, what will the world look like in 2050? For us, this question depends above all on how our climate trajectory will develop. And that evolution will mainly be defined by one parameter: the speed with which we as a society and our industries can drive decarbonization and digitalization.

As the world's thirst for energy rises, we do not only need to expand green energy generation with wind and solar. After all, the greenest energy or kWh is one that is never consumed – which means that we also have to increase energy efficiency and reduce energy dissipation wherever possible to achieve the Paris Climate Goals. Together we can still mitigate the effects of climate change. The only question that remains: How?

2 Infineon's Role and Responsibility to Shape a Better Future

We believe decarbonization and digitalization are the two defining challenges of our time. We may not be able to solve all the issues they bring with them at once. However, this is exactly what keeps us going. We at Infineon are passionate about innovating and developing the best technologies and doing our part to shape a future that is worth living – for ourselves, and for the generations to come. The firm belief that technical development should not be an end in itself, but should make life better, protect the future of humanity, and maybe even make the world a safer and greener place, is the guiding principle of our work. It is our conviction that driving decarbonization and digitalization forward is a joint effort and every one of us can contribute.

Regarding decarbonization, energy efficiency is one of the key contributors to meeting the goals of the Paris Climate Agreement. At Infineon, we try to find solutions that handle energy smarter and more efficiently at all stages of the electrical energy chain, from generation of electricity to transmission to consumption. Our climate strategy is based on the pillars of reducing our own emissions and contributing to climate protection through innovative products and solutions that improve resource management. In total, Infineon's products and solutions helped reduce emissions by a net total of 97 million tons of CO2 equivalent last fiscal year after considering our own emissions. With reference to the first strategic pillar, we know that as a key player with more than 55,000 employees, a generated revenue of €14.2 billion in the 2022 fiscal year (Infineon Technologies AG, 2022a) and integral part in the supply chain of various industries that rely on semiconductor solutions, we know we have our own contribution to make to meet the challenge of decarbonization. Energy efficiency and intelligent manufacturing concepts, which help reduce CO2 emissions, have long been central to Infineon's business model. Infineon is already one of the most sustainable semiconductor producers. It has made CO2 avoidance and resource efficiency in production a priority for many years, such as through the adoption of 300-millimeter thin wafer technology. With our goal of becoming carbon-neutral, the company is increasing its efforts using renewable electricity and investments in exhaust air treatment that go beyond industry standards. By the end of the 2022 fiscal year, Infineon's scope 1 and scope 2 emissions were 23.4% below the emissions of the base year 2019 (Infineon Technologies AG, 2022b). Factors contributing to this reduction include the expansion of smart abatement concepts, the implementation of energy efficiency programs, and the switch to green electricity in Europe and North America. With reference to the second strategic pillar and thanks to our products and solutions, Infineon's customers were able to avoid 33 times more CO2 last fiscal year than was generated during production of these products. Infineon is responsible for maintaining close contact with its customers and demonstrating the value of its products. With Infineon's system solutions, our customers can produce and efficiently use products for renewable energy production, reducing the need for fossil fuels. These offerings are urgently needed considering the climate crisis. Infineon's semiconductors enable higher energy efficiency throughout the entire transformation process. Chips are a key component of renewable energy and are necessary for a transition to a low-carbon future. Infineon Technologies AG is a world-leading provider of semiconductor solutions that make life easier, safer, and more sustainable. To market Infineon's microelectronics is key to a livable future. Here, digitalization and the digital customer engagement play a decisive role.

3 Infineon's Ambition to Redefine (Digital) Customer Engagement

Digitization and digital technologies are revolutionizing the way we live, work, and interact with each other. From controlling cars with voice and gestures to smart self-driving vehicles that are changing the way we travel, the potential of digitization is enormous. Not only are our personal lives changing, but businesses and relationships are being transformed as well. Digital technologies enable efficient, distributed, connected, cross-functional processes that help companies to become more agile and adapt to their in the most cases rapidly changing environment. New technologies are transforming the way people interact and the way businesses operate because they enable work to be done across different countries and organizational boundaries. Our goal is to leverage the potential of digitalization for ourselves, our partners, and our customers all over the world.

Digital customer engagement is a key part of this transformation. It is the act of communicating with customers through various digital channels in order to intensifying the relationship with them and offering the highest value in the exact moment they are searching for solutions. Digital customer engagement is important because it allows businesses to communicate with their customers in a personalized manner and build relationships through digital channels such as websites, communities, platforms, social media, and messaging apps. This is especially important in today's digital age, as more and more customers appear to be open to use these channels to communicate with businesses and make purchasing decisions. By enabling our customers and partners to engaging with us digitally, we are able to address customer inquiries and complaints before they can express it and thus leading to increased satisfaction. Digitalizing customer engagement improves customer retention by helping us building long-term relationships with our customers by scaling personalization to unprecedented levels.

Also, by engaging with our customers digitally, we can identify opportunities to upsell and cross-sell products and services, ultimately leading to increased sales. At the same time digital customer engagement can be more cost-effective than traditional methods of customer communication, such as phone or in-person support. But ultimately, it will be only successful if we leverage both traditional and digital customer engagement and use it in a seamless fashion.

Overall, digital customer engagement is important because it allows us to connect with our customers in a meaningful and effective way leading to increased satisfaction, retention, and sales.

4 Structure of the Book

This book is a comprehensive guide on how to effectively use digital marketing to improve the customer experience in the automotive semiconductor industry and to market key products on the path to decarbonization. It provides valuable insights from practice as well as managerial guidance for companies looking to successfully transition to digital customer engagement.

In Part I of the book the authors discuss the opportunities and necessities for a digital transformation in sales and marketing in the automotive industry. With rapid advances in technology development and the increasing importance of sustainability, there is a growing need for companies in the automotive semiconductor industry to embrace digital marketing and digital customer engagement to increase time-to-market. In particular, digital customer engagement can help companies through more seamless collaboration methods to address societal challenges such as decarbonization and digitalization efficiently by providing innovative solutions and thus ease their time-to-market pressure.

One of the key pillars of digital marketing discussed in the book is the conversion of the customer journey from analog to digital. This shift has opened up new business opportunities for both electronics suppliers and B2B customers, as it allows for more personalized and efficient communication and engagement with customers. The authors also provide ambidextrous design guidelines for overcoming digital marketing barriers in the automotive electronics industry, taking into consideration contextual factors for digital marketing in B2B.

In Part II of the book, the authors delve into organizational design, marketing strategy and operation, and the implementation of a target model for digital customer engagement. They provide a practical guide for setting and achieving digital marketing goals using a plan-do-check-act approach which helps companies to define their objectives, develop a plan to achieve those objectives, implement the plan, and then evaluate the results. This approach can be used to ensure that digital marketing efforts are aligned with business goals and objectives.

The authors also examine the importance of a focused and standardized model in managing digital customer engagement. Well-defined model helps to ensure that all aspects of digital customer engagement are aligned and working towards a common goal. The authors present a framework for orchestrating higher-level processes for successful digital customer engagement, including an integrated model that maps all relevant elements and interactions of their successful approach in the automotive electronics industry.

In Part III, the authors cover campaign design and optimization, as well as creating meaningful marketing content for automotive customers. Campaign design and optimization is a crucial aspect of digital marketing, as it helps companies to effectively reach their target audience and achieve their desired results. The authors provide a process guide for modular, buyer persona centric and channel optimized content creation which guides readers to create relevant and engaging content that resonates with their audience.

The authors also examine the importance of scaling channel optimization in B2B. In the automotive electronics industry, B2B sales often involve long and complex purchasing processes, and it is important for companies to have a clear and effective strategy for reaching and engaging with potential customers. The authors discuss the various channels that can be used for digital customer engagement such as social media, email marketing, and website optimization and provide insights on how to effectively optimize these channels to reach and engage with customers.

In addition to discussing insights from academia and other industries, the respective authors also provide a conclusion and outlook on the future of digital marketing in various industry. As technology continues to evolve and the importance of sustainability grows, it is clear that digital marketing and digital customer engagement will play an increasingly important role. Companies that are able to effectively leverage these tools will be well-positioned to succeed in this rapidly changing market.

References

Faranda, D., Bourdin, S., Ginesta, M., Krouma, M., Noyelle, R., Pons, F., Yiou, P., & Messori, G. (2022). A climate-change attribution retrospective of some impactful weather extremes of 2021. *Weather and Climate Dynamics, 3*(4), 1311–1340.

Infineon Technologies AG. (2022a). *Annual Report 2022.*

Infineon Technologies AG. (2022b). *Sustainability at Infineon Supplementing the Annual Report 2022.*

Rhodes, C. J. (2016). The 2015 Paris climate change conference: COP21. *Science Progress, 99*(1), 97–104.

Sheehan, M. C. (2021). Climate change and human well-being in the 2020s: Lessons from 2020. *International Journal of Health Services, 51*(3), 281–286.

Shultz, J. M., Berg, R. C., Kossin, J. P., Burkle, F., Jr., Maggioni, A., Escobar, V. A. P., Castillo, M. N., Espinel, Z., & Galea, S. (2021). Convergence of climate-driven hurricanes and COVID-19: The impact of 2020 hurricanes Eta and Iota on Nicaragua. *Journal of Climate Change and Health, 3*, 100019.

Singh, J., Ashfaq, M., Skinner, C. B., Anderson, W. B., Mishra, V., & Singh, D. (2022). Enhanced risk of concurrent regional droughts with increased ENSO variability and warming. *Nature Climate Change, 12*(2), 163–170.

Thieken, A. H., Bubeck, P., Heidenreich, A., von Keyserlingk, J., Dillenardt, L., & Otto, A. (2022). Performance of the flood warning system in Germany in July 2021–insights from affected residents. *EGUsphere*, 1–26.

Tymstra, C., Jain, P., & Flannigan, M. D. (2021). Characterisation of initial fire weather conditions for large spring wildfires in Alberta, Canada. *International Journal of Wildland Fire, 30*(11), 823–835.

Van Oldenborgh, G. J., Wehner, M. F., Vautard, R., Otto, F. E., Seneviratne, S. I., Stott, P. A., Hegerl, G. C., Philip, S. Y., & Kew, S. F. (2022). Attributing and projecting heatwaves is hard: We can do better. *Earth's Future, 10*(6), e2021EF002271.

Digital Customer Engagement in the Automotive Semiconductor Industry: Leveraging Continuous Disruption

Uli Schneider and Jürgen Hoika

1 Introduction: Customer Engagement in a Changing Marketplace

Megatrends such as digitalization or decarbonization or market shifts triggered by end customer behavior and new business models have revolutionized numerous industries. These disruptive developments are leading to fundamental changes in all industries, and the automotive industry will be no exception. These changes are profound in nature and affect all areas of the automotive value chain. And what was that again about old dogs and new tricks?

In this transformation every market entity has an important role to play: Legislators will continue to set the legal framework for the industry, existing industry leader, new players, and partnerships will shake up the market with their disruptive technologies and business models, and end customers will continue to determine the acceptance and speed of adoption of innovations with their behavior. The panacea for facilitating all the interactions of these players is still sought in digitization, which is believed to reconcile the influencing factors in all these areas and make the impossible possible.

However, the COVID-19 pandemic in particular showed us how far the road to digitization and the digital transformation in the automotive industry still is. Hofstätter et al. (2020) emphasize that other industries had already taken far-reaching digitization measures before the pandemic, while this happened in the automotive industry primarily as a result of and during the COVID pandemic. The authors conclude that the automotive industry is lagging behind and that the typical automotive company has a clear need for digitization. Specifically, on the sales side, while the automotive industry is aware that the digitization of remote customer

U. Schneider (✉) · J. Hoika
Infineon Technologies AG, Neubiberg, Germany
e-mail: Uli.Schneider@infineon.com; Juergen.Hoika@infineon.com

U. Schneider, J. Hoika (eds.), *Digital Marketing in the Automotive Electronics Industry*, Management for Professionals,
https://doi.org/10.1007/978-3-031-30720-1_2

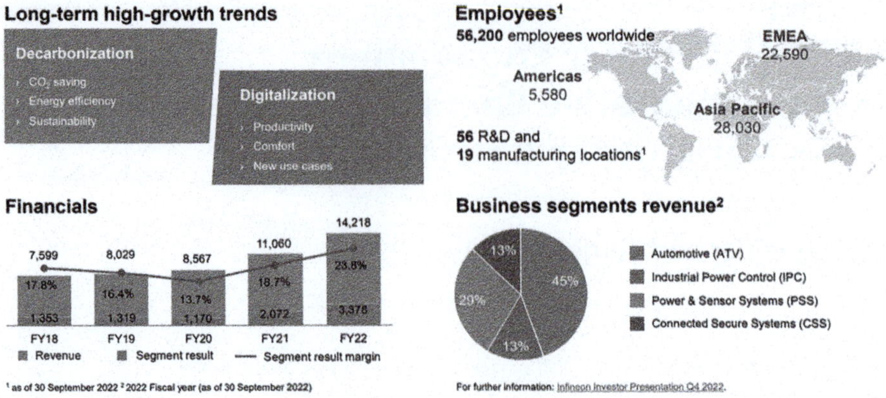

Fig. 1 Infineon Technologies in numbers

engagement models is primarily beneficial, it still has some catching up to do in terms of current customer sentiment, which is now twice as high for digital customer engagement as it is for traditional models. We at Infineon Automotive view this (digital) customer engagement as the fundamental marketing strategy that aims to increase customer loyalty to our products and solutions by providing a personalized yet value-added experience by interacting with customers through their preferred digital or traditional channels.

Against this background, the aim of the chapter is to describe the dynamics in the automotive industry triggered by disruptions and to derive implications for a fundamental rethink from the traditional to the digital approach to customer loyalty. The chapter is structured as follows: The first part describes the company and the internal corporate environment. This is followed by explanations of the various trends and for customer engagement relevant disruptions in the automotive electronics market and, finally, the implications for the (digital) customer approach are described.

2 Infineon's Ambition to Shaping the Automotive Industry

Infineon's vision to link the real world with the digital world through our solutions is the ultimate goal that inspires and motivates an entire company and its more than 55,000 employees to keep moving forward. We have a clear focus on mitigating climate change and shaping a better world tomorrow. That's why our goal is not just to enable decarbonization and digitalization, but to drive and shape these megatrends. In four business divisions, of which the automotive division's business accounts for the largest share, we are making digital transformation a reality by enabling the Internet of Things, artificial intelligence and Industry 4.0, deep machine learning, and intuitive sensor technology. While we do not fully design and implement the applications of these technological developments, it is our semiconductor solutions that form the backbone of them (Fig. 1).

At Infineon, we also look back on more than four decades of success and proven expertise in supplying dependable semiconductors for electronic systems in the automotive industry. We address the entire control loop of automotive systems with our broad product range: sensors as the eyes, nose, ears, and haptics of the car, microcontrollers as the automotive brain, power semiconductors as the muscles and thus actuators of the vehicle, and connectivity ICs and security products for secure communication between the elements of the control loop and the infrastructure. Thus, we support automotive manufacturers worldwide and contribute to the automotive trends of safety, intelligent and electrified as well as automated driving and to achieve manufacturers' increasingly demanding goals in terms of safety, affordability, and efficiency.

We have defined three core beliefs to summarize and communicate to our automotive customers and the industry our deepest assumptions about the automotive market, the world, and ourselves. The first core belief "zero emission becomes real" refers to powertrain electrification as the new normal. Our second core belief, "a driver becomes a passenger," expresses our conviction that driver assistance systems will continue to grow strongly in the coming years and contribute to Vision Zero.[1] The last core belief states "a car becomes a smart car" and underlines that the user experience will become a key differentiator and therefore safety, comfort, and connectivity features will continue to proliferate. As a prerequisite new vehicle architecture will reshape vehicle electronics.

These automotive core beliefs help us not only to communicate our deep convictions to the market and our customers, but also to provide our internal stakeholders with a secure orientation in a complex business environment regarding the "what" and "why" of our offering. This strategic alignment helps us as a market leader to focus on the "how" we consistently pursue our goal of delivering premium products and premium services for more than 3000 products, 30,000 automotive customers, and a total of more than 7 billion parts delivered per year. The strategic alignment reflected in these core beliefs enables strategic subsidiarity in the business units and automotive functions without getting bogged down in strategic complexity. Especially for our digital customer engagement approach and the required marketing content and materials, it is helpful to have a simple messaging and direction framework that summarizes the relevant market changes in a simple concept. Like all other departments in the automotive division, this framework helps us focus on value creation and complexity reduction, i.e., how to simplify interactions between us and the large number of customers, products, and deliveries within the digital customer approach.

In summary, requirements for our digital customer engagement approach can be derived from the previous internal circumstances. These include the following requirements:

[1] "Vision Zero," the global project's goal to achieve zero fatalities in traffic

- **Competitive edge**: The digital customer engagement approach must help to underpin our leading position in the automotive semiconductor market.
- **Strengthen unique selling points**: As with traditional sales and marketing tasks, the digital customer engagement approach must differentiate our company from the competition through premium services and products.
- **Scalability to customer base**: The digital approach must be scalable and thus accessible to all 30,000 customers or reinforce the growth trajectory.
- **Scalability to entire portfolio**: Scalability refers not only to customers, but also to the broad product and solution portfolio which we offer.

3 A Disruptive Market Environment as a Continuous Source for Innovation

Although our core beliefs are comprehensive and postulate the major changes in the automotive electronics industry, there are still developments within the belief framework that are not explicitly or only indirectly covered. Although the belief framework provides directional stability, it is insufficient in representing the convoluted and dynamic external market developments to derive requirements that affect all players in our market environment, such as customers, end users, and partners to be served by digital customer engagement.

These complex and dynamic external market developments are discussed below in the sections on shifts in customer behavior through market shocks, technology trends, and new entrants. It is noticeable that the impact of legislators and end customers as stakeholders is not treated separately. However, these are not ignored. The impact of these segments is critical to the future path of the automotive industry, and is therefore addressed in the following three sections.

3.1 Shifts in Customer Behavior and Needs Through Market Shocks

The automotive industry is characterized by a complex and a global opaque, intertwined, and multi-tiered global supply and value chain. Among the many industries on which automotive supply chains depend are electronics and semiconductors, which are also characterized by the same features and reliance on opaque global supply chains (Manley et al., 2022). Far from being a problem, this is also a consequence of the focus on just-in-time, just-in-sequence, and low-inventory logistics concepts to ensure competitiveness in the automotive industry (Harrison, 1994, p. 151). While these so-called "world class manufacturing" concepts are comprehensive and holistic supply chain concepts, they are not designed to deal with "black swan" events with extreme impacts outside of normal expectations (Zarghami & Dumrak, 2021). The problem arises when world-class manufacturing encounters precisely these rare phenomena, which in recent years have included numerous events (in the semiconductor industry) that occur infrequently but have major industry impacts.

As a result, drastic strategic decisions such as destocking or closing production facilities have a significant operational impact, especially when demand later recovers (Udenio et al., 2015). The initial disruptions impact the business, spread up the value chain, and, if necessary, worsen over time, leading to inventory dynamics and sales declines if not addressed quickly enough to manage demand recovery (Jaenichen et al., 2021). These disruptions, which cause large fluctuations in the upstream supply chain, are referred to as the bullwhip effect (H. L. Lee et al., 1997) and can come from a variety of sources, such as severe weather events, geopolitical tensions, or epi- and pandemics, and are almost impossible to predict. Expected losses from such (rare) supply chain disruptions can average 42 percent of a year's EBITDA over the course of a decade. In the automotive industry it is 7.3 percentage points of EBITDA and in the electronics industry 5.9 percentage points of EBITDA (Lund et al., 2020).

Prominent examples of these rare disruptive events that trigger bullwhip effects include the 2011 earthquake in Japan, which slowed global automobile production because a major chip supplier was forced to close its factory (Leslie, 2021a). Other similar events in 2021 included a fire at the same Japanese factory that closed after the 2011 earthquake or the February 2021 freeze in Texas that led to a power outage (Leslie, 2021b). Uncertainty also arises from a variety of geopolitical tensions. For example, European-Russian relations suddenly deteriorated in early 2022, and since then other relations such as Sino-European relations and any sign of dependence have been viewed with caution (Teer & Bertolini, 2022).

But the COVID pandemic has arguably caused the biggest and most far-reaching shock to the value chain in a long time, and the cost to automakers alone was estimated at $210 billion in 2021 (Leslie, 2021a). It all started when the COVID-19 pandemic and the associated lockdown, which varied in severity from country to country, led to a sudden plunge in auto sales of up to 80 percent in Europe, 70 percent in China, and nearly 50 percent in the United States. As a result, automakers canceled 15% of orders, and just-in-time concepts and low inventories were suddenly confronted with average lead times for semiconductors that exceeded 4 months. The pandemic and the associated lockdown caused immediate disruption to the entire automotive industry. At the same time, consumer electronics manufacturers ordered more capacity to meet the increased demand for devices that could be used during the lockdown. For many semiconductor companies, this led to a capacity shift that ultimately resulted in a prolonged chip shortage in the automotive industry, with dire consequences for automakers (Ramani et al., 2022).

This text is about digital marketing and digital customer engagement, so why are supply chain and market shocks so relevant anyway? Precisely because the consequences of these aforementioned incidents are so far-reaching, and at the same time, there is an opportunity to reshape the understanding of the purpose of digital marketing. Upon closer examination, the understanding of digital marketing in the automotive electronics industry should be redefined toward digital customer engagement based on three elements: first, content scope; second, functional scope; and third, customer behavior.

As for the first element, the content scope of digital marketing, all of the above examples of disruptive events have shown the importance of finding solutions to these events as they become more frequent and have an increasingly strong impact. It makes sense for our customers to take prophylactic measures to protect themselves against these events and to choose a semiconductor vendor that is able to mitigate the consequences of such events. How do customers find out which suppliers are a suitable partner for them to survive market shocks? As a trusted supplier, many of our efforts and investments relate to our manufacturing and supply chain capabilities that help our customers withstand market fluctuations. As an integrated device manufacturer, Infineon has historically focused primarily on product-related communications rather than marketing communications related to supply chain or operational excellence. In the context of these market shocks and supply chain disruptions, customers increasingly value dependable suppliers to help them hedge against them – apart from the right, high-quality, safe, and secure solutions – with globally excellent and robust supply chains. That's why our dependable solution and partner offerings are an integral part of our content scope in campaigns.

The second element, functional scope, refers to the ability to enable digital customer engagement through a variety of online tools and features that can be accessed remotely. All of the previous examples of disruption show that while digital customer engagement does not increase robustness against market shocks, it does increase an industry's ability to withstand, manage, and survive disruption by enabling digital customer interaction at all times and from all locations, and thereby increasing industry resilience (Munoz et al., 2022). One of the compelling examples was the continuous interaction with customers during the pandemic, which showed how system developers in the automotive industry could design semiconductors into innovative vehicle systems by having the tools and information needed for semiconductor development available online. Digital tools such as virtual development labs, workbenches, or platforms that enable transparency for product or sample availability and delivery status allowed development engineers to continue their development activities regardless of geographic location and travel restrictions.

The third element, the behavioral change of automotive customers and developers in particular, is closely related to the second element and the ever-increasing functionality of digital customer engagement. The Corona pandemic has shown us that large parts of the automotive industry can continue to work from home. This does not mean that the industry and its multi-layered supplier industry can be entirely managed from the home office or that face-to-face customer contact has become less important for building trust. It just means that many players in the industry are more aware of their work environment and that more emphasis is being placed on the remoteness of development engineers and need for accessibility of online tools. Some changes in work processes and customer behavior that occurred during the pandemic will persist or even take hold, opening up pathways to new and existing markets (Bauer et al., 2020).

Digital marketing and digital customer engagement will further open up new markets and distribution channels to mitigate the impact of the increasing number of events that put pressure on markets and supply chains and in summary the following requirements can be derived:

- **Promoting dependability and reliability (content scope)**: Digital customers engagement practices have to ensure transparency about the availability of products, incidents, and cases that can enable or hinder the chip design-in process.
- **Enabling a virtual design process (functional scope)**: Required tools, information, and simulation inputs as well as interfaces must be digitalized to enable virtual and remote design-ins.
- **Enabling remoteness (behavioral change)**: The digital customer approach must enable remote access to all information and tools required for the development of automotive systems.

3.2 Disruptive Innovations

In addition to market disruptions, the emergence of new technologies, sustainability legislation, and changing consumer preferences are also presenting the automotive industry with significant changes. While these changes are challenging, the industry also sees them as opportunities, to which it is responding with disruptive innovations. Currently, the biggest leaps include powertrain electrification, autonomous driving systems, and the software-defined car, all of which have reshaped the competitive dynamics in the automotive value chain.

The pursuit of zero-emission driving has gained tremendous momentum in recent years. Many governments have set conditions to accelerate the adoption of electric vehicles to reduce transportation emissions and are now setting tight deadlines for the elimination of internal combustion engine vehicles (Lee, 2022). Although there are still many unanswered questions in the industry, such as the role of hydrogen-powered vehicles (Dash et al., 2022), the widespread deployment of smart charging infrastructure (Arora et al., 2021), and the lifecycle environmental impact of electric vehicles (Messagie, 2014), it seems inevitable that powertrain electrification is only a matter of time. For the semiconductor industry, this means that experts must be ready on a large scale to address technical issues, and our expertise must enable designers to optimize high-voltage power conversion applications to achieve the best efficiency and performance, including the proper use of higher cost wideband gap technologies (silicon vs. silicon carbide) (Bhalla, 2021).

Another leap in the industry is due to the changing role of the driver and the adoption of more driving functions by the car itself. Advanced driver assistance systems (ADAS) have become prevalent in cars in recent years, but the road to driverless autonomous driving (AD) is still long. To achieve a higher level of autonomy, several basic consumer needs must be met to achieve the ultimate system goal-a dependable system that drivers can rely on to save their lives. These basic needs are that driver assistance systems are safe, reliable, and highly available. For the electronics industry these needs translate into requirements, which can only be achieved through the appropriate technology and the development of dependable electronics that suffice automotive specific quality, security, and functional safety standards and norms. Only then will consumers be willing to trust AD vehicles.

However, consumers not only want their basic needs for physical integrity and safety, but their expectations for the driving experience are also rising. They are taking their cue from consumer electronics, and the in-car user experience must measure up. By 2020, an entire generation will have grown up with cell phones, (high-speed) Internet, cloud services and apps for everything at their fingertips on a smart device, and the car of the future will therefore be expected to function much like a mobile device and be easy to use. The car of the future will enable new safety features via software updates over the air (OTA), and new apps and subscriptions can optionally add user experience features, such as autonomous driving features or heated seats. The underlying goal is a software-defined vehicle that requires the decoupling of hardware and software to provide exactly the flexibility that consumers demand. Yet the challenges on the hardware side are enormous for OEMS and suppliers alike. This means continuing making sensors and actuators smarter, increasing the computing power of the processors in the car, and implementing a completely new electrical and/or electronic (E/E) architecture. The latter requires the transition from a domain architecture, as is often the case today, to a zone architecture with a central computing cluster (Bandur et al., 2021).

As you can see: Whether autonomous driving, electric driving, or the digitization of the car – these trends have our industry fully in their grip. An average vehicle runs several hundred million lines of software code (Charette, 2009), so value creation in mobility is rapidly shifting toward software. In addition, the transition to new drive components and technologies is also shifting the potential for new value creation activities within the automotive value chain. Not surprisingly, many manufacturers and suppliers in the value chain are finding that they have been overtaken by development. Neither OEMs nor suppliers are really ready to master the change that needs to be managed in terms of software and hardware development on an industrial scale (Ohlsen, 2022). Extensive investment in talent and capability building and organizational change takes time, and those pursuing this goal also face a significant risk of failure as they enter terrain that is new to the established players in the automotive industry. At the local level, neither skills nor resources are available on the scale needed to compete. Experts agree that this creates undeniable pressure, as not all players will be able to adapt to the new situation in time (Hofstätter et al., 2020). Therefore, open, collaborative approaches of engagement to innovation in this area, as well as processes and access to platforms that make the complexity of development manageable, are crucial for success.

The role of a digital customer engagement must be to enable innovation in the marketplace by making necessary cross-functional expertise (on, e.g., technology, products, functional safety, software, etc.) easily accessible on a large scale, thus ensuring organizational robustness that leverages existing talent while protecting it. The following requirements can be derived:

- ***Cross-functional expertise at fingertips***: Digital customer engagement must provide easy access to all relevant development fundamentals from various cross-functional areas.
- ***Know-how at scale***: Digital customer engagement must provide easy access to information for all relevant stakeholders, regardless of their geographical location.
- ***Mitigation of expert scarcity***: The scope of retrieval of information on know-how conserves the scarce resource coverage of experts.

3.3 New Market Entrants and Value Chain Disruptions

The third disruptive force is closely linked to innovation: Every innovative leap also simultaneously needs a carrier to bring innovative solutions to market. In the past, however, market entry barriers in the automotive sector were high due to capital-intensive initial investments, complicated supply chains, and the complexity of the internal combustion engine, and incumbents were able to leverage their competitive advantage over newcomers for decades, thus providing these innovation carriers (Candelo, 2019; Cho & Shin, 2022). However, digitalization and the increasing focus on software, the simpler architecture of the e-motor in e-vehicles, and also changing consumer preferences are making it increasingly difficult for the large incumbents to keep market entry barriers high. As a result, many new, often smaller players (start-ups and scale-ups) and tech players from all regions of the world are entering the market with software- and hardware-related value propositions. They do not stick to the previous rigid automotive value chain order, redefine the playing field by transforming the value chain from scratch, and enter either as new OEMs, mobility providers, or horizontal platform providers. In the following, three different start-up and scale-up companies are explained as examples.

In order to reduce the contribution of transportation to climate change, energy consumption, and pollution from conventional fuel vehicles, and to promote the adoption and sales share of electric vehicles, China has introduced extensive subsidies (Deng & Tian, 2020; Olle et al., 2016). This subsidy policy has undeniably contributed to the rapid development of the electric vehicle industry (Deng & Tian, 2020), and as a result, Greater China has become a powerhouse for electric vehicles, providing favorable conditions for new entrants and opportunities for investors. One of these new players in the automotive industry is NIO Inc., founded in late 2014, which launched its first supercar (EP9) in 2016 after only 18 months of development and gradually entered in 2018 mass production with the ES8 (Zhang & Zhang, 2020).

And by 2022, the company has already reached another production milestone, with rolling out its 200,000th electric car in an unprecedented record time from its incorporation, rivaling incumbents in the global automotive industry, some of whom have dominated the market for decades (Shanthi, 2022). Of course, access to capital, including Tencent Holdings Ltd. a Chinese multinational technology group, is also an important factor in the company's rapid success. But it would be presumptuous to reduce success to that. Rather, the company convinces customers, predominantly through its business model innovations. These are a clear focus on the user experience. NIO Inc. claims to define all processes that serve customers in such a way that they provide them with a more pleasant experience than expected. Another focus of the company's business model is Battery as a Service (BaaS) solutions. NIO Inc. has introduced a battery rental model where users can choose an interest-free loan for a battery rental program, following the paradigm of "power separation in the car." The third important pillar of its business model is the Joint Manufacturing Arrangement, in which NIO Inc. and Jianghuai Automobile signed a framework agreement on manufacturing cooperation. According to this manufacturing cooperation framework agreement, both partners will benefit, and NIO will be able to fully integrate itself and, more importantly, its resources into the development and design of the vehicle (Zhang & Zhang, 2020).

Technology companies, which were already a serious player in the automotive industry before COVID-19, are putting additional pressure on the established OEMs (Hofstätter et al., 2020). Meanwhile, large IT companies such as Alphabet (Google), Apple, and their Chinese counterparts Baidu and Tencent have the financial and technical capabilities to enter the automotive industry. However, as it becomes apparent that control over IT platforms in the automotive industry will be more valuable in the long run than manufacturing the car itself, especially as individual ownership of cars declines significantly, technology companies are choosing a different path and value proposition in the automotive industry (Perkins & Murmann, 2018). However, this realization has not escaped small companies, which have now also realized how they can benefit from the changing value chain and lower barriers to entry. Lyft, for example, has been very successful in attacking established cab companies as so-called mobility platforms (Hind et al., 2022) and focuses on a single mission: transporting people in the inner cities of the United States. The company relies on its large customer base to analyze the mobility needs of these customers. Lyft operates exclusively in the United States and focuses on ride-hailing and bike-sharing. Although the company is still making significant losses, it and its investors are clearly betting on a bet and the importance of data in the automotive market. Over the past decade, the company has carried more than 112 million Lyft passengers on more than 3 billion trips (De Chant, 2022). This means they are collecting unimaginable amounts of driving data, which is essential for developing software for autonomous driving and is not yet available in this form from established OEMs and suppliers.

The last example refers to automotive platforms, which used to be the exclusive domain of OEMs. An automotive platform is a structure on which the car is built and a common set of shared design, engineering, and production efforts and major components for a wide range of different car models. Originally, platforms were introduced by incumbent OEMs to reduce complexity in production and the manufacturing network as the number of variants increased (Lampón et al., 2019). In the context of autonomous and electric driving, opportunities are now emerging for new players to focus on such platforms. One example is Israeli startup REE, which offers completely flat modular platforms, or skateboards, in various sizes for electric vehicles and vans. Providers like REE are thus pushing far ahead in the value chain and changing existing boundaries. Their offering opens up completely new possibilities for start-ups without their own production capacities to develop a car with modular plug-and-play components with the help of contract manufacturers and bring it to market after a short development period.

These three company examples so far impressively show how the value chain is changing. Whereas a few years ago it was clear what role and position a company occupied within the automotive value chain, today this is more blurred and may no longer even play a role for new market players thanks to new business models and lower barriers to market entry. New forms of collaboration are emerging in the market, leading to the development and manufacture of systems and even vehicles becoming independent. However, this has huge implications for the customer interaction of semiconductor and electronics manufacturers. Before, or if ever, clearer structures emerge, we will have to adapt to new development speeds, new geographic markets, new customers, and different business models. Certainly not all of the countless newcomers will survive, and even the traditional players have proven to be very adaptable despite their size. Digital customer engagement must therefore strike a balance between serving existing customers, with whom we want to continue to grow, and new players who are future growth drivers and are redefining the rules of the game in the industry.

- **Unconditional digital enablement**: Regardless of company size and category, digital customer engagement must ensure all relevant stakeholder groups have access to key information to bring innovations to market quickly.
- **Serve both legacy and future business partners at highest-quality levels**: The digital customer engagement approach must provide both a premium service for premium products for new and existing players.
- **Account for digital affinity**: The digital customer engagement must integrate off- and online channels in order to account for the different degree of digital affinity.

4 Implications for Digital Customer Engagement

The previous comments on the customer behaviors, new market players, and technological change underline the thesis formulated at the beginning that the automotive market is in a state of upheaval. Mary Barra, CEO and Chairman of General Motors, was therefore right when she claimed at the World Economic Forum in 2016 in Davos that "the automotive industry will change more in the next five to 10 years than it has in the last 50" (Barra, 2016). It would therefore be naïve to believe that the same traditional sales and marketing approach to customer engagement will be able to overcome these very challenges and lead the automotive industry into a future characterized by speed to market and innovation. Fortunately, the field of digital marketing (as the wider field of digital customer engagement) offers many new opportunities in terms of scalability of customer base and personalization of customer targeting to meet the challenges (Anzén & Ekberg, 2020). However, these opportunities offered by technical capabilities can only be efficiently exploited if they are aligned with the right industry requirements, and digital marketing practitioners in this field often lack the necessary understanding of the B2B automotive context or the understanding of design-in processes. The requirements derived above are intended to fill this gap and thus cover the "WHAT" of strategic alignment.

To capture the requirements of the automotive industry in a suitable framework for addressing customers digitally, we make use of the basic mechanisms of digital marketing that apply regardless of the industry. These consist of reaching a broad existing and new customer base, engaging them with relevant content, and ultimately converting them in their customer journey and turning them into customers.[2]

Reach continues to be important in both the digital and traditional space and refers to increasing awareness, website users, and mobile and social media visits through digital and traditional marketing channels (Chaffey & Ellis-Chadwick, 2019; Smart Insights, 2010; Yasmin et al., 2015). Compared to traditional marketing, the "reach" component of digital customer targeting can now be much more targeted and reach a smaller but exclusively relevant group of potential automotive customers. For example, slight parameter or keyword configurations in digital marketing measures and campaigns now make it easy to avoid wastage. However, against the backdrop of an existing target group of several 10 thousand potential customers, this number is still enormous. In addition, we have to ensure that we offer new and existing customers as well as other potential partners' scalable expertise while fulfilling the requirement to offer transparent and easily comprehendible information in a complex field of automotive electronics.

Engagement refers to the set of activities that build customer relationships through multiple customer (user) interactions across the lifecycle to drive customer value and enhancing their user experience (Bala & Verma, 2018; Chaffey & Ellis-Chadwick, 2019). These activities can be applied throughout the entire automotive customer journey, from awareness, sales (online and offline), customer retention, and growth. However, achieving a high level of engagement and superior user experience with our approach is highly dependent on how we can scale the value we add to the user across the entire product portfolio in terms of the functional expertise we can offer virtually in the context of information or tools.

While engagement refers to the customer enabling activities, conversion refers to the successful and focused set of activities that result in transitioning possible customers through the customer journey within the marketing and sales funnel (Bala & Verma, 2018; Chaffey & Ellis-Chadwick, 2019). For our approach to digital customer engagement, this means that regardless of preferred customer channels and

---

[2]This marketing mechanism is always the same in principle, but is summarized in the marketing literature in various, only slightly different forms. One example is the RACE (Reach-Act-Convert-Engage) concept of (Smart Insights, 2010) or the REAN (Reach-Engage-Activate-Nurture) concept of Jackson (2009). All are based on a funnel concept that aims to move a broad potential customer base through the sales funnel.

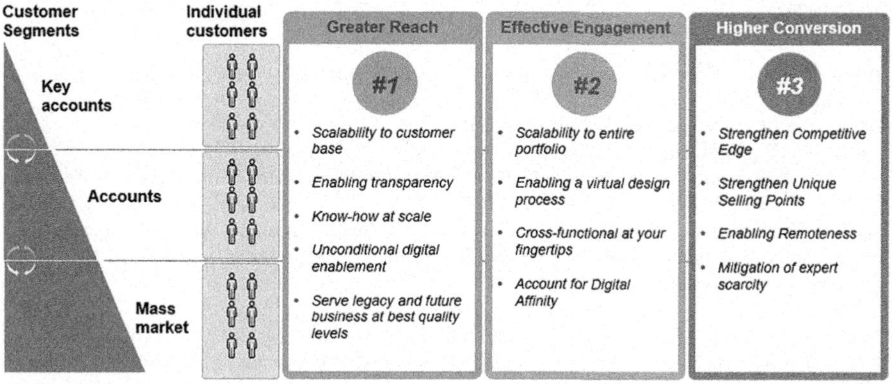

Fig. 2 Reference frame for automotive digital customer engagement requirements

customer location, it must help strengthen our leading position through our key differentiator as a trusted partner in the automotive market, without being hampered by a lack of experts. A summary of the reference frame for the automotive digital customer engagement approach is shown in Fig. 2.

5 Summary

The aim of this chapter was to explain the radical changes currently facing the automotive industry. To this end, questions and practical examples relating to market players and the shifts in customer behavior and technology were discussed, and requirements for future digital interaction with customers were derived. Finally, these requirements were summarized in a practical reference frame to set the direction of our approach to digital customer engagement, which encompasses all digital channels and thus inbound and outbound measures. The reference to digital channels does not mean that traditional marketing and sales channels are left out. On the contrary, digital and traditional channels must be closely coordinated.

Above all, the chapter has shown that the opportunities for adaptive players, for new players, for the customer, and for the industry are enormous and that change is fascinating. At the same time, new approaches are required, which fortunately are also enabled by new marketing tools and platforms. The challenge for our business division seems enormous: to serve more than 30,000 customers annually with several thousand premium products, while delivering more than 7 billion products, all while maintaining a premium level of service or user experience. The necessary prerequisite for innovation in digital marketing is given, but it can only be exploited if we meet the sufficiency and combine customer and market requirements with technological prerequisites.

References

Anzén, E., & Ekberg, L. (2020). *Understanding how automatized personalization with AI can drive value in B2B marketing: A case study of a Swedish industrial equipment manufacturer.*

Arora, A., Niese, N., Dreyer, E., Waas, A., & Xie, A. (2021). *Why electric cars can't come fast enough.* Boston Consulting Group.

Bala, M., & Verma, D. (2018). A critical review of digital marketing. *International Journal of Management, IT & Engineering, 8*(10), 321–339.

Bandur, V., Selim, G., Pantelic, V., & Lawford, M. (2021). Making the case for centralized automotive E/E architectures. *IEEE Transactions on Vehicular Technology, 70*(2), 1230–1245.

Barra, M. (2016, January 21). *The next revolution in the auto industry.* World Economic Forum, Davos.

Bauer, H., Burkacky, O., Kenevan, P., Mahindroo, A., & Patel, M. (2020, April). *Coronavirus: Implications for the semiconductor industry.* McKinsey & Company. https://www.mckinsey.com/industries/semiconductors/our-insights/coronavirus-implications-for-the-semiconductor-industry

Bhalla, A. (2021). Silicon carbide semiconductors with wide bandgap for electric vehicles. *ATZelectronics Worldwide, 16*(4), 18–21.

Candelo, E. (2019). Is disruption taking apart the carmakers'. In *Marketing innovations in the automotive industry* (pp. 117–129). Springer.

Chaffey, D., & Ellis-Chadwick, F. (2019). *Digital marketing: Strategy, implementation & practice.* Pearson.

Charette, R. N. (2009). This car runs on code. *IEEE Spectrum, 46*(3), 3.

Cho, M., & Shin, J. (2022). Identifying a combination of key resources to overcome the entry barriers in the electric vehicle market. *IEEE Access, 10*, 60373.

Dash, S. K., Chakraborty, S., Roccotelli, M., & Sahu, U. K. (2022). Hydrogen fuel for future mobility: Challenges and future aspects. *Sustainability, 14*(14), 8285.

De Chant, T. (2022, October 20). Lyft co-founder says autonomous vehicles won't replace drivers for at least a decade. *Techcrunch.* https://techcrunch.com/2022/10/20/lyft-co-founder-says-autonomous-vehicles-wont-replace-drivers-for-at-least-a-decade/

Deng, Z., & Tian, P. (2020). Are China's subsidies for electric vehicles effective? *Managerial and Decision Economics, 41*(4), 475–489.

Harrison, A. (1994). *New wave manufacturing strategies. Organisational and human resource management dimensions: An introduction* (pp. 175–203). Paul Chapman.

Hind, S., Kanderske, M., & van der Vlist, F. (2022). Making the car "platform ready": How big tech is driving the platformization of automobility. *Social Media + Society, 8*(2), 20563051221098696.

Hofstätter, T., Krawina, M., Mühlreiter, B., Pöhler, S., & Tschiesner, A. (2020). *Reimagining the auto industry's future: It's now or never.* Retrieved from McKinsey & Company: Https://Www.Mckinsey.Com/Industries/Automotive-and-assembly/Ourinsights/Reimagining-the-auto-industrys-future-its-now-or-never

Jackson, S. (2009). *Cult of analytics: Driving online marketing strategies using web analytics.* Routledge.

Jaenichen, F.-M., Liepold, C. J., Ismail, A., Martens, C. J., Dörrsam, V., & Ehm, H. (2021). Simulating and evaluating supply chain disruptions along an end-to-end semiconductor automotive supply chain. In: *2021 Winter Simulation Conference (WSC)*, pp. 1–12.

Lampón, J. F., Frigant, V., & Cabanelas, P. (2019). Determinants in the adoption of new automobile modular platforms: What lies behind their success? *Journal of Manufacturing Technology Management, 30*, 707.

Lee, H. L., Padmanabhan, V., & Whang, S. (1997). The bullwhip effect in supply chains. *Sloan Management Review, 38*, 93–102.

Lee, R. (2022). *Electric vehicles: A fair way to go.* University of Sheffield.

Leslie, M. (2021a). *Pandemic scrambles the semiconductor supply chain.* Elsevier.

Leslie, M. (2021b). *Texas crisis highlights grid vulnerabilities*. Elsevier.
Lund, S., Manyika, J., Woetzel, J., Barriball, E., & Krishnan, M. (2020). *Risk, resilience, and rebalancing in global value chains*. McKinsey & Company.
Manley, R. L., Alonso, E., & Nassar, N. T. (2022). Examining industry vulnerability: A focus on mineral commodities used in the automotive and electronics industries. *Resources Policy, 78*(102), 894.
Messagie, M. (2014). Life cycle analysis of the climate impact of electric vehicles. *Journal of Life Cycle Assessment, 2014*, 14.
Munoz, A., Billsberry, J., & Ambrosini, V. (2022). Resilience, robustness, and antifragility: Towards an appreciation of distinct organizational responses to adversity. *International Journal of Management Reviews, 24*(2), 181–187.
Ohlsen, J. (2022). The software-defined Vehicle Is Overwhelming the Automotive Industry. *ATZelectronics Worldwide, 17*(6), 56–56.
Olle, W., Plorin, D., Vogel, D., & Wächtler, A. (2016). The automotive agenda of the future – automotive suppliers face immense challenges. *Autoland Sachsen, 2*.
Perkins, G., & Murmann, J. P. (2018). What does the success of Tesla mean for the future dynamics in the global automobile sector? *Management and Organization Review, 14*(3), 471–480.
Ramani, V., Ghosh, D., & Sodhi, M. S. (2022). Understanding systemic disruption from the Covid-19-induced semiconductor shortage for the auto industry. *Omega, 113*(102), 720.
Shanthi, R. (2022, April 26). Nio rolls out 200,000th ev in record time, says on track with 2022 plans. *Benzinga*. https://www.benzinga.com/news/22/04/26804733/nio-says-hefei-plant-rolls-off-200-000th-ev-in-record-time-confirms-2022-plans-are-on-track
Smart Insights. (2010). Introducing RACE: A practical framework to improve your digital marketing. *Blog Post by Dave Chaffey*, p. 15.
Teer, J., & Bertolini, M. (2022, October). *Reaching breaking point: The semiconductor and critical raw material ecosystem at a time of great power rivalry*. The Hague Centre for Strategic Studies. https://hcss.nl/wpcontent/uploads/2022/10/Reaching-breaking-point-The-semiconductor-and-critical-raw-material-ecosystem-at-atime-of-great-power-rivalry-October-2022-1.pdf
Udenio, M., Fransoo, J. C., & Peels, R. (2015). Destocking, the bullwhip effect, and the credit crisis: Empirical modeling of supply chain dynamics. *International Journal of Production Economics, 160*, 34–46. https://doi.org/10.1016/j.ijpe.2014.09.008
Yasmin, A., Tasneem, S., & Fatema, K. (2015). Effectiveness of digital marketing in the challenging age: An empirical study. *International Journal of Management Science and Business Administration, 1*(5), 69–80.
Zarghami, S. A., & Dumrak, J. (2021). Unearthing vulnerability of supply provision in logistics networks to the black swan events: Applications of entropy theory and network analysis. *Reliability Engineering & System Safety, 215*, 107798.
Zhang, G., & Zhang, M. (2020). Innovation in new energy vehicles-take NIO as an example. In: 2020 International Conference on Social and Human Sciences.

The Key Role of Disruptive Digital Marketing Approaches in the Automotive Electronics Market

Jürgen Hoika and Uli Schneider

1 Preface: Change of Sales and Marketing in the Automotive Electronics Market

1.1 The Roles of Sales and Marketing in the Automotive Electronics Market Facing New Challenges

The key roles supporting the decision-making process of customers in B2B markets like automotive electronics are sales and marketing. Customer contact and support are one of the most relevant tasks to gain expertise about the market, applications, and hence positioning of the products like semiconductors. Sharp lines between sales and marketing could not be drawn often, and the missing competence of one role has to be compensated by the other role. Marketing communication in B2B was established to attract customers, specifically at face-to-face events like trade fairs. The times have changed. The consumer market pushed new ways mainly by digital channels to inform consumers about new products. The B2B industry followed the trends to adapt and take advantage of the new user behavior. Nowadays the decision-makers in the companies like to gain the same experience in their professional lives like they do in their private ones. New generations of decision-makers see company web pages and social media as a normal way of dealing with suppliers in contrary to the old times when arranging a meeting with the suppliers was the preferred way to become aware of new products or solution during their R&D phase. The pandemic has accelerated the change from what we can call analog to digital customer engagement.

J. Hoika (✉) · U. Schneider
Infineon Technologies AG, Neubiberg, Germany
e-mail: Juergen.Hoika@infineon.com; Uli.Schneider@infineon.com

U. Schneider, J. Hoika (eds.), *Digital Marketing in the Automotive Electronics Industry*, Management for Professionals,
https://doi.org/10.1007/978-3-031-30720-1_3

1.2 Roles of Sales and Marketing Supporting the Customer Decision Process

In an ideal organization the responsibilities are well split between sales and marketing. Typically, the business or buying funnel which is reflecting our customers' buying decision starts with marketing and ends with sales being responsible to achieve a positive decision-making of our customers (Fig. 1).

This is a very common set-up in many companies, but we are experiencing the hand-off point is changing with increasing digital customer engagements. As well we see digital and analog interactions with the customer going hand in hand.

2 The Analog-to-Digital Conversion of Sales and Marketing in B2B Markets

The digital transformation of the traditional customer interactions is leading to digital customer engagement which is demanding a different split of sales and marketing responsibilities. The so-called touch points the customer has had with different types of media and personal interactions with a company's personnel – especially with sales and marketing – are now either supplemented or substituted by digital offerings (Fig. 2). Digital offerings can range from advertisement on a web page, price indications to digital self-services like ordering samples of a product online.

Long-lasting business relationships are key for business growth of a supplier in the B2B domain, especially in an environment like the automotive market. Excellent support of the supplier's sales and marketing team to its customer base are one of its fundaments. The digital transformation of sales and marketing has to result in the same positive perception of a supplier towards the customers. One solution for this is providing excellent digital customer engagement. Excellent customer interactions are those that create a value to the customer.

An important value to customers is trusting their suppliers. Trust is created by the quality of information provided over a longer period of time. There is of course no difference to the importance of information quality in the analog and digital domain. Interaction with sales managers who are reliable partners, respectively, providing reliable information, is valued significantly. Reliable information is key, especially in B2B markets like automotive electronics where the quality of the information has a big commercial impact to the customer. This dogma can be proven empirically by observing positive and negative interactions with customers over a longer time frame.

In the automotive electronics industry, you can observe following decisive information for a customer designing and manufacturing electronic control units that demand a high level of reliability of information by the supplier of electronic components (Table 1).

The empirical knowledge from this example can be very likely copied to similar B2B relationships in other markets. The effects of the quality of information in B2B

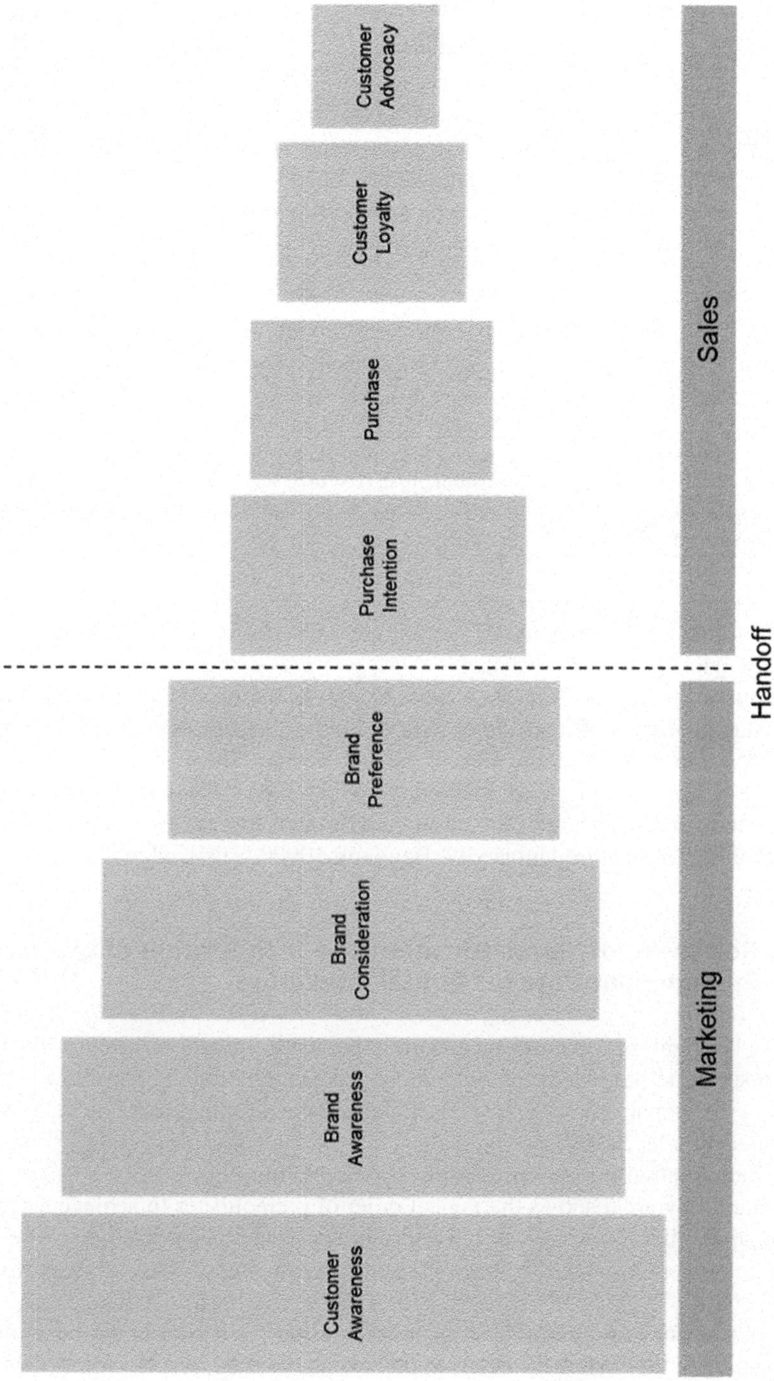

Fig. 1 The buying funnel and typical areas of responsibility for sales and marketing (Kotler et al., 2019)

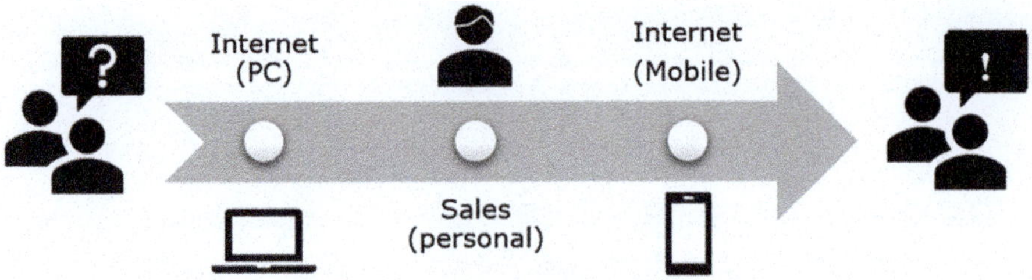

Fig. 2 Touch points of a customer today along his decision process – analog and digital

Table 1 Examples of decisive information and impact to customers

Information	Impact of information quality to the customer
Price indication	Reliable calculation for the customer's product towards his customers (e.g., Tier1 to OEM)
Availability of samples	Ensuring time-to-market with creating prototypes in time (according to agreed time schedules for testing at OEMs)
Technical parameter in documentation and software	Fulfilling the product specification of the customer towards the OEM

can be found in publications such as one from the Michigan State University (Mcknight et al., 2017).

Information quality and responsiveness belong to the factors which gain trust in the digital engagement of a customer with a supplier besides many other important factors like security and functionality of the web design. There are publications that describe how a trust management roadmap for e-commerce could be built on defined quality criteria and feedback of the customers through surveys (School of Information Technology, Sripatum University, Bangkok 10900, Thailand et al., 2014).

2.1 Relevance of Standardization and Stabilization of Customer Engagement Data for Digital Marketing

Providing the right information and ensuring that the information is right is the base for a proper digital knowledge development process. One model that can illustrate the knowledge management process well is the Data-Information-Knowledge-Wisdom model (Rowley, 2007).

One interpretation for our corporation is presented in Fig. 3.

This digital pyramid shows the logical order of prerequisites to achieve a certain level of capabilities. You need to have a stabilized and standardized database that you can connect in a standardized way if you like drawing conclusion, e.g., from a KPI dashboard.

This is true for any kind of data of a corporation. Hence, it is the base of the understanding of the customers' decision process and criteria, too. Customer data can be categorized into the following four groups (Dam et al., 2022):

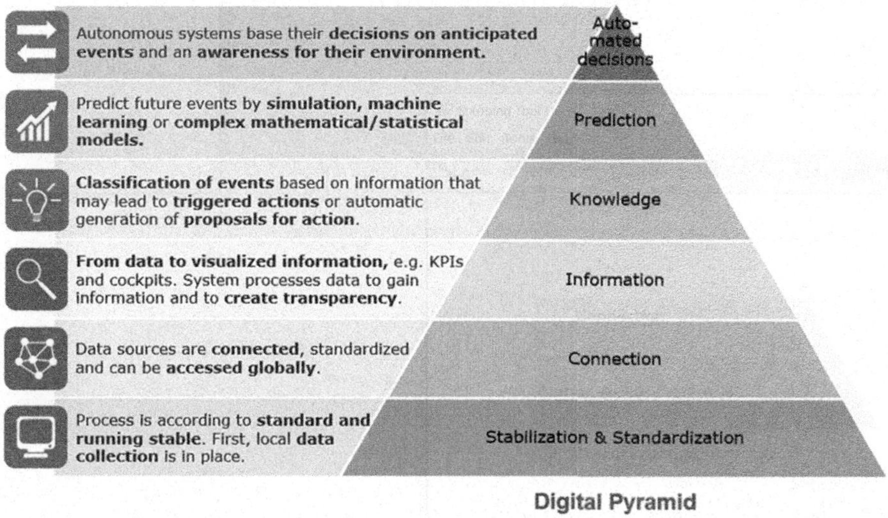

Fig. 3 Interpretation of the Data-Information-Knowledge-Wisdom model (Infineon Technologies)

Table 2 Examples of customer data

Customer data	Examples
Behavioral data	Visit of a product web page Application of a technical online training for a specific solution Download of a technical white paper
Transactional data	Purchase of an evaluation board Purchase of a product sample Quote for a product for a certain volume (for volume production)

- Demographic data
- Behavioral data
- Transactional data
- Psychographic data

The main pillars for digital marketing in B2B are behavioral and transactional data. The behavioral data considers the digital customer engagement. This data consists of information about which content or deliverable of a supplier a customer has used and what led her/him successfully to her/his buying decision. The transactional information will give insights about what products the customers have purchased finally. This information is an important insight in the decisive engagements of the customer with the supplier.

In the domain of B2B in the automotive electronics, you can find in Table 2 examples for these two data groups:

Standardization and stabilization in the defined data is key to climb up in the digitization pyramid to the level information and beyond. The role of digital

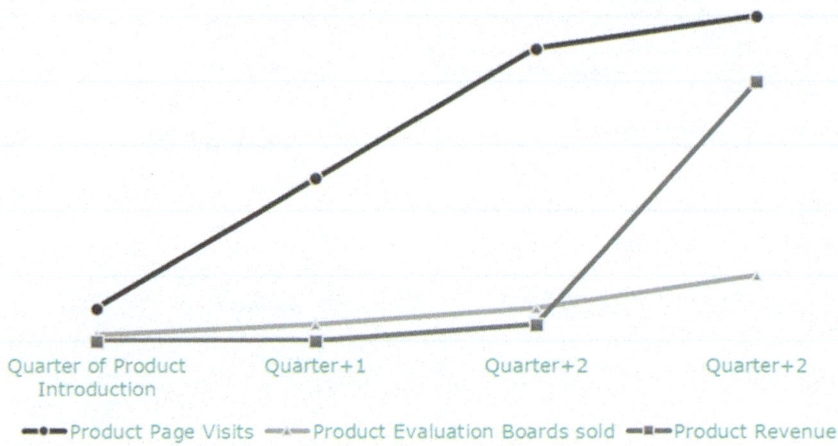

Fig. 4 Examples of descriptive analysis of the digital customer engagement

marketing is to ensure that a clear definition of this data and a description that ensures standardization is available.

Descriptive analytics on historical data can lead into a reporting that generate findings about the customers' digital engagement.

The result of the analysis can be compared across different product groups to gain the knowledge needed to understand the performance of the customer engagement first and then to drive actions to improve the outcome (see Fig. 4 for reference). The outcome is finally of course determined by the revenue generated for the specific product. Descriptive analysis is the core of what marketing has used to understand markets, competitors, and customers. In the B2B the knowledge about customers was usually transferred from the customer and/or sales to marketing to drive improvements.

A simple example is the correlation of the availability of product samples and the successes of engaging with a customer in the automotive electronics market. Marketing learned to track the availability of samples to drive more projects from design-in phase to design-win.

Descriptive analysis is the fundament for digital marketing. Examples and methods will be further explained in the following chapters.

The next level of wisdom in the area of customer engagement is prediction. It is the way to develop from customer information to customer intelligence. This level of wisdom was and will be in the hands of the sales and marketing teams of a corporation. The number of customer interactions on the digital side is requiring digital means to build up this intelligence. The primary goal for a supplier is to support the customers with the right information at the right point of time that finally leads to a positive buying decision. There are different angles to describe customer intelligence; one possible way is these four groups (Dam et al., 2022):

Customer intelligence focusing on:

1. Product-aware intelligence/requirement capturing
   - Provides customer insights in products and services needed (e.g., through surveys, interaction in communities or support tickets, etc.)
2. Customer DNA/personalization
   - Gives insights about the customer segmentation (e.g., small to big corporation, information about the professions of the users/persona)
3. Customer experience
   - Understands the customer journeys, how to attract customers, convert them to buying customers, and keep them as loyal customers over time
4. Customer value
   - Describes the value a customer offers (important – usually meant the other way around): The value created economically (revenue and profit), socially (reference to other customers), or cognitively (knowledge and experience)

This segmentation is not new to the traditional sales and marketing world. We see many responsibilities of the sales and marketing teams described at the beginning reflected in gaining customer intelligence. The intelligence is created, maintained, and communicated by these organizations. Strategic positioning is usually kept in presentations shared across the entire corporation. The objective is taking advantage of it and getting the buy-in of all stakeholders who take this intelligence into their strategy to drive actions for a successful customer development. This has clear limitations in terms of scalability and utilization of this important knowledge. In the digital domain we face magnitudes of more customers, and especially more individuals of the targeted companies, and many more touch points of these individuals, too.

Hence, we need to invest in modeling the customer decision process deriving the right prediction of the customers' digital engagement based on the data.

The basis to achieve the levels of wisdom of prediction, knowledge, and information of the presented digital pyramid is standardization. In the domain of customer engagement, standardization can be achieved by two important measures:

1. **Standardized customer journey** – standardized understanding how the customers buy and become a loyal customer to a supplier
2. **Standardized persona** – standardization of the main decision-makers – describing the profession of the individual who are undertaking the customer journey

3 Modeling the Customers' Buying Process

3.1 The Customer Journey

There is history describing the steps a customer is doing from becoming aware of a product to the decision to buy the product. The roots are going back to the Elias St. Elmo Lewis in 1898 where a first "AID" model was defined. This model was further refined in the following years like the famous "AIDA" model (Barry & Howard, 1990). The motivation of a standardization of these models was in identifying the effectiveness of advertisement to the buyer's decision.

As simple as this model is, it already creates a nice foundation to structure the buying process or what we can call customer journey.

In a B2C environment the model of a customer journey was introduced before the Internet shopping became a standard as a further development of the AIDA model. Buying products through multiple channels that partially include channels with non-personal interaction like catalogue buying demanded a model to understand the buyer behavior in order to optimize each buyer's journey to a positive buying decision (Harris et al., 2021).

It was a logical development that this model was used when digital customer engagement including e-commerce, email campaigns, company web pages, and social media became popular. Examples of a customer journey with exemplary touch points for the customers are visualized in Fig. 5.

Hence, the first and most fundamental step is standardizing the customer journey. It starts with the naming convention and the understanding of each phase. This includes the clear definition of the person who is taking a buying decision to structure the decision process into important phases. For each phase you have to standardize which decisive touch points, also called "moments of truth," support the customer to move from one to the next phase. As a supplier you like to drive the person not only to buy, but you like to win the person as a loyal customer who is starting as many new customer journeys again in the future.

The customer journey mapping is also an important instrument for the entire organization of a company to understand what the market perceives as standard touch points that you have to fulfill, but also where your company can create a

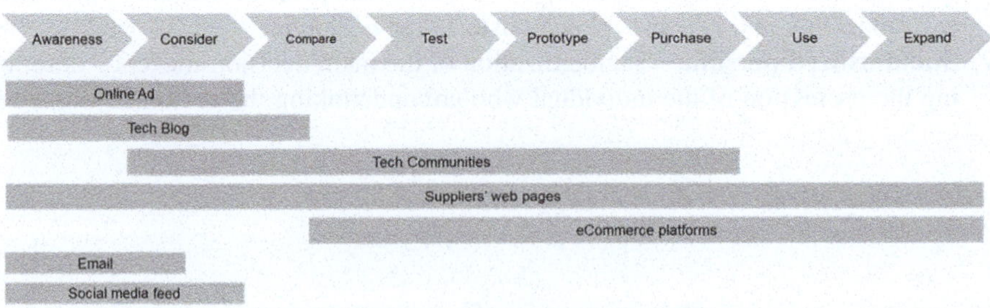

Fig. 5 Examples of a customer journey with different digital channels

Table 3 Required elements of a customer journey map (Temkin, 2010)

Required elements	Definitions
Customer processes	How customers interact with the company across the life cycle of the relationship. What are the stages of the relationship? What are the specific interactions or touch points within each stage?
Customer needs	What customers want from the company during each interaction? What do they want to accomplish? How do they want to feel and be treated? Do they have unrecognized needs that could be addressed?
Customer perceptions	What customers think and feel about current interactions with the company. Do they feel their needs are being met? Are they satisfied? Do they view interactions as adequate or particularly valuable?

difference to your competition (Table 3). Digital marketing is a key role in this activity and is in most organizations considered the center of knowledge for a competitive customer journey mapping.

3.2 The Buyer Persona

It is important to clarify who at the customer side will be addressed before the customer journey map is created. The definition of a so-called buyer persona can help to illustrate it better. In the B2C environment the definition of buyer personas is established as a fundamental method to identify the goals, desires, and the limitations of the target group of buyers and users, called persona (Akre et al., 2019). Usually the characteristics of a persona are age, location, and gender. Some of these attributes can be taken over from B2C to B2B, but some are very specific to B2B, especially considering the more complex way of decision-making. In addition, the method of buyer persona cannot be seen totally separated to the analog way of capturing the attributes of a buyer persona.

Value selling methods in sales organization strive for a thorough understanding of the decision-makers for the respective customers. Based on the know-how of many customers, the target groups can be as well clustered and seen as personas.

A persona study is one measure to conclude about the personas. The main objectives of such a study are:

- **Identify main decision-makers** of your customers.
- Give them a **representative name.**
- Provide guidance on how to **improve customer engagement across the whole customer journey**, especially in terms of:
  - **Content**: relevant collaterals and assets that support the persona to progress in its customer journey
  - **Channels**: characteristics and relevance of information channels (website, email, social media, communities)

Table 4 Examples of buyer personas in the B2B market

Buyer persona "developer"		Buyer persona "purchaser"	
	• R&D engineer for electronics, 20–40 years old • Electrotechnical university or similar education background • Driving whole or significant part of the development process, from defining requirements to the final product design • Typical decision criteria are system fit of the component, real life performance, availability, support, costs, and time to market	• Procurement manager for electronics, 30–45 years young • Business or/and technical university degree • Identifying the optimal solution from components suiting the company's products' target specification, level of support, pricing, delivery, and quality performance	

– **Support and services**: characteristics of personalized support (tech community, personal contact, digital self-service)

A snapshot of two important buyer personas can be found in Table 4. More attributes can be added to support the mentioned objectives. The level of understanding of the personas and hence the definition of the right attributes can be part of the differentiation between different suppliers.

3.3 The Moments of Truth

The next step of modeling the customers decision-making process is to define the touch points, or so called "moments of truth" (Temkin, 2010), especially those who support the start of the customer journey or the conversion from one phase to the next one.

The customers are shifting more and more from personal to digital interactions. Due to this reason marketing responsibilities shifted from traditional to digital marketing or were complemented by it (Desai, 2019). Marketing needs to concentrate on selecting the right measures to create digital touch points and measure their effectiveness. Some examples about digital marketing measures are:

- **Social media marketing** – invest to create the right awareness in digital channels (Facebook, Twitter, YouTube, etc.)
- **Email marketing** – advertisement through emails/newsletters to support customer nurturing
- **Content marketing** – focusing on of generating brand awareness, web page traffic, and lead generation by content on digital channels – especially focusing on

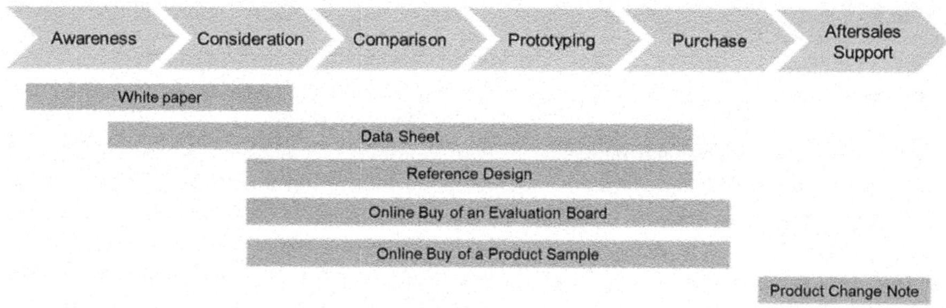

Fig. 6 Example of a customer journey and digital touch points

content for the company's product web pages, but also including community posts, ebooks, whitepapers, etc.
- **Search engine optimization** (SEO) – invest that customers find the supplier's web pages best

The final step of modeling the digital decision process of the customers is to bring the customer journey for the defined persona and the digital touch points together and finally measure the effectiveness of each measure.

In a B2B environment like automotive semiconductors, content marketing is an important measure to cover the demands of the two mentioned personas developer and purchaser. In B2B the product is a deliverable to the customer to complete his product for the end customer compared to B2C where the final product is in focus. One example is a semiconductor power switch for an electric water pump that is an end product purchased by a car OEM. In this context the persona developer is not searching for the semiconductor power switch only, but for all collaterals and services that are necessary to complete his task in designing an electric water pump.

Hence, the content around the product "semiconductor power switch" is as important as the product itself. It is obvious that the moments of truth will resonate well with the persona developer if the relevant content connected to the product is satisfying the requirements of the persona.

In addition, self-services need to be defined by digital marketing that enables the persona to master certain touch points autonomously and thus fast and at the right time.

Figure 6 is showing examples of decisive content and self-services for the defined persona "Developer" mapped to the phases of his digital customer journey.

The definition of the decisive touch points and their effectiveness in driving a customer from awareness to buy is the differentiating know-how in the digital marketing.

Following the example of the developer who needs to develop an electric water pump, the digital touch points will turn into a positive customer experience that will have a positive impact for the developer. Typically, the benefits of the touch points provide an advantage in terms of innovation, cost, and time to market.

Table 5 Standard elements of a successful digital marketing approach

Buyer personas	Standardization of the targeted buyer
Customer journey	Standardized model that describes the buyer persona buying process
Portfolio of digital touch points/moments of truths (mainly content and services)	Portfolio of content and services that are decisive for the respective buyer persona
Portfolio of digital channels	Portfolio of digital channels the buyer persona uses for her/his customer journey (e.g., company's Internet page, YouTube, communities, ecommerce platforms, etc.)

It is essential for digital marketing to differ non-effective customer journey from those that delight the customer. Digital marketing needs to host this intelligence to drive best-in-class content and services as well as understanding which digital channels are the right ones used by the customers.

Non-effective customer journeys consist of so-called "broken moments of truth" (Temkin, 2010). In an analog way these moments are identified usually at a customer meeting, when the customer complains to his account manager what content or service was unsatisfactory and did not lead into a solution, respectively did not bring the customer in the next phase of his customer journey.

In conclusion digital marketing needs to standardize and investigate the following domains of Table 5:

4 Learning from the Data and Outlook on Digital Marketing

4.1 Return of Investment of Digital Marketing Activities – Growing Prospects, Suspects, and MQLs

One responsibility of digital marketing in B2C and B2B is to win more customers, especially individuals at companies – primarily belonging to the buyer persona – through digital marketing activities.

The return of investment (RoI) of digital marketing activities is usually determined by the number of potential and not yet personally known customers (suspects), known possible customers who have agreed to get further information (prospects), and prospects that have indicated a clear interest in the supplier's offering (marketing qualified leads/MQL).

The effectiveness of digital campaigns and digital content can be determined by measuring the generated suspects, prospects, and MQLs. Therefore, the measurement framework of digital marketing has to include these KPIs.

What is finally essential is how the digital marketing activities attract customers to buy the product and therefore generate business for the supplier.

4.2 How Does the Business Funnel Connect to the Customer Journey?

The business funnel is one common practice especially in the B2B market to follow up the business. It is an important instrument, because the time from the decision point of a customer and the revenue resulting out of it is relatively long. In the automotive semiconductor market, this time lasts between about a quarter of a year to 3 years, depending on the complexity of the semiconductor and thus the complexity of the customer's R&D project. In addition, the time until a positive decision is determined by the decision and release process at the end customer side – the automotive OEM. The decision is typically done faster for a commoditized and rather simple semiconductor products, compared to a product that impacts massively the cost of the customer's product and time to market.

Sales and marketing are monitoring the business performance in respect to:

- How many projects at the customers are currently evaluating the products and what is the estimation of the entire business value of all projects? This is what is typically called **projects in design-in stage**.
- How many projects are won at customers and what is the estimation of their business value and revenue projection in the future? This is what is typically called **projects in design-win stage**.
- What is the **final revenue** generated with the customers? Not all projects which were won are successful in the market. The customer or the end customer can either fail in the market or progress much faster and better than expected.

In the analog domain organizations were set up, mainly in sales and marketing, to review the business funnel regularly. Business targets from top down are set to drive the business successfully, i.e. targets are set mainly for design-win and revenue. Business reviews are installed to constantly check if enough business is won to fund the R&D of products, the manufacturing capacity to produce them and the sales of the products while hitting the targets of profitability to ensure continuous growth.

In the digital domain the model of the customer journey helps in this respect, because not all customer interactions can be followed up personally. On the one side the customer likes to experience a satisfactory customer journey, and on the other side the supplier likes to gain revenue by providing efficient customer journeys.

In the digital domain it is meaningful to connect now the customer journey to the business funnel like what is shown in Fig. 7.

All customers that start a R&D project to design a product for their customers will start and end their customer journey. The objective of the supplier is to make the decision-makers (buyer persona) aware about its solution and convince the customer to purchase it. The steps towards a positive buying decision are split into the discussed phases of the customer journey.

That means all customer journeys connect to the business funnel. Therefore, the final and major business indicators for digital marketing are design-win value and revenue generated by digital customer journeys. This is a challenge, because the

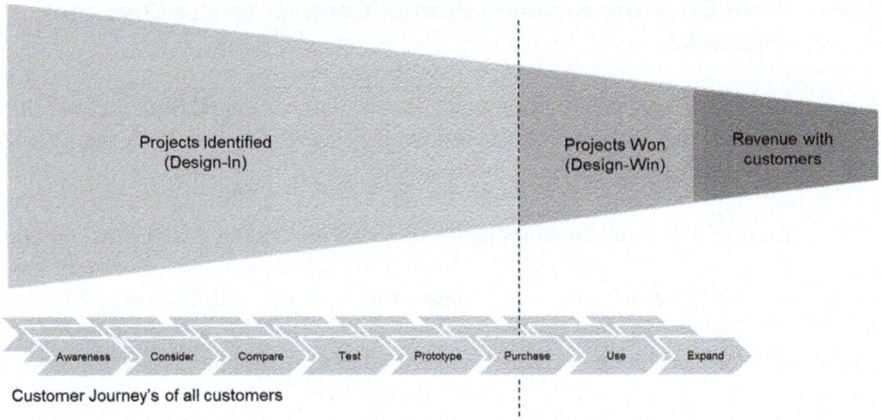

Fig. 7 Connection of the customer journey and the business funnel

Table 6 Example of conversions in a customer journey of buyer persona "developer"

Phase:	Awareness	Consider	Compare	Test	Prototype
Digital touch point:	Google search of a developer ended up at product web site of the supplier	Developer spends time on specific product pages of the supplier and downloads a specific data sheet of a semiconductor product	Developer is downloading a digital simulation model of the product and compares the results with best next alternatives	Developer is ordering an evaluation board online to test the performance of the product	Developer is ordering samples online

decision-making is not done by digital touch points only, and it is not easy to connect every digital touch point to the final result like revenue or design-win value. Nevertheless, it is obvious that the conversion of a customer from one phase of his customer journey to the next phase is increasing the probability of a positive buying decision, respectively a design-win. Personalized digital interaction with the customer like a customer portal simplifies the analytics of the conversion beside offering a personalized and thus efficient experience to the customer.

The conversion of the buyer persona from one phase to the next one is a clear sign that the customer is succeeding in his decision process and thus also an important indicator for the supplier to offer the right content or service that is beneficial. Some examples of customer's digital touch points and correlation to the phase of the customer are shown in Table 6.

In the measurement framework of digital marketing, the quantitative analysis of how the digital touch points resonated with the customers is an important base to understand the conversion, especially if the customer journey is personalized. Qualitative measurements about the feedback of the customer, e.g. by a developer

Table 7 Three types of voice of the customer data and examples from digital channels (Jain, 2022)

Direct feedback	Indirect feedback	Inferred feedback
Online survey	Online community	Performance of digital touch points (e.g., datasheet downloads)
"5-star" rating	Support requests	Online purchase

about the quality of a digital touch point, can be retrieved by direct and indirect feedbacks, like explained in Table 7.

Digital marketing needs to take over the analytics of the effectiveness of the digital customer journeys in both aspects:

1. **Quantitative analytics** – measures how the defined customer journey with their digital touch points, content, and services is yielding in higher digital customer engagement and finally providing the growths of the business funnel
2. **Qualitative analytics** – measures how the customer/persona values the digital touch points, content, and services derived from direct and indirect feedback from the customer ("voice of the customer")

In this respect a stable measurement framework and KPIs will help to drive the right activities to promote the products in the right way to create value at the customers' side.

When we now compare the areas of responsibilities of sales and marketing in 1.1 and convert it to the digital domain, we will realize that there is no hard hand-off point anymore. Digital marketing is not covering the early phases of customer awareness only, but gains know-how that is instrumental to ensure best digital customer engagement (Fig. 8).

The hand-off points between digital and human interaction can happen in all phases of the buying funnel starting with the purchase intention. The difference in the digital domain, especially in a B2B market, is that standard interaction and services will be driven more and more through digital channels and digital self-services and the human interaction will cover the so-called premium service. The premium services cover all non-standard technical and commercial support which are not offered digitally. In addition, sales will learn about the customer journeys and digital touch points of their customers to decide where premium services are valuable to the customer.

The objective of the collaboration between the digital marketing and the sales organization is to grow the business by providing benefits to the customers in terms of cost, performance and time to market. Digital customer engagement will offer more scalability to a company's sales organization to learn fast from the moments of truths of a magnitude of customers interacting on digital channels to proceed in their customer journeys. Furthermore, marketing will accelerate in the learning of what digital touch points, content, and services resonated well with the target customers.

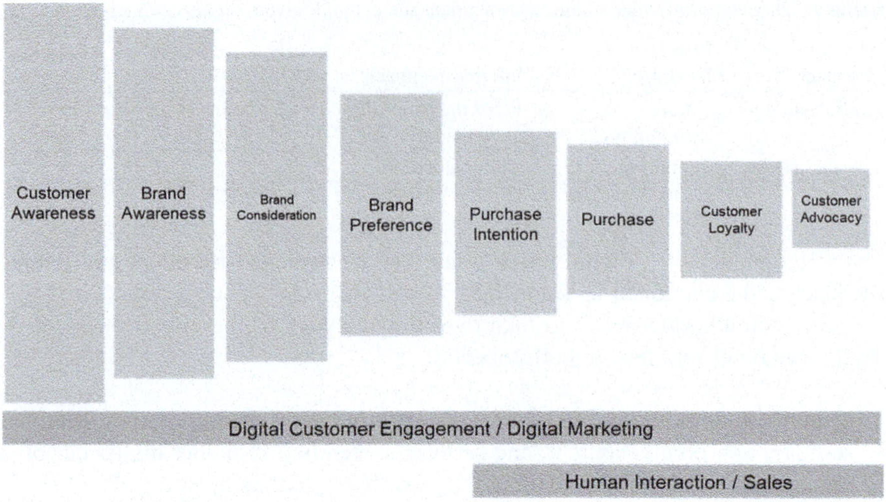

Fig. 8 The buying funnel and typical areas of responsibility for digital and human customer interaction

References

Akre, V., Rajan, A., Ahamed, J., Al Amri, A., & Al Daisi, S. (2019). Smart digital marketing of financial services to millennial generation using emerging technological tools and buyer persona. In: *2019 Sixth HCT Information Technology Trends (ITT)*, pp. 120–125. https://doi.org/10.1109/ITT48889.2019.9075106.

Barry, T. E., & Howard, D. J. (1990). A review and critique of the hierarchy of effects in advertising. *International Journal of Advertising, 9*(2), 121–135. https://doi.org/10.1080/02650487.1990.11107138

Dam, N. A. K., Dinh, T. L., & Menvielle, W. (2022). The quest for customer intelligence to support marketing decisions: A knowledge-based framework. *Vietnam Journal of Computer Science, 09*(03), 349–368. https://doi.org/10.1142/S2196888822500208

Desai, V. (2019, March). Digital marketing: A review, *Special Issue, 196*.

Harris, P., van der Veen, G., & Pol, H. (2021). Customer journey: From practice to theory. In *The Routledge companion to strategic marketing* (pp. 67–90). https://doi.org/10.4324/9781351038669

Jain, A. (2022, March 16). 3 ways to use voice of customer data in B2B marketing. *Gartner*. https://www.gartner.com/en/digital-markets/insights/voice-of-customer-data-b2b-marketing

Kotler, P., Rackham, N., & Krishnaswamy, S. (2019). *Ending the war between sales and marketing*, 16.

Mcknight, D., Lankton, N., Nicolaou, A., & Price, J. (2017). Distinguishing the effects of B2B information quality, system quality, and service outcome quality on trust and distrust. *The Journal of Strategic Information Systems, 26*, 118. https://doi.org/10.1016/j.jsis.2017.01.001

Rowley, J. (2007). The wisdom hierarchy: Representations of the DIKW hierarchy. *Journal of Information Science, 33*(2), 163–180. https://doi.org/10.1177/0165551506070706

School of Information Technology, Sripatum University, Bangkok 10900, Thailand, Jairak, R., Praneetpolgrang, P., & Chirawichitchai, N. (2014). A roadmap for establishing trust management strategy in E-commerce services using quality based assessment. *International Journal of Information Engineering and Electronic Business, 6*(5), 1–9. https://doi.org/10.5815/ijieeb.2014.05.01

Temkin, B. D. (2010). Mapping the customer journey. *Forrester Research, 3*, 20.

Overcoming Barriers to Digital Marketing in the Automotive Electronics Industry Through Ambidexterity Design Guidelines

Uli Schneider

1 Introduction

The success of digital marketing[1] among business-to-customer (B2C) companies is undisputed, and many of the leading companies in many industries such as fashion and retail have not only embraced digital marketing, but are using it as a competitive advantage (Leeflang et al., 2014). In contrast, digital marketing in the business-to-business (B2B) sector seems to still be in its infancy, even after several years. The characteristics of digital marketing in B2B industries have been researched for several years, and as early as 2012, Järvinen et al. (2012) described the application of digital marketing as an emerging field. In their research, B2B companies did acknowledge the value of digital marketing efforts such as email marketing, but the value was primarily attributed to awareness and marketing communication aspects rather than digital customer engagement. At the time, the authors saw the barriers to a successful transition to digital marketing primarily as a lack of resources (human resources, time, and expertise).

One would think that this dynamic field of digital marketing has also penetrated the B2B sector within 10 years and that research is now in a position to derive a status, if not recommendations for action, in this rapidly growing field. However, a look at the literature shows that even after 10 years, with a few exceptions, relatively little knowledge has been researched in the B2B area (Brink, 2017; Karjaluoto et al., 2015; Leek et al., 2019; Setkute & Dibb, 2022) and the need to generate new insights

[1] Digital marketing refers to a set of practices that involve the use of digital communication channels, such as websites, search engine marketing, digital advertising, social media, and email. The practices range from market communications and promotions to digital customer engagement, which helps move customers through the sales funnel (Setkute & Dibb, 2022).

U. Schneider (✉)
Infineon Technologies AG, Neubiberg, Germany
e-mail: Uli.Schneider@infineon.com

U. Schneider, J. Hoika (eds.), *Digital Marketing in the Automotive Electronics Industry*, Management for Professionals,
https://doi.org/10.1007/978-3-031-30720-1_4

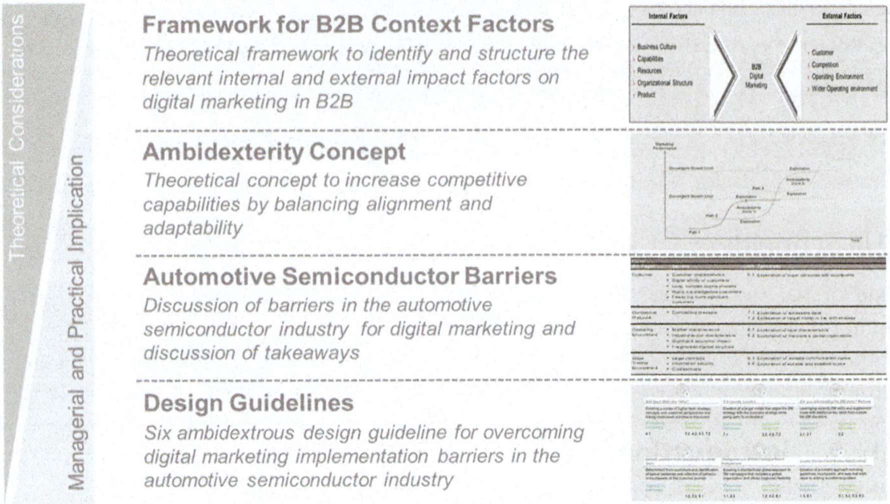

Fig. 1 Outline of the article structure

into digital marketing in the B2B context has been reiterated by (Kim & Moon, 2021).

Why is it worth looking into this, even though management research in this area seems to be making little progress? Management research is a welcome source of solutions from neighboring industries whose challenges are common in practice and often transferable to other industries and contexts because of their similarity. In our practice in the B2B automotive semiconductor industry, we see challenges or resistances for the use of digital marketing and specifically digital customer engagement practices that seem to exist not exclusively for our company. For example, we see that the automotive electronics industry is still characterized by strong personal customer relationships. These relationships are deep, long-lasting, and often complicated (Burkacky et al., 2022). In particular, the longevity and long design-in cycles mean that it is difficult to demonstrate the mediate impact of digital marketing on strategy. In addition, product-related communication inside and outside the company appears to be highly technical, much like corporate culture.

These circumstances often result in the perception of practitioners outside of the digital marketing function being the same as that of researchers 10 years ago. Accordingly, while the value of digital marketing is recognized, it is usually limited to awareness and marketing communication measures that do not make a tangible or measurable contribution to the success of the strategy.

While the current state of research does not yet provide specific guidelines to overcome challenges in the B2B automotive industry, if it can do so at all for an industry, it does provide an overview of the current state of research and a taxonomy. To address this gap for practitioners, we will analyze in this article the factors that influence digital marketing in the automotive semiconductor industry and derive design guidelines to overcome barriers to successful digital marketing practices. Figure 1 outlines how the article is structured and the managerial and practical implications are built upon theoretical frameworks.

2 Theoretical Foundations

2.1 Context Factors for Digital Marketing for B2B Firms

One of the few recent studies that examines influencing factors and barriers on digital marketing in the B2B sector comes from (Setkute & Dibb, 2022), where the authors describe how the B2B approaches still resembles an "old boy's club" with strong reliance on existing networks. The authors conclude that a "one-size-fits-all" approach is not suitable for the successful use of digital marketing measures and an approach contingent on a firm's context is advisable. Although the scope of the study differs in that it is conducted in a different industry and for small- and medium-sized enterprises, it still provides a suitable framework because the scientific basis on which it is based is not as restrictive and applies to B2B companies in general.

Already in our company, where we serve other semiconductor markets in addition to the main automotive market, we can confirm the realization that a "one-size-fits-all" approach to digital marketing is not applicable. This suggests that the study also provides a sufficiently precise framework for our B2B subject of study and derives influencing factors and barriers to success for our industry. In doing so, we also follow the common view that influencing factors are context-dependent (Coviello & Brodie, 2001) and describe them in the context of the automotive semiconductor industry. We distinguish between internal factors and external factors that influence the adoption of digital marketing. While internal factors relate to resources, capabilities, corporate culture, and product and organizational structure, external factors relate to variables such as the customer, the competition, and the (wider) operating and trading environment (see Fig. 2).

Fig. 2 Context factors in B2B marketing based on Setkute and Dibb (2022)

2.2 The Concept of Organizational Ambidexterity

The illustration in Fig. 2 shows that digital marketing operates in a field of tension between the multitude of defined context factors (as well as the barriers that can be derived from them). As much as this field of tension in the corporate context represents a challenge for the digital marketing function, it is also the potential source of corporate capabilities. For example, the management literature describes the corporate context in which employees operate as an enabler or inhibitor of a company's competitiveness (Birkinshaw & Gibson, 2004; Day, 1994; Duwe, 2021; He et al., 2021; O Reilly & Tushman, 2004; Tariq et al., 2022). Accordingly, Birkinshaw and Gibson (2004) refer to the ability of making use of organizational context as an overarching organizational capability. This is consistent with Day (1994), who describes capabilities as a set of skills and collective learning exercised through organizational processes that ensure powerful coordination of functional activities that characterize market-oriented organizations.

Birkinshaw and Gibson (2004) describe two strands of these overarching capabilities that can be derived from context. The first is adaptability (often referred to as exploration) – the ability to engage quickly with new opportunities. The second strand is alignment and states that it is not a focus on mere innovation and proactivity that makes companies successful, but an orientation (often referred to as exploitation) that focuses very well on leveraging the value of assets and coordinating and streamlining activities to create value. The authors further go on to state that for any company which aims at succeeding in the long run "it must master both adaptability and alignment - a trait sometimes referred to as ambidexterity" (Birkinshaw & Gibson, 2004, p. 1).

These capabilities also refer to the design and implementation of marketing capabilities (He et al., 2021), and these very digital marketing capabilities are becoming critical for companies to remain competitive in global markets (Low et al., 2020). Especially in the context of digital marketing for B2B companies, this approach appears suitable because digital marketing, as a young field in its infancy, is on the one hand susceptible to innovations that need to be tapped (exploration), and on the other hand represents a cross-organizational B2B environment that often, and in our case certainly, requires alignment. For a better illustration, we use the following figure.

Figure 3 describes a generic path of marketing performance over time for digital marketing performance, adopted and adapted based on the work of Duwe (2021). Path 1 in the figure describes the traditional marketing approach, such as a highly tailored and personalized face-to-face sales and marketing approach. This approach has proven very successful for our automotive business in the past and has made us a market leader. However, in view of our growth ambitions and a changing market environment, this traditional marketing is no longer sustainable and will sooner or later reach its limits. We cannot, for example, grow indefinitely using the support of personal sales and marketing approaches without this growth being eaten up by the complexity of corporate structures and processes.

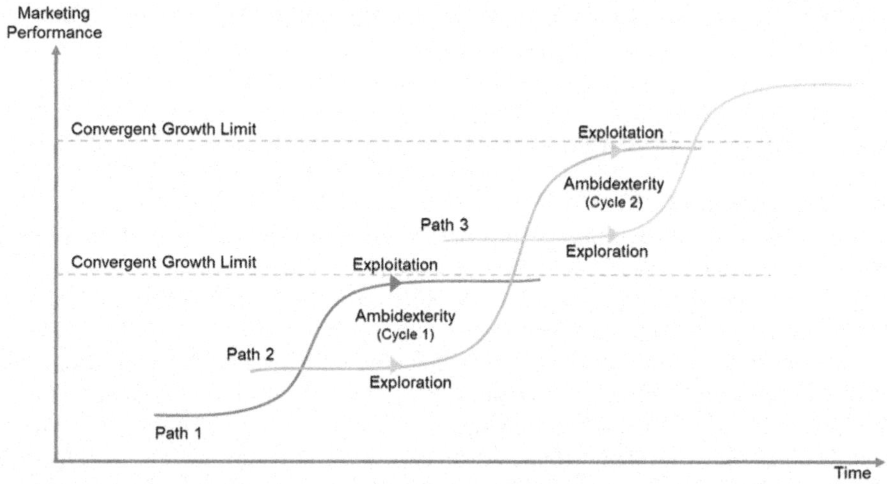

Fig. 3 Marketing performance based on ambidexterity management (Adapted from Duwe, 2021)

Therefore, we need a second path to ensure our sustainable growth, where we explore new tools and marketing and sales approaches without leaving the first path (Path 1). During this exploration, we are not able to fully leverage the newly discovered approaches and tools, and therefore need to manage the ambidexterity between Path 1 and Path 2 imposed by the context. The greater the ambidexterity we can manage, the greater the leap in performance. Once we get a handle on ambidexterity, we can start a new cycle with Path 3.

In the design part of the chapter, we will be reconsidering this very concept of ambidexterity[2] and the capability of balancing exploration and exploitation.

3 Impact Factors and Barriers of Digital Marketing in the Automotive Semiconductor Industry

In the following section, we use Setkute and Dibb's (2022) framework to match B2B contextual factors with the reality of our digital marketing practice in the automotive semiconductor market to identify barriers and ultimately important implications for our digital marketing design guidelines that will ensue at the end of this article. The following section is consistently structured in such a way that each internal and external influencing factor and the resulting barriers are explained in one section, in another section these are contrasted with our company's (Infineon Technologies)

[2]For completeness, we focus on contextual ambidexterity, where individual workers choose between alignment orientation and adaptation orientation in their activities, not on structural ambidexterity (Birkinshaw & Gibson, 2004).

context and practice, and then in a concluding section in each case the takeaways are explained.

3.1 Internal Factors

3.1.1 Business Culture

The first element of the internal factors that shape the contextual environment of B2B companies is corporate culture, which in turn is shaped mainly by two aspects. First, the corporate culture of a typical B2B company places great emphasis on relationship marketing rather than transaction marketing (Grönroos, 1997). This is most evident in the emphasis on personal selling and face-to-face interaction. The backbone of this relationship is creating value for the customer (Karjaluoto et al., 2015). As a result, seller-buyer relationships can seem more difficult than purely transactional, one-off relationships, but on the other hand, they are rewarded by trust and longevity and their frequent occurrence. Therefore, companies that are able to effectively establish, manage, and maintain this mutually beneficial relationship have a competitive advantage over other companies in their industries (Avlonitis & Karayanni, 2000). The second aspect typical of B2B business culture is the technology and production orientation that makes a B2B relationship necessary in the first place.

This description and its implications also apply to Infineon Automotive. A significant part of Infineon's and Infineon Automotive's business is direct-to-customer business with a few major customers (Infineon Technologies AG, 2021). This business has developed over a long period of time with customers who, for example, have entered into partnerships with us or have jointly developed important products with us. In addition, it is typical for the automotive industry that only a limited number of automotive platform orders are placed each year with semiconductor suppliers capable of delivering on a large scale and meeting the stringent quality standards of the automotive industry. To become a supplier of choice for these platforms and continue to successfully serve existing customers, the focus must be on individual interaction tailored to customer needs and the creation of added value. To meet these requirements, comprehensive technical competencies are needed, which require an in-depth understanding of the products as well as production and logistics.

Infineon Automotive's success story, which has played a major role in shaping our culture, does not necessarily determine the company's future path and may require new hybrid marketing approaches. Following the idea of ambidexterity, the success factors that have made us competitive in the past should be exploited and improved while we look for new approaches and tools or combine the success factors with them. The conclusion from the barriers imposed by our business culture is that personal selling, such as individual face-to-face contact or direct interaction, is still required in areas where scalability is not possible or is vehemently demanded by the customer. At the same time, we need to explore tailored and value-added solutions specifically for digital channels, which are often technical in nature and require exploitation of technical product and application understanding.

3.1.2 Marketing Capabilities[3]

The second element of the internal impact factors relates to (marketing) capabilities, which translate into two different types of barriers hindering the successful implementation of digital marketing practices in B2B companies. As mentioned earlier, digital marketing is a young and ever-growing field, but this mainly refers to the B2C sector. In B2B, digital marketing is still in its infancy, and the widespread lack of application experience in B2B digital marketing leads to a lack of expertise and possibly even popularity to attract talent in the field. This lack of expertise within companies means that there are few experts and professionals who understand the mechanics of selling in their respective B2B industries, or specialized experts outside the digital marketing (DM) function who understand the mechanics of the DM function. This leads to the common misconception that DM does not support business strategy and objectives.

The automotive semiconductor industry is no exception in this respect. On the contrary, the industry represents a niche in the digital marketing B2B field where the already scarce pool of digital marketing experts is even more limited. While there are enough experts in the field of digital marketing (from the B2C sector and other B2B industries), the knowledge of these experts can only be used to a limited extent for the DM field in B2B automotive. Specialized knowledge is necessary because, for example, content marketing in the semiconductor and automotive industries is more technical, industry-specific channels and platforms are used, and the lengthy sales process with automotive B2B customers follows completely different rules. As in other industries, this lack of knowledge at the interface between business and the DM function means that DM's contribution to business strategy is unclear and underutilized. To remove this ambiguity and unlock the potential, capabilities are needed to bridge the functional and business issues: On the one hand, these capabilities can help sensitize the business-managing departments (business units) to the opportunities and possibilities of promotions and measures in digital channels, and on the other hand, understanding the business-relevant strategies and possible goals of the business units helps to tailor the right digital measures.

The conclusion is that the pool of possible suitable digital marketers is too small and that it is unlikely to hire the few digital marketers who have exactly the DM skills needed in the automotive industry. Of course, it makes sense to draw on the expertise of digital marketers even if they do not have a specific automotive or semiconductor background. However, in this case, complementary skills are needed

[3]In this section, we do not refer to the above definition of capabilities (see Sect. 1.2.2), which represent the collective ability of an organization to coordinate its functional activities to achieve a competitive advantage. Here, we refer to the lower level of specific marketing-related capabilities required to implement and embed digital marketing activities in an organization. This is also the reason why we deviate from the original term used in the literature of Setkute and Dibb (2022), where authors only refer to capabilities, in order to avoid duplication definition of the term.

such as stakeholder management, which can foster understanding between digital marketers and business units, and analysts who can express the DM's contribution to strategy and goals in numbers.

3.1.3 Availability of Resources

Another element that hinders the digital marketing area in B2B companies is the availability of resources, namely, time, money, and manpower. Järvinen et al. (2012) describe that it is common and preferred in the B2B sector to allocate resources to traditional marketing areas, and that in the case of allocating resources to the digital marketing areas, they are regularly overloaded and overused.

Although Infineon is a large company with a global workforce, the company strives to use resources efficiently and sustainably. Accordingly, resources are dedicated to maintaining core marketing processes, such as analyzing revenue and profit trends, developing growth businesses, and more.

To overcome this barrier of lack of resource availability, it is necessary to leverage marketing resources from other traditional areas. This also means identifying short-term overlaps with strategies and objectives, such as product launch strategies, to create shared resource strategies and resolve any resource shortage as well as creating integrated processes between traditional and digital marketing.

3.1.4 Organization Structure

The organizational structure presents further barriers to the B2B digital marketing function. These barriers are, on the one hand, the misalignment of professional purchasing with the digital marketing approach and, on the other hand, organizational complexity. The disconnect between the DM function and the purchasing process stems from the multitude of interactions customers have with companies, which often require experts to manage them. In a B2B environment, managing the different types of interactions across a variety of organizational levels and people involved in the communication processes adds further complexities (Setkute & Dibb, 2022).

At Infineon Automotive, the barrier of the misalignment of the customer purchasing process and the DM approach also exists, and the cause is the experience gap of employees at the interface between the automotive semiconductor industry and the DM function described earlier. The second barrier of organizational complexity relates not only to the knowledge gap between departments, but also to the fact that departments are not organized in a uniform manner and communication must be coordinated across multiple levels.

These barriers, which are caused by the clearly delineated and small-scale responsibilities within a large organization and the frictional losses in coordination communication, can only be overcome by developing a DM strategy that is oriented to higher-level strategies of the overall automotive area. This DM strategy must then contain information on value-adding types of interactions to which DM contributes, directly and indirectly, to higher-level automotive objectives and clearly measurable metrics and targets.

3.1.5 Product

The product itself is the final internal influencer that sets up barriers to B2B digital marketing. In particular, the nature of the product (service or product) or its characteristics have a critical impact on B2B marketing. B2B products tend to be more complex and require more time to develop. In addition, today's sales and marketing activities place more emphasis on physical performance and personal selling than consumer goods, where psychological attributes and advertising are critical to success (Urban & Hauser, 1980).

In our company, we are aware of the unique characteristics of the automotive semiconductor industry, such as the long development cycles and focus on product performance and features, as well as the complex products, which require marketing communications and customer engagement to take place at a more technical level than in other industries or B2C segments. This fact is also reinforced by the specific technical requirements of the automotive industry, such as automotive quality requirements and the size of the portfolio of sensors, microcontrollers, memories, and power electronics.

In our industry, we need to exploit know-how for technical communication to promote a product. We need to meet customers' information needs through knowledge-rich content and accuracy in delivery, but we also need to explore where (in which channel) we best promote what content, what simplification of approach and abstraction in channels is sufficient to grow or further penetrate the existing customer base.

3.2 External Factors

3.2.1 Customers

The first and certainly most important (external) factor in any company is the customer, because all DM activities must ultimately serve the customer and must not be an end in themselves. The challenge, however, is to understand the various prevailing B2B customer characteristics that arise from questions such as the following: Where is the customer located in the supply chain, is he served directly or indirectly in the supply chain? What value does he place on the business relationship? What are the customer's information needs? What affinity do customers have for digital media? How many key customers have an influence on the company's business? Only companies that master these various characteristics while being able to scale their marketing efforts will be able to realize the full potential of DM.

It is indeed a challenge for Infineon Automotive to identify the right characteristics of target customers, especially because we are dealing with large customers that are not necessarily monolithic or homogeneous and whose workforce therefore has different behaviors and information needs. From empirical data, we can see that there are companies that have a greater affinity for Infineon's digital offerings and platforms. In addition, we also need to differentiate the importance of these customers, as there are existing, profitable, and growing customers that are more strategically relevant than others. We do not want to overload them with irrelevant and excessive information so as not to strain our existing long-term omnichannel relationships. Customers know their needs very well and usually evaluate the various alternatives objectively.

To deal with this effectively and overcome the customer inhomogeneity, we explore buyer personas which represent behaviors and features of typical customer individuals and that can be found in different companies. Additionaly, we continuously explore all relevant touchpoints where customers interact to satisfy their information needs in the design-in process. In this way, we detach ourselves from the customer's firm and at the same time are able to personalize the experience we can offer customers digitally, regardless of their size.

3.2.2 Competitive Presssure

Setkute and Dibb (2022) describe competitive pressure as the overall competitive dynamics caused by changes and shifts in the competitive landscape. Whether B2B competitive pressure has a positive or negative impact on digital marketing depends on whether a company is complacent, eager, combative, or weak, which in turn depends on the company's efficiency level (Boone, 2000).

Although efficiency levels in the semiconductor industry have increased continuously over the years, competitive pressures in the industry vary widely depending on the immediate market environment and the dynamics therein (Bauer et al., 2020). Infineon, although a leader in the automotive semiconductor market (Infineon Technologies AG, 2021), has had to contend with extreme dynamics in recent years, first with the Covid-induced decline in demand (Bauer et al., 2020) and then with the shortage of automotive chips (Burkacky et al., 2022). This volatility complicates digital marketing planning and marketing plans, but at the same time can present an opportunity if DM is positioned as a scalable approach and adaptable marketing model.

Indeed, it is impossible to predict market dynamics and thus to assess whether the market environment is favorable or unfavorable for DM at any given time. However, the investment and support within the company for the DM approach should ideally be continuous and sustainable, but in reality depends on its assumed business contribution. Therefore, the following aspects are important: First, digital marketing is a very transparent field, and benchmark data from direct and indirect competitors (e.g., by monitoring social media reach, or through online traffic monitoring tools) is readily available. This data should be used to show how competitors and other companies are using DM successfully. Second, it is important to highlight the DM's contribution to competitiveness by showing how digital customer engagement activities resonate with customers, in terms of metrics that matter to the business (e.g., lead-to-sale conversion rate, size of sales opportunities).

3.2.3 Operating Environment

The operating environment refers to industry and market characteristics, including market structure, and their impact on the company within its operational context. B2B markets can be similar to B2C markets in that they can be local and global, but markets in both areas differ significantly in their transaction volume and target audience.

Our operating environment influences the DM approach of Infineon Automotive in many ways. As a globally operating company, we need to also be able to address local and regional specifics in terms of digital marketing measures. This includes understanding local specifics such as the channels used, their use by users, as well as the competitive situation on a regional level. For example, in China the social media app WeChat has permeated everyday life with various functions. Unlike other global social media platforms, WeChat offers several additional features for businesses and individuals beyond messaging, such as payment or customer services, which you should consider if you want to do business successfully in this market.

Exploring these local and regional channels and specifics, which we then use to meet customer needs, is one pillar of leveraging our global presence; the other is building a distributed global organization. This globally distributed DM organization has the task of understanding precisely these specifics, but aligning them with the globally applicable DM strategy.

3.2.4 Wider Trading Environment

The final external influencing factor of the wider trading environment refers to contractual matters, information security, and confidentiality. Contractual issues that ensure a company's confidentiality and information security relate to the fact that legal issues can become challenging for the free disclosure of product or business information and thus limit the usability of DM approaches and platforms (Jussila et al., 2014).

With the development of advanced (automotive) technologies and applications in confidentiality areas, more and more semiconductor companies are recognizing the need for tighter and more systematic control of corporate information (Zhao et al., 2015). This seems to be at odds with digital marketing and marketing communication activities, which are all about getting as much information out to as many customers as possible at the right time and through the right channel to provide value to customers.

But this is actually only a contradiction in theory, because by selectively focusing on appropriate communication topics and focusing on scalability of communication (e.g., provisioning content suitable for one-to-many communication), this contradiction can easily be resolved for communication with customers.

4 Ambidextrous Design Guidelines for Digital Marketing

After describing the influencing factors and barriers of digital marketing in the semiconductor market and deriving the results in Sect. 1.3, this section synthesizes the findings into clusters to formulate the design guidelines. Figure 4 shows the synthesis of the findings listed in Tables 1 and 2 into new clusters. Substantively related findings are often at different ends of the continuum between exploration and

Fig. 4 Summary of six ambidextrous design guidelines

Table 1 Internal impact factors for DM adapted based on the work from Setkute and Dibb (2022)

Factor Int. Factor	Barriers	Code	Take-away
Business Culture	• Focus on personal selling • Focus on complex relationships • Culture driven by manufacturing/ technology	1.1 1.2 1.3	Exploitation of value-add through personal selling Exploration of value-add through digital selling Exploitation of technical know-how for content
Capability	• Lack of digital know-how • Misconception of DMs lack in contribution	2.1 2.2	Exploitation of digital marketing skills Exploration of analytical and stakeholder management
Ressources	• Allocation of resources to trad. marketing	3.1 3.2	Exploitation of traditional marketing resources Exploration of common strategies and goals
Organization Structure	• Organizational complexity • Misalignment of professional purchasing with DM approach	4.1 4.2 4.3	Exploitation of business strategy Exploration of DM strategy Exploration of a DM Target framework
Product	• Product types • Products characteristics • Complex products	5.1 5.2 5.3	Exploration of simplification areas Exploration of channel communication for technical content Exploitation of technical know-how and accuracy

Table 2 External impact factors for DM adapted based on the work from Setkute and Dibb (2022)

Factor Ext. Factor	Barriers	Code	Take-away
Customer	• Customer characteristics • Digital affinity of customers • Long, complex buying process • Highly knowledgeable customers • Fewer but more significant customers	6.1	Exploration of buyer personas and touchpoints
Competitive Pressure	• Competitive pressure	7.1 7.2	Exploitation of accessible data Exploration of target model in line with strategy
Operating Environment	• Market characteristics • Industry/sector characteristics • Significant economic impact • Fragmented market structure	8.1 8.2	Exploration of local characteristics Exploitation of the scale a global organization
Wider Trading Environment	• Legal contracts • Information security • Confidentiality	9.1 9.2	Exploitation of suitable communication topics Exploration of suitable and scalable topics

exploitation. The 6 design guidelines describe how these should nevertheless be reconciled and how supposed contradictions are resolved.

4.1 Still Start with "Why"[4]

For some, the idea of starting with the "why," which originates from popular mainstream literature theory, may be familiar or even worn out; for others it is new and fascinating. Regardless of how the concept is perceived, the idea of emphasizing purpose at the beginning of any change is still valid. Even in the current context, where a group of relevant stakeholders needs to be won over to innovative approaches in digital marketing, they are more easily mobilized if they can understand the normative elements of the purpose (the "why"), the motives, and the strategic goals. However, the challenge in large organizations is often that these normative elements are often different for different stakeholder groups, such as business unit technical content providers, tactical digital marketing, or traditional marketing resources. Therefore, it makes sense to create a comprehensive big picture that includes all overarching frameworks and processes, such as an exploratory digital marketing strategy that exploits all relevant aspects of the business strategy that are important for the relevant stakeholder groups. This picture should also be aligned with a digital customer view (buyer persona) in terms of usage, as this is the key stakeholder for purpose and underpinned by a target measurement construct. The clearer this bigger picture connects the different strategic perspectives of all stakeholders, the easier it is to identify the common "why," derive concrete goals, and measure them.

4.2 If it Counts, Count it

It is precisely this construct for measuring performance management that is crucial for engaging all stakeholders and supporting them through digital marketing activities. Therefore, it is important that certain criteria are met for a suitable performance measurement framework. First, it must relate to the business strategy; second, it must be understandable to stakeholders who are not part or experts of DM field; and third, it must reflect the purpose of digital marketing. In theory, these criteria seem easy to meet, but in practice, you often see measurement constructs that are too granular and more appropriate for DM experts to evaluate a specific measure (e.g., open rates to assess a newsletter performance) and therefore not suitable for this purpose. It is also important to realize that there is a huge amount and variety of data in the digital space, as each digital user of a platform leaves behind multiple to countless data. For this reason, people often fall back on existing business intelligence solutions from platform providers (e.g., Google Analytics). However, this is exactly where the danger exists that one measures and optimizes the existing and easily accessible data and not the data that determines the success of the strategy

[4]The idea is based on the work of Simon Sinek (2009) who argues that if we want to mobilize resources for innovations, leaders should start with why and particularly communicating an idea's purpose.

implementation. For this reason, one is well advised to follow the sequence of identifying relevant and influenceable elements of the business strategy, conceptualizing the DM strategy, operationalizing it in terms of measurability, and working with a data analyst to develop a business intelligence concept that is descriptive in nature, easily understood by key stakeholders, and enriched with publicly available benchmarks to place the construct in its competitive context. Measurement constructs should also be developed successively for subject matter experts and for detailed evaluation of individual measures, but only if they contribute to the overall measurement construct in the context of the DM strategy.

4.3 Are you Still Looking for DM Skills? Rethink

Clearly, relying on digital marketing talents is paramount for the success in the field, even if the people who have it have little or no experience in B2B or the semiconductor industry. DM professionals, covering a very broad spectrum of expertise, understand the technical DM context, they understand the proper purpose-driven use of a POEM channel strategy,[5] and they have at least a vague understanding of success measurements and benchmarks. What employees with DM experience often and most likely lack is experience of how a typical customer relationship and traditional buying mechanisms work in the automotive semiconductor industry, they lack an understanding of the relevant buyer personas and target groups, and from experience they invariably lack an analytical understanding that goes beyond business intelligence and the interpretation of simple descriptive statistics. However, even profiles with these capabilities are not yet sufficient, as an ideal profile also requires sufficient stakeholder and change management experience and expertise to cover the semiconductor purchasing process, strategic and process-related issues, and the customer perspective of internal knowledge holders. Of course, the ideal candidate doesn't usually exist, and so this challenge can only be solved through a balanced team composition that emphasizes stakeholder management, analytical skills, and digital marketing expertise in equal measure. As if that were not enough, the team must also function well among themselves. This means that the talent must bring an even more important prerequisite: The most important ingredient is still the willingness and openness to work and learn together in such a diverse team with different experiences. From our experience, we do not see this willingness and open-mindedness as an additional requirement, but rather as a necessary quality of team members that allows us to make sacrifices in subject-related skills.

[5]The PEOM strategy refers to a balanced and targeted mix of paid, owned, and earned media that a company uses for its digital marketing efforts (Lovett & Staelin, 2016).

4.4 Detach Yourself from Customers to Ultimately Serve Them

A not inconsiderable proportion of internal requests for digital marketing support relate to tasks that do not have an intention to scale, but a pure digitalization intention. The latter are requests that aim to digitalization customer communication with one or a very limited group of customers, while tasks with scaling intent pursue the goal of reaching or addressing as many customers as possible. For precisely this scaling, it is necessary to break away from customers and identify types of people across companies who have an affinity for digital platforms and digital offerings. Describing these people with characteristics, traits, and behaviors of different market segments that are relevant to the companies is called buyer personas (Revella, 2015). The buyer persona analysis ensures the scalability of measures by targeting a class of relevant people, even if they are active in different companies. Another important tool for addressing and fulfilling customer value is the development of a generic customer journey, which helps to show the purpose and stage the customer is at in the buying process, with typical touchpoints (Ludwig et al., 2017). With both concepts, it is possible to address a customer type at one or more stages of the customer journey. This scalability decouples digital marketing from the customer and frees up resources to serve a variety of users. While this use essentially relates to digital marketing resources, it also helps to free up unnecessarily tied-up resources from traditional or technical marketing or from areas that can be used elsewhere.

4.5 Be Omnipresent without Being Present Everywhere

Developing the buyer persona in conjunction with the customer journey shows how customers behave during their digital interactions and ensures that personalization can be applied in addition to the scalability of the approach. To do this, it is important to understand the key touchpoints and, in particular, how the relevant information needs of users are met by analyzing the touchpoints in detail, including the type of content (technical or informational) and format (e.g., whitepapers, webinars, promotional videos, posts). This is the foundation for an omnichannel marketing strategy that aims to create seamless, effortless, and high-quality customer experiences within and across channels (Bianchi et al., 2016). It's important to work with both exploring digital channels and exploiting in-person selling. Only then will the right omnichannel approach enable customers to move further down the sales funnel and have a more positive customer experience. Especially in the context of an omnichannel marketing strategy, there may be global differences in the use of different channels (e.g., WeChat in China) as well as the affinity to the digital medium (e.g., Japan with high value on the relationship level (Schaede, 1995)). Therefore, it is important to develop a standardized global digital marketing campaign and customer engagement approach involving a global organization and regional experts who can design and ultimately implement a regional strategy. Standards must include the use of specific tools such as personas, customer journeys, predefined metrics of the measurement framework, and objectives that highlight the contribution of campaigns to the big picture and DM strategy. In this way, a globally standardized marketing approach can be ensured that allows for regional flexibility, enabling the greatest possible global reach with the greatest local impact.

4.6 Create Content that Builds Relationship

Good content is anything that adds value to solving a customer problem. In the automotive semiconductor industry, the first challenge for the customer is often technical. The commercial aspect is also of great importance, but only arises if there is a technically suitable product or the skills to develop it. The marketing content (digital or traditional) must therefore answer, for example, the question of how to develop the right, reliable product with little effort and at low cost. This can be achieved through an appropriate content strategy. This in turn must be connected to the big picture and contain the company's core messages and missions. In addition, the buyer personas need to be linked to the customer journey to identify the right content for the persona, in the channel, and at each stage. Benchmark numbers for typical performance must also be defined to set performance expectations for content. Most importantly, the guidelines define individual pieces of content (e.g. webinars, blogposts, white papers) that meet specific information needs. It should be noted that there are formats that require a lot of technical depth and knowledge. Other formats require simplification, depending on the stage and persona.

Figure 4 shows a summary of all design guidelines related to the two ambidexterity stances.

5 Summary

In this chapter, we have presented design guidelines for the successful implementation of DM in the semiconductor industry. To this end, we described the context of the B2B industry in terms of internal and external factors. These nine factors were so general, but at the same time so precise, that they provided a framework for transferring them to the automotive semiconductor industry. From these, we derived the barriers to DM in our context and a set of insights from which we formulated the six design guidelines.

Because digital marketing is a young but innovative field that requires adaptability, and meets an established industry in a large company that requires a lot of alignment, these guidelines are in an area of tension that requires ambidextrous skills to leverage this tension as a source of competitive advantage.

The implication for managers is that they have to build both ambidextrous capabilities (higher-level capabilities) of the organization and ambidextrous skills (lower-level capabilities) of employees. This means challenging the status quo of the organization while continuously improving it at the organizational and professional levels.

The limitations of this article are that it relates to Infineon Automotive and is therefore, at best, a single case study. In a different context (e.g., a possibly differentiated corporate culture), parts of the above guidelines may therefore need to be adapted to the specific barriers (e.g., the implication of the prevailing culture). Furthermore, the individual guidelines only describe what fields of action are; the design of the fields of action requires a comprehensive description of the concepts, the respective environment, and the relationships between these elements (e.g., performance measurement framework: which KPIs are measured based on which data collection methods).

References

Avlonitis, G. J., & Karayanni, D. A. (2000). The impact of internet use on business-to-business marketing: Examples from American and European companies. *Industrial Marketing Management, 29*(5), 441–459.

Bauer, H., Burkacky, O., Kenevan, P., Mahindroo, A., & Patel, M. (2020, April). *Coronavirus: Implications for the semiconductor industry*. McKinsey & Company.

Bianchi, R., Cermak, M., & Dusek, O. (2016). *More than digital plus traditional: A truly omnichannel customer experience*. McKinsey Insights.

Birkinshaw, J., & Gibson, C. (2004). Building an ambidextrous organization. *MIT Sloan Management Review, 45*(4), 47–55.

Boone, J. (2000). Competitive pressure: The effects on investments in product and process innovation. *The Rand Journal of Economics, 31*, 549–569.

Brink, T. (2017). B2B SME management of antecedents to the application of social media. *Industrial Marketing Management, 64*, 57–65.

Burkacky, O., Deichmann, J., Pfingstag, P., & Werra, J. (2022, June). *Semiconductor shortage: How the automotive industry can succeed*. McKinsey & Company.

Coviello, N. E., & Brodie, R. J. (2001). Contemporary marketing practices of consumer and business-to-business firms: How different are they? *Journal of Business & Industrial Marketing, 16*, 382.

Day, G. S. (1994). The capabilities of market-driven organizations. *Journal of Marketing, 58*(4), 37–52.

Duwe, J. (2021). *Ambidextrous leadership: How leaders unlock innovation through ambidexterity*. Springer.

Grönroos, C. (1997). Value-driven relational marketing: From products to resources and competencies. *Journal of Marketing Management, 13*(5), 407–419.

He, P., Pei, Y., Lin, C., & Ye, D. (2021). Ambidextrous marketing capabilities, exploratory and exploitative market-based innovation, and innovation performance: An empirical study on China's manufacturing sector. *Sustainability, 13*(3), 1146.

Infineon Technologies AG, I. R., Accounting, Consolidation &. Reporting. (2021). *Annual Report 2021* (pp. 1–249) [Annual Report]. Infineon Technologies AG. https://www.infineon.com/dgdl/Infineon+Annual+Report+2021.pdf?fileId=8ac78c8b7d507352017d622b5bfb0161

Järvinen, J., Tollinen, A., Karjaluoto, H., & Jayawardhena, C. (2012). Digital and social media marketing usage in B2B industrial section. *Marketing Management Journal, 22*(2), 102.

Jussila, J. J., Kärkkäinen, H., & Aramo-Immonen, H. (2014). Social media utilization in business-to-business relationships of technology industry firms. *Computers in Human Behavior, 30*, 606–613.

Karjaluoto, H., Mustonen, N., & Ulkuniemi, P. (2015). The role of digital channels in industrial marketing communications. *Journal of Business & Industrial Marketing, 30*, 703.

Kim, K. H., & Moon, H. (2021). Innovative digital marketing management in B2B markets. In *Industrial marketing management* (Vol. 95, pp. 1–4). Elsevier.

Leeflang, P. S., Verhoef, P. C., Dahlström, P., & Freundt, T. (2014). Challenges and solutions for marketing in a digital era. *European Management Journal, 32*(1), 1–12.

Leek, S., Houghton, D., & Canning, L. (2019). Twitter and behavioral engagement in the healthcare sector: An examination of product and service companies. *Industrial Marketing Management, 81*, 115–129.

Lovett, M. J., & Staelin, R. (2016). The role of paid, earned, and owned media in building entertainment brands: Reminding, informing, and enhancing enjoyment. *Marketing Science, 35*(1), 142–157.

Low, S., Ullah, F., Shirowzhan, S., Sepasgozar, S. M., & Lin Lee, C. (2020). Smart digital marketing capabilities for sustainable property development: A case of Malaysia. *Sustainability, 12*(13), 5402.

Ludwig, T., Wang, X., Kotthaus, C., Harhues, S., & Pipek, V. (2017). User narratives in experience design for a B2B customer journey mapping. *Mensch Und Computer 2017-Tagungsband.*

O Reilly, C. A., & Tushman, M. L. (2004). The ambidextrous organization. *Harvard Business Review, 82*(4), 74–83.

Revella, A. (2015). *Buyer personas: How to gain insight into your customer's expectations, align your marketing strategies, and win more business*. Wiley.

Schaede, U. (1995). The "old boy" network and government-business relationships in Japan. *Journal of Japanese Studies, 21*(2), 293–317.

Setkute, J., & Dibb, S. (2022). "Old boys' club": Barriers to digital marketing in small B2B firms. *Industrial Marketing Management, 102*, 266–279.

Sinek, S. (2009). *Start with why: How great leaders inspire everyone to take action*. Penguin.

Tariq, E., Alshurideh, M., Akour, I., & Al-Hawary, S. (2022). The effect of digital marketing capabilities on organizational ambidexterity of the information technology sector. *International Journal of Data and Network Science, 6*(2), 401–408.

Urban, G. L., & Hauser, J. R. (1980). *Design and marketing of new products*. Prentice Hall.

Zhao, S., Zhu, S., & Guo, S. (2015). The information security in semiconductor industry. In: *2015 IEEE international conference on industrial engineering and engineering management (IEEM)*, pp. 1782–1785.

Part II

Deep Dives into Organizational Design, Strategy and Operations as Well as Target Model Implementation

A Practical Guide to Setting and Achieving Digital Marketing Goals Following a Plan-Do-Check-Act Approach

Theo Göpfert, Kati Zieger, and Uli Schneider

1 Introduction

Similar to how they are valuable in many other fields, the words of Austrian Management author Peter Drucker in *The Frontiers of Management* (Drucker, 1986) serve also as a guiding beacon in the field of digital marketing: "you can't manage, what you can't measure." This mindset convoluted with us defining marketing performance management (Järvinen & Karjaluoto, 2015) in the context of the automotive semiconductor company Infineon Technologies motivated by a target model which will be described in the following chapter. To this end, the methodology of quantifying the improvements by setting up a basic digital marketing success measurement framework will be described using the plan-do-check-act framework (Fig. 1) in line with Shewhart (1939).

During the pandemic situation in the beginning of 2020, we could identify an increasing usage of offerings on our company's webpage. Despite that, the digital marketing activities to provide the visitors relevant content with the aim leading to unique and valuable on-site experience have still been driven by people: the digital marketing team. Challenges arose, due to expectations to scale, where the call after support of automation grew louder within the company. With automation in this context, marketing automation is meant, which Bagshaw (2015) describes as the "use of software to automate marketing processes [. . .] with far less human resource and at much lower costs." In some committees efficiently using this kind of automation was seen as long overdue to keep and improve the position against competition. We experienced that initiating this change did not take place from one day to the other.

T. Göpfert (✉) · K. Zieger · U. Schneider
Infineon Technologies AG, Neubiberg, Germany
e-mail: Theo.Goepfert@infineon.com; Kati.Zieger@infineon.com; Uli.Schneider@infineon.com

U. Schneider, J. Hoika (eds.), *Digital Marketing in the Automotive Electronics Industry*, Management for Professionals,
https://doi.org/10.1007/978-3-031-30720-1_5

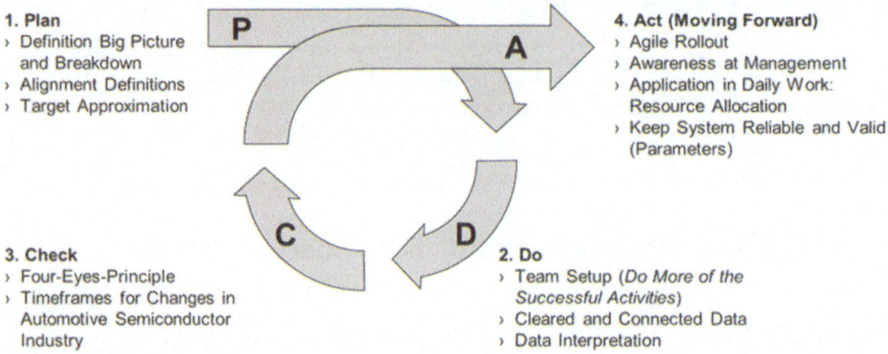

Fig. 1 Moving forward along PDCA cycle framework to create a success measurement framework

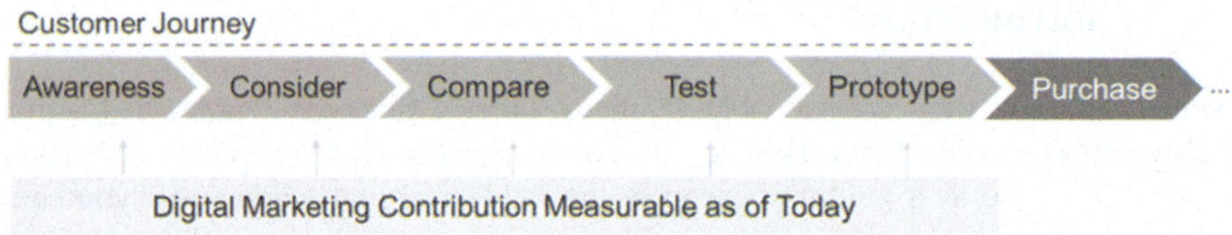

Fig. 2 Infineon's representation of a customer journey and a general mapping of digital marketing activities

In the environment of semiconductor automotive industry, we experienced every day that timeframes of a quarter to half a decade are no exceptions – starting from development cycles of products, over designing-in evaluation cycles of products in customers' projects, to long-term agreements regarding pricing. The planning cycles for digital marketing activities in contradiction where shorter, but before the target operating model was developed and applied, an annual planning cycle was the reality. Also, the development and the change to bring the digital marketing team up to speed to make at least use of the success measurement framework in a manual manner was planned for two digital marketing planning cycles.

To come back to marketing automation: Our approach was that only the right actions can be automated when it is clear what we consider to be the right actions. To make sure that the automotive division's vision and mission are reflected in the digital marketing team's doings, the strategy to contribute, but also make it measurable, was broken down as "reach and convert." Therefore, the mental picture of stepping in the shoes of a potential customer, where this individual is sequentially getting more and more engaged with the company's offerings, is depicted in Infineon's representation of a customer journey (Blomkvist et al., 2010, Fig. 2). Conversion in the sense of being measured by the success measurement framework can be understood as identifying from the set of unknown individuals we see on our webpage the most relevant buyer personas among roles of employees of our customers (Revella, 2015) to further play on them and anticipate their interests and next steps.

To implement the strategy, the whole set of digital marketing doings we started with consists out of single external and internal firm-initiated activities (Dash et al., 2021), which one could either cluster in campaigns or other names for the work-packages, which in sum result in the execution of the strategy. The way the word campaign is understood at Infineon is as an umbrella of activities, broken down into its individual aspects: search engine advertising (SEA), mailing or social media posts, where the company pays for the execution, as well as internal activities like creating the content, which is shared via different channels. There are also activities existing, which have more an indirect or lagging influence, which is also subject to policies of organic search machines like search engine optimization (SEO). The mental picture is that each activity is contributing to one or more stages pushing the customer further in the customer journey.

We will see later, that for us giving these activities (everything that creates costs regarding money or time for the company) a digitalized structure was key to implement the success measurement framework as a model to describe how to achieve digital marketing goals. For such an instrument, also the direct connection to each responsible was seen as valuable input; since not all team members are in the management group, the execution group was represented, as well. The activities mentioned are leading to results, which are measured by the success measurement framework. Slicing the results actually is a multi-dimensional matrix. The four measuring points, which are introduced in this chapter to start describing the customer journey, are only the first dimension. The optimization methodology is universal. Drilling along the roles and activities in the digital marketing (team) is an additional dimension, as well as the company's organizational structure and the online presence structure with the content provided there.

The digital marketing environment is an often used example to describe the difference between output, e.g., the (amount of) content published on the web, and the outcome, how the influenced person (potential customer) is reacting (Lobacher & Jacob, 2020). The activities ranked by the outcome, as preparation for the business impact, describe the reporting approach of thinking in descending sorted lists. That's why Pareto's basic principle was one of the main concepts for the manual approach, which we have colloquially named as "do more of the successful activities" mindset. With this approach, the perception is that the involved digital marketing team is able to quantify the individual contribution, which sums up the overall direction to move forward.

2 Plan

As indicated before, the chosen digital marketing strategy "reach and convert" is not focusing on taking a look into impressions shown on searching machines, or clicks and on-site activities on the company's homepage. Behind every click, there is a person working for a company – a potential contact working on our customers' projects. What do we know regarding this person? What can we do to learn more regarding this individual? And where can we identify levers to bind this one to our company? The framework we have in mind is starting from the basic economic principle of a maximal principle. We only have limited resources regarding budget and especially time of the executing specialists, so there is a need to allocate this budget in a way that it optimizes the result (Eichhorn & Merk, 2015). How we measure the result and describe the possible activities within the budget will be described in more detail later.

2.1 Target Operating Model

Furthermore, the approach with a target operating model by setting ambitious targets and knowing that without a global success measurement framework as single source of truth in place, the targets won't be achieved, was the team's motivational basis to create a sense of urgency for focusing to get better and reach the targets. In terms of measuring, describing, executing, and integrating digital marketing activities, we interpreted "better" in this case to mean "different" from how it was previously done.

An often-experienced expectation, on management level, as well as on working level, is to find an easy connection from digital marketing activities, or even on-site activities, to materialized revenue. Having this as end in mind helped us to benchmark the department's contribution to the corporate strategy. But what we experienced also from data-driven point of view, why various groups within the company have failed, when they wanted to connect digital touchpoints with turnover, was that measuring points being too far away from each other were tried to be connected and the various paths from a to b consisted out of too many unforeseen detours like customer granularities. So, starting from the digitalize-able end, namely, customer projects, and identifying possibly some success stories (the one business out of one thousand, which we can link to digital activities in maximum half-digitalized ecosystem), we have had in the back of our mind. But the lever is in this chapter on measuring the digital activities and describing the discoveries along the funnel of materialization: In the automotive semiconductor industry, starting point for the digital marketing team was slicing the big picture from awareness to qualified contacts, who the respective responsible sales community can further work on and which then later can materialize into business opportunities (customer project pipeline digitalized), which might in the latter lead to quotes, orders, and finally revenue.

What is also meant with the big picture is taking a step back and viewing the overall result from bird's eye view: the sum of all results which we see. And when we drill down, which share are we further evaluating? We esteemed this feedback loop to not get lost in evaluating details, which did not have a lever. Moreover, while developing the model we described success in terms of: to become confident, that we can say, we are on the right track.

With the word result, we mean the pure numbers in terms of fulfillment, independent on what they were triggered by. The result view was seen as worthless, in case the team was not able to describe, what triggered the results: What was executed? How can we then improve with a best-in-class mindset? We could sharpen the understanding that even a structured set of slides is not sufficient to describe what activities are performed and how they are to be described. Digitalization in the field of describing the activities in a digital tabular way was identified as key to apply the target operating model, even though it was a challenge, because it meant change not only in the digital marketing team's behavior. Such a transition was not seen as only to be done by assisting functions too far away from the business context like information technology (Hunsberger, 2017).

With what was described so far, the only need was to have a manager in place, who can map basic economic principles in a performance management environment. The manager afterwards decided that on the digital marketing context content-wise experts were required to bring the activities and the expected outcomes together. And in the very end, the team was enriched by data experts. The content-wise expert team's understanding was that not each activity will perform strong on every outcome. Digital marketing experts brought in their expertise, which types of activities are existing and what the theory says that they are good at, seen from their academic background. The approach was to bring experts from campaign management and execution, from marketing communications regarding content to publish on the website, as well as website experts together. This was seen to ensure that the relevant involved parties along the digital marketing processes in a stock listed company gave their inputs and it fitted to the possibilities a digital marketing team – who are no experts on the complex products – had.

The company's central sales and marketing supporting function for various business models communicated that a generic digital success measurement framework adds value. The number of possible touchpoints along the customer journey was broken down by the described committee of content-wise experts for the automotive section within the company, since the automotive business in the company is perceived with particularly long design-in cycles and long-lasting deep customer relationships (Burkacky et al., 2022). As stated, there was practical confidence on the one hand side that the relevant touchpoints are measured, but on the other hand side that the overview was not lost, such that only a hand full of KPIs were considered.

To retrieve, the basis was the customer journey from awareness to sales. The following describes the simplification along this framework, how the expert committee broke it down. Within the marketing aspect of leveraging the number of contacts to further play on, we defined the starting point as the amount of suspects we see on-site (KPI 1), who open up the funnel. The pure number of suspects, who are leaving their touchpoints on-site, is relatively high. But we know much more about the subset, which is quantified by the number of newly registered contacts in our contact data base (KPI 3). Last but not least, the number of qualified contacts was seen as relevant to describe the development of the amount of these persons to potentially follow up on (KPI 4). To enhance the knowledge regarding these individuals, it was seen valuable to describe their interactions, on suspect level, via

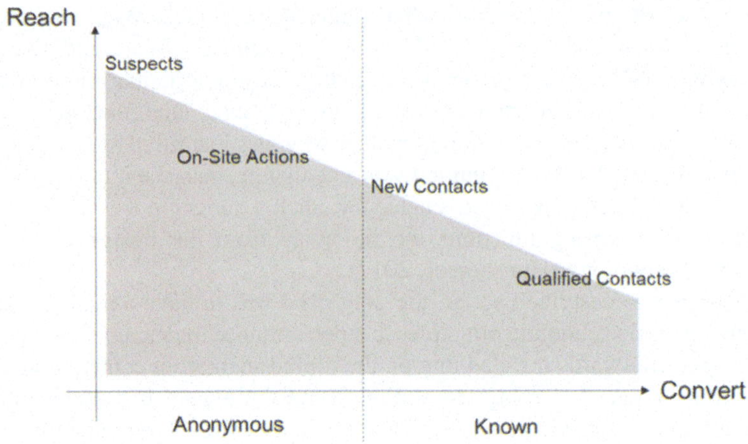

Fig. 3 Digital strategy "reach and convert" with the measures mapped in a funnel

the number of relevant on-side actions (due to a good mapping of content and their relevance for the business – KPI 2).

The relevant target group of digital marketing was defined as focusing on engineers, who check technical specifications, which can be derived from technical documents. For the registered contacts, we directly have the information, which activities have triggered certain behavior, such that we have way more clarity on this smaller set of persons. Although it would have been possible to explore various other touchpoints in more detail, we decided to focus on the ones mentioned as a starting point within the existing reporting ecosystem at that time. This was done to avoid losing sight of the personas and to maintain an overall perspective.

Regarding meaningful and precise definitions, the team was able to align that it was not required to be on the same detail level how definitions are required, e.g., in the academic probability theory. But less interpretation given by the communication of the KPI definition supported the discussions with the stakeholders. No time was lost in bringing the whole organization to the same understanding of the numbers and their statements. To reflect the levers along the overarching "reach and convert" strategy (Fig. 3), we aligned on the definitions for the four already mentioned KPIs in Fig. 4 as a starting point.

With the Automotive division being one part of the entire company and with the existence of central sales and marketing supporting functions, those definitions have been aligned with the central process owners to guarantee consistency top down. Three out of four measures are counting individuals, which are so-called "semi-additive" measures. This means, e.g., one suspect triggered via several digital marketing activities still remains only one person, that we reached. So, we needed to be very careful, when evaluating the result of our activities, to not overestimate the amount of persons, who are interested in our content, by aggregating numbers since their values cannot be directly summed (Bhaskara et al., 2018). That's why we

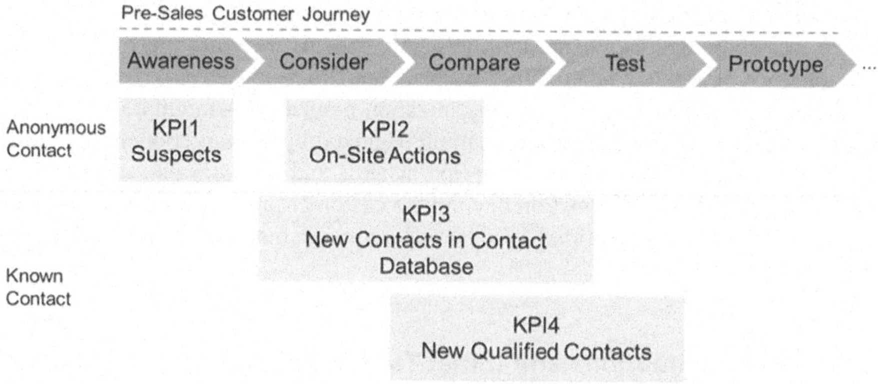

Fig. 4 Starting set of digital marketing KPIs mapped to Infineon's representation of a customer journey. KPI1 – suspects: Unique users and yet unknown individuals traceable/measurable through any kind of on-site activities on the company's website. KPI2 – on-site actions: Number of on-site activities by suspects on the company's website. KPI3 – new contacts from our (potential) customer base: Unique known contacts added to the contact database, identified by their e-mail address, which we are allowed to contact after they have given their consent in accordance to currently valid GDPR. KPI4 – new qualified contacts: Known and "sales-ready" contacts in the contact database, who have indicated a specific interest in our offerings based on a defined lead scoring system

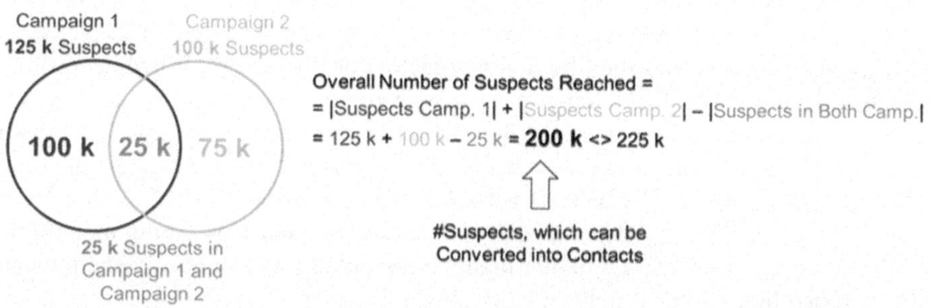

Fig. 5 Example of the semi-additive measure suspects reached by two campaigns with intersection of the suspects

decided when drilling down, the aggregated numbers become invisible because the semi-additive measure cannot be simply summed up across all slicers (Fig. 5).

Despite the technical challenges, the slicing and dicing was seen as the value-add, starting from the big picture and drill down into the details, which can be mapped to individual activities. Clustering the activities and restricting the number of groups to maximum ten and clustering the rest in an "other bucket" was valued by the team as key for the usability of visualizations. Here, we also made the experience that the stakeholder management is important to benchmark the theoretical digital marketing clusters with the importance of certain activities perceived in the marketing community. Considering the case that the data quality is never perfect, we identified that this is an area to get the buy-in by describing the past pragmatically by using lookups. There was some data available, but the required fields were not (yet) filled, due to lack of sense of urgency or a process. Some connections needed to be maintained for a longer time via lookups, until the organization moved. This might be seen as hard manual work, but keeping the end in mind triggered by the target operating model, this was seen as a suitable way to get first insights and get early into the actionable mode. To link further information beyond the customer projects the digitalization of customer interactions supported by sales was required, but elaborating on this is out of scope for this chapter.

2.2 Approximations and Initial Target Setting

What we have described so far was moving away from presentation slides. The buy-in was supported by giving the stakeholders some dashboards, which they can click through. Even though the management intelligence was seen in the economic principle convoluted with the performance management mindset, the described approach was supported by repeating the model on and on, as well as the concrete visualizations, numbers, and actions derived are shared. But how did we come up with a first version of ambitious but realistic targets?

Measured touchpoints and evaluating historic numbers on top level we mentioned. The thought must be allowed, that without performance management in the past, every increase in the numbers must have been either "organic" or depicted the market interest, or was driven by external factors or distractors. When acquiring a competitor and integrating their pages, of course the numbers measuring suspects and on-site activities are increasing. But to remain then on the same level of growth, one would need to acquire every year such a company, which might not sound realistic. So, what we did was taking these external influences out of the long-term rate of increase. The approach was that with setting the focus on "doing more of the successful activities" a target higher than the organic growth can be reached, where the cleansed historic trend defines a first lower boundary.

We have talked about the lower boundary, but how about a realistic upper boundary? Industry standards were taken into consideration. Knowing that in certain industries the absolute amount of contacts might be restricted, especially the amount of valuable contacts was not expected by us to be infinite. The calculation approach can be described with using conversions: three out of four KPIs mentioned are a number of people, where estimated conversions from the industry were used as a feasible indicator, what could be possible. Benchmarking the real numbers against industry standard numbers led to vast deviations in some areas. Of course, a lot of processes along, e.g., the contact qualification or hurdles in the registration process, were the reason for the numbers, which are not showing the expected result. This exercise also led to depicting these situations, but going into more detail is not in scope here.

Nevertheless, the initial targets described were set, due to the boundary conditions, in the middle of the upper and lower boundary. Furthermore, hard numbers have been identified as the more stable increase factors compared to percentage increases. Avoiding percentage increases year over year we decided to use to ensure the understanding that long-term targeting is not modeled as exponential growth with even increasing percentage factors.

We experienced that external factors can make a target a vulnerable instrument, especially, when targets are linked to annual personal targets. It turned out that an open discussion culture (e.g., in team jour-fixes) helped to get the buy-in, since the entire digital marketing organization is dealing with the topic that this change along the motivation triggered by the target operating model needs to be performed. The level of the sum of all campaign-related activities in practices turned out to be a feasible level to check the match of top-down and bottom-up targets, because here each specialist was able to relate to the activities in the own area of responsibility, and yet had the chance to improve the mix of activities for the next planning period.

2.3 From Reporting to Analytics

What has been described so far was an approach for a performance management environment supported with advanced reporting functionalities. But the way to apply the often-used word of analytics is not trivial. We have talked about the performance management mindset and this was key for the entire methodology: This supported us in defining the decision variables to optimize on our KPIs. The lever we have are the activities, so the sentence of "do more of the successful activities" became central. Digitalization was key to describe what happened in terms of digital marketing activities. To the activities, we added the results measured via KPI 1–4 (and, e.g., weighted by the budget used), and we got for the start a four-dimensional model to optimize the decision for successful activities on. This gave us the what (was successful).

But what made these activities successful? The end in mind was, while performing so many activities, which a single person cannot know each of them in detail, that an intelligence supports us in predicting and proposing, how to design the activities and on which activities to focus. Therefore, we needed to be able to learn from the past, in the following subsequent way: describe the activities with as many relevant columns as possible: up to a certain degree, the more information digitalized, which give us insights, how different activities are designed, the more variables an (artificial) intelligence can use to build a model on (Frost, 2013). The criteria to characterize the successful activities were the columns of the second table, which described the activities content wise. This gave us the why (was it successful).

What has been described is deriving insights from quantitative criteria. In addition, we considered it advantageous to leverage knowledge about future trends that may not be evident in the described model. To achieve this, we proposed a collaboration between engineers, who have direct contact with some of the targeted personas, and digital marketing experts, who have a comprehensive view of the digital marketing results and can identify an aligned go-to-market approach. Sharing the digital marketing views already during the development with a larger audience took take time because of the questions, which appeared, but we were able win the technical marketers. Furthermore, we experienced that stakeholders in the organizations pushed into the direction, on which they are incentivized, but what we describe here is the lever of digital marketing activities along the measures the entire automotive division's management was confident with and have been broken down by digital marketing experts.

We stated that as a starting point the currency "valuable contacts" was defined. When joining customer projects' opportunity value or revenue figures, which are not fitting, then the described optimization can lead to diverging results, which might not be optimal in the sense of the digital marketing strategy, measured by the four digital KPIs. But we agreed that a model is nothing, which was stable forever. So, during the cycles, we evolved during a steep learning curve to match those numbers and then improve the optimization model with adding a fifth dimension, since only parameters needed to be recalculated, but the methodology remained the same.

3 Do

After sharing the initial framework and the mindset, we emphasize that we think it is crucial to get the hands dirty and spend the time digging into the numbers and crawling through the data.

3.1 Setup

We thought outsourcing might enable certain other levers. But having significant data insights in the digital marketing team itself supported the approach described. Additionally, this was seen as value-add to get the buy-in from the stakeholders, when questions can be answered by persons with in-detail understanding directly, without stating that we have to get further information and will come back later.

One sentence, which might not like to be heard: data engineering and data cleansing were not the most attractive job. Nevertheless, it needed to be done. Neither could our team perform analytics nor derive information, on which decision can be based on without meaningful, connected data. However, our team did marketing. Even if the data was not perfect (and most likely never will be perfect), implementing methodologies and learning about the approach was something we did not wait for. Especially when the data then was available and not enough time would have been spent to evaluate methodologies, then the result would have been poor.

During the conceptualization phase, the lever became clearer and clearer that the key decision criterion was doing more of the successful activities. And therefore, understanding results, which were derived from the evaluations, needed to be readable. We decided for descending sorted lists, sliced by the digital marketing activities, then sorted by the result measured with the KPIs. This was directly shared and benchmarked with the cross-functional stakeholders from business lines, sales, and also the marketing management. Every employee, who has worked in a central

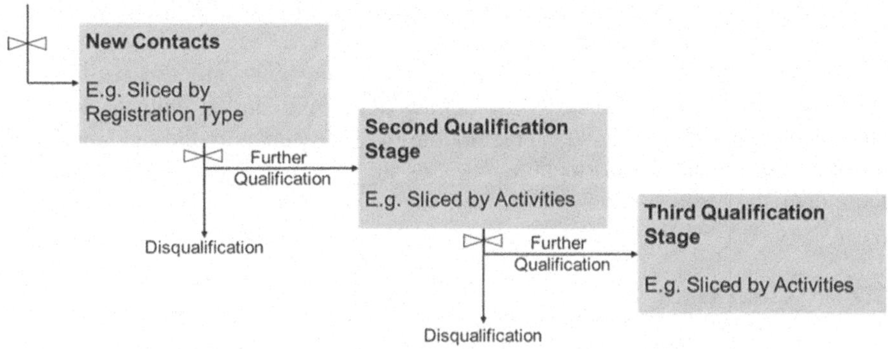

Fig. 6 Contacts stock and flow through lead qualification based on Sterman (2000)

reporting (supporting) function, knows the challenge with reported numbers. There needed to be the one number to be in place, which is the truth within the whole organization. Otherwise there is too much time and energy lost in explaining the number from the own organization's point of view. That's why alignment with the central functions was seen as very important, even though they might have their own agenda. The central function's number was always taken as given after they were aligned and concepts like the semi-additive measures learned by heart, but we were able to slice it down along our expertise and the activities, which we knew in more detail.

We already elaborated on the KPIs. Once we understood the mathematical challenges involved in counting possible contacts with the measures, we were faced with content-related challenges in determining whether we were truly optimizing ourselves on the right touchpoints. One challenge we experienced was the differentiation between registrations and new contacts. After finding out in exchanges with the IT department that a suspect can register more than one time, we had to clarify that we are optimizing along new contacts and the focus is on activities, which lead to real new contacts in our contact data base, and not the amount of registrations button clicks. Because checking the numbers in detail showed us that the amount of registrations and the amount of new contacts behaved differently and thus might have led to totally different conclusions. What also enabled a strong buy-in, especially in the digital marketing team itself, was describing the qualification of contacts in our contact data base by the stock and flows model after John Sterman's *Business Dynamics* (Sterman, 2000): One person at a time can always be only in one status (one bucket). But over the time, one person can be qualified and flows from one bucket to the other one (Fig. 6). Our contact-KPIs were measuring the conversions along those flows.

Another personal requirement to implement what was described was having team members in place, who speak two languages, namely, the business and the IT language. Other departments experienced that without such a translator in place, too much energy and time was wasted, when requirements could not be described properly and just a huge set of requirements was handed over, which was not needed in the end and overloaded the IT department.

We also made the experience that learning along our journey of rolling out the information was not seen as a blocking point. We started with the best that was at the time available. The methodology was seen complicated enough to translate the available information in views along our activities. With more and more data, the results converged to a few statements.

3.2 Clear Data

Thinking from the end in mind was also seen as key for the beginning of the data engineering part. From the very beginning, we focused on having meaningful numbers in place in terms of magnitude. Therefore, sharing the logics with the direct stakeholders, as well as touring through the company's marketing analytics communities supported the minimum four eyes principle for each step of the data blending. What we started with and shared with the organized, after we made sure that no inflated or deflated results are provided, we called "dashboards." But actually, these were small databases within themselves. On the one hand side the complexity in the calculations to reflect the measures supporting the digital strategy did not allow flat lists which can be exported to spreadsheets, and on the other hand side the views provided were required to be broken down for further evaluation to a certain level. The levels we broke down are explained below.

There is an organization existing, and as long as the company is organized and incentivized along a business line structure, we decided that this needs to be reflected in the evaluations, as well. Even though there were and are still challenges to compare two totally different business models, the internal comparison facilitated discussions about digital marketing approaches. This supported the buy-in to spend efforts in digital marketing within the line organizations, because the managers were able to ask, what the other managers were doing different or were setting digital marketing focus, at all.

Additionally, the digital marketing activities are taking place in most of the cases on the company's website. So, identifying the success on different areas of our homepage was seen as key, especially the product structure communicated to the outside world. The combination of the two mentioned dimensions organization hierarchy and homepage hierarchy initially was solved with lookups before implementing the success measurement framework. With the pure number of products, this was identified as one of the few areas, where lookups were not the way to go, when they are not maintained centrally and automatically.

Furthermore, we identified levers and regional specifics are important to be identified in matrix-organization, especially when there are counterparts in the regions, who have a significant autonomy. "What can we learn from regional activities?" and "is in other parts of the world the language a criterion?" appeared as discussed questions and found their way into the evaluations. Filtering was also required along the digital marketing activities, specially to focus in the stakeholder management on the activities for a certain campaign. The activity view will be described in the following paragraph in more detail.

As previously mentioned, campaigns are composed of a collection of activities. Initially structuring campaigns in detail assisted the entire team in comprehending the individual components, such as activity groups, timeframes, and affected webpages. Moreover, breaking campaigns down by their financial implications in terms of expenditures facilitated an additional use case. In a second step, incorporating the KPI results from the previous year allowed for the weighting of individual activities. Now in a third step, the best-in-class activity quantified by the maximal KPI value result per activity group (e.g., from all social media posts) could be identified to know which activities and activity groups have performed best. Using the most successful activities from data point of view also provided us a basis for detailed campaign target setting, which paid into the overall target fulfillment along the target operating model.

We related to the fact that long enough timeframes are required to determine the long-term trend to answer the questions, whether we are on the right track. To be able to fully decompose an economical time-series properly, (Kleijn & van Dijk, 2006) state that four cycles are required for a proper description of the dynamics. However, using on the long-term linear trend worked out as a good starting point, especially, since the journey to implement, roll out, and apply performance management was a more year cycle, in the meantime, the data was collected. Beside business cycles, in the communication we made our stakeholders aware that sometimes a lag appears until an activity unfolds its full potential; SEO was the most often communicated example.

3.3 Connect Data

We had on our mind that the strategy was called "reach and convert" – into possibly interesting contacts. So, making sure that all the measures were in sync meant: reduce the sources to make sure you do not get biased by double counting persons to overestimate certain influences (e.g., one person first on a third party's webpage and later on our own webpage still remains one person to convert into a contact).

For most of the required data, there were already all master data drill downs available in the corporate data warehouse. For the general buy-in and the automation, it helped a lot to use those tables. Therefore, exchanges with employees, who have worked in central reporting of revenue or other figures or in finance before, were seen as a value add. For customer master data, product master data, and even calendared master data in the corporate data warehouse, we did not need to reinvent the wheel. It was even seen as dangerous to have own lookups in place, since organizations changed, especially with the fiscal year changes.

In the digital marketing team in the automotive division, we felt like being caught between the chairs. On the one hand side, departments like IT or central marketing strived for fully end-to-end implemented data pipelines and processes with a first-time-right approach, and we felt the business lines were too far away from the technical and legal challenges. What was described above can be broken down data wise that we are tracking two types of information: the anonymous web activities and the personalized contact information. The full and automated connection of these data sources was a corporate project and was not solved within a division's digital marketing department within 1 year. Taking the audience from the business lines with us on this journey along user stories and pilots was seen as valuable. Furthermore, this also created awareness that the connection with other data points in preparation for a customer data platform was only successful, when the entire organization moved and spent the effort. Therefore, management and their executive assistants were involved right from the beginning. But even in the initial environment with a separated web and contact reporting, one practical challenge our team faced was sticking to the campaign name coding on the activity side and assigning the campaign codes in the results to the result side. To align such coding on result side, a clear understanding that a holistic aggregation is required helped to move different supporting functions to use the same campaign coding, which then helped us a lot.

3.4 Interpret Data

One question that appeared was regarding the explicit users of such views described. The plan was that every team member and executor of digital marketing activities should use it along their use cases. However, we realized, it was the team leads and above who used it first. It was seen as crucial that the overall approach was understood by the operative team members, too, and that questions on benchmarking were allowed. Nevertheless, we experienced that the management support helped to bring the data-driven mindset into the digital marketing organization.

For example, in the business line organizations, who are focusing more and more on digital measures, the question was allowed: Which levers were existing for them? Checking a development of KPIs with clear actionable possibilities to improve the situation was identified as useful, since it supported the roles and responsibilities introduced with the digital marketing departments. The digital marketing teams have been able to identify distorted information, to the benefit or the disadvantage of the organization, which have been communicated and subtracted out. Even with not 100% accurate data, the right group of questions appeared with the insights provided.

A totally different, but possible also worth knowing aspect was the comparison to the recent previous business cycle. An additional value add was seen in the quantifiable amount of contacts reached in the near past and possibly to be reached, when taking a look outside the company and not restricting oneself to internal data only. The success measurements framework's aim was not to model the customers' employee fluctuation but to describe the current state in the market, and providing the sales community insights, which they have not known before and not already digitalized in the customer project funnel.

4 Check

It was seen as helpful to understand the moment, when it made sense to start verifying that the approach described leads to the first results. As stated, we interpreted "better" as "different," and when we experienced that there were really the activities done differently, the whole organization understood the approach of doing more of the successful activities beard fruits. Otherwise, in the past external factors must have been the reason for the different results. Of course, also we experienced that during the manual process of setting the attributes, which described, e.g., the groups of campaign activities, some touchpoints were not set with the correct values or have even been forgotten to be set. This led to a shorter timeframe, where numbers could be evaluated. In some cases, further one-time lookups in the past could be done for corrections, but when a touchpoint was just not set, then there was no chance to link the results.

Again, different results were derived from different activities: In the automotive semiconductor industry, there is a lot of planning done for timeframes, which last several years (Burkacky et al., 2022). Even though the digital marketing activities are set up in shorter cycles, those cycles have also been annual cycles in the past. Planning took time and processes with several stakeholders were established over the entire business division. Regarding the timing challenge depicted, better results based on the approach described could only be expected, when the (annual) planning has been adjusted after learnings of doing more of the successful activities. Regular performance reviews with the digital marketing experts have been established, where the digital marketing approach was not stopping by showing a red, yellow, or green traffic light in terms of target fulfillment, but also pointing to the best-in-class activities to learn from them.

When the success measurement framework was first shared, the time horizon was seen as a foot note. But the 3 years mentioned to establish the success measurement framework and bring the system up to speed became more and more realistic. Even though processes and clear roles and responsibilities have been implemented before, the target operating model approach was shared for the first time. The same behavior was experienced, when taking a first look into the results after the first year. They only showed what we called "organic" growth. Why? We did not do more of the successful activities, because when planning the first year's activities, the team has not been aware, which have been the successful and best-in-class activities. This could only be derived with the lag or agile interventions. So, the understanding, where one is in the cycle, was seen as crucial. An agile mindset might have positively influenced this area, as well (Hunsberger, 2017). We experienced that performance reviews during the planning cycle enabled corrections up to a certain degree during the year.

To mention an additional challenge, which we faced, was that the enablers' systems like search engines also led to additional lags. To unleash the full potential of digital marketing activities, a time-dependent tracking until the big search machines' algorithms started to turn into results, in some areas led to an additional delay of some quarters (Fig. 7).

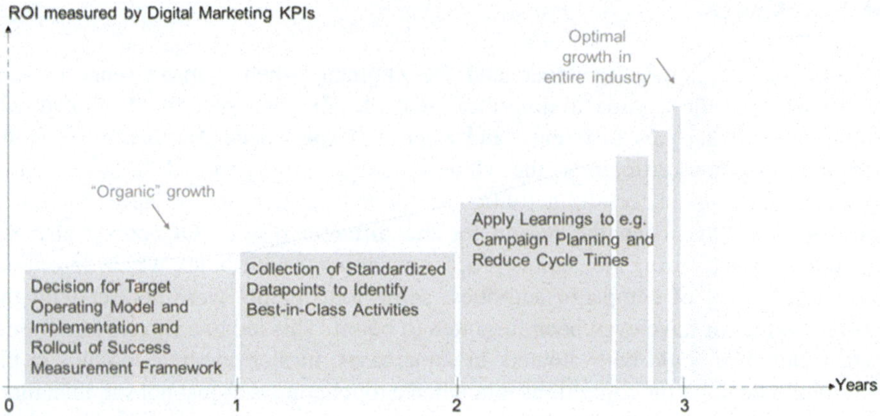

Fig. 7 Implementation of success measurement framework, performance management cycles

5 Act

Once the first success stories could be provided, the entire organization could make use of the success measurement framework, and we valued that the business lines spent the time to follow us on this journey. It was totally clear that there are the leading departments, as well as the departments, for whom it was more challenging to change their approach or even did not have the digital marketing agenda on top of their minds. We also experienced: Do not forget the stakeholders or team members, which you think that they are informed anyhow, because they are relatively close – but not close enough. For example, the entire digital marketing team, who were identified as important multiplicators, but were not in the project's core team. One of the biggest levers we identified in the digital marketing team itself was moving oneself in the mode of using the information derived from success measurement framework and by that restricting other sources from which we knew that they were insufficient. As described, it was very useful to have the user in mind while conceptualizing the views, but the team needed to use it, as well. Therefore, triggers were set by providing centrally on regular basis a data-driven evaluation for the digital marketing functions. Those evaluations' read out in team jour fixes created certain awareness and helped to solidity the approach, because the hypotheses, which buzzed around verbally, then were written down. In follow-up tests, these hypotheses could be refuted or supported within the own tooling and only few additional statistical efforts.

For the success of the success measurement framework, it was very helpful to be very close to the dedicated use cases, which the business line organizations knew and had understood before. During the development of the success measurement framework, we identified that a huge set of users have worked with views in the past, which have used only slightly different measures. So, we guided them from the approach they had used in the past to the views we had created specifically along the digital strategy. The basic data remained unchanged, but the same information sliced by additional attributes were provided. Especially bringing the concept of suspects being a semi-additive measure into the organization opened their eyes, which large deviations have been overlooked without the success measurement framework in place. So, we could convince them that using only one measure pruned the amount of information, which would have led to less focus otherwise. We called this the "fighting guide" to use, whenever someone came around the corner with evaluations based on impression or was asking for reporting of pageviews because when for one activity the suspects measure indicated good results and another measure for awareness bad results or vice versa, we overcame the situation by focusing on suspects and knew which suggestions to present.

Moreover, with the state-of-the-art technical reporting front-end environment provided by our IT department, we started to send out a standardized reporting via e-mail on regular basis to penetrate the own organization, especially to have the big picture of the own area of responsibility on regular basis.

6 Summary and Outlook

The essence of this chapter lies in the methodology of modeling. We pointed out that the model was and is a living model. As this journey evolved, the touchpoints coming closer to the center of the company's business model have been taken into consideration: additional KPIs can be connected, their results to the activities can be added, and it can be optimized on then six and so on measuring points. The methodology remains the same, and the model is just getting more precise with time and of course leads to new insights and thus different suggestions and decisions taken by the digital marketing managers.

Digital marketing at Infineon is seen as targeting a market with dedicated go-to-marketing categories. On the market there are business opportunities, with individuals being active and working on those customer projects. Behind every individual our understanding is that there is an individual customer journey, so opportunities and individuals are seen as to be crossed from result's perspective. The concept of an attribution model, which credits the individual activities driving the contact through the journey (Shao & Li, 2011), can be applied and the respective logics fed with the data used in the success measurement framework to take the next step identifying best-in-class activities, e.g., in the way (Dalessandro et al., 2012) estimate activity performance.

Furthermore, we are working on predictions for business opportunities, which are identified, clustered, and worth to be pursued by the salesforce and where it was in the current environment not able to identify them with the existing approach. Then the success measurement framework's successor is not only supporting to achieve digital marketing goals, but also giving our stakeholders in the sales area an information they did not know before.

References

Bagshaw, A. (2015). What is marketing automation? *Journal of Direct, Data and Digital Marketing Practice, 17*(2), 84–85.

Bhaskara, I. M. A., Suardani, L. G. P., & Sudarma, M. (2018). Data warehouse implemantation to support batik sales information using MOLAP. *International Journal of Engineering and Emerging Technology, 3*(1), 45–51.

Blomkvist, J., Holmlid, S., & Segelström, F. (2010). *Service design research: Yesterday, today and tomorrow* (pp. 308–315). BIS Publishers.

Burkacky, O., Deichmann, J., Pfingstag, P., & Werra, J. (2022). *Semiconductor shortage: How the automotive industry can succeed.* McKinsey Insights.

Dalessandro, B., Perlich, C., Stitelman, O., & Provost, F. (2012). Causally motivated attribution for online advertising. In: *Proceedings of the sixth international workshop on data mining for online advertising and internet economy*, pp. 1–9.

Dash, A. Z., Mero, J., & Laukkanen, T. (2021). From suspect to customer: Using marketing analytics data to study the effectiveness of digital marketing channels in the B2b sales funnel. Industrial Marketing Management. *Available at SSRN 3935497.*

Drucker, P. F. (1986). *The frontiers of management: Where tomorrow's decisions are being shaped today* (1st ed.). Truman Talley Books.

Eichhorn, P., & Merk, J. (2015). *Das Prinzip Wirtschaftlichkeit* (4th ed.). Springer Gabler.

Frost, J. (2013). Multiple regression analysis: Use adjusted R-squared and predicted R-squared to include the correct number of variables. *Minitab Blog, 13*(6).

Hunsberger, S. (2017). The next era of HR: Digital marketing. *People & Strategy, 40*(4), 26–31.

Järvinen, J., & Karjaluoto, H. (2015). The use of web analytics for digital marketing performance measurement. *Industrial Marketing Management, 50*, 117–127.

Kleijn, R., & van Dijk, H. K. (2006). Bayes model averaging of cyclical decompositions in economic time series. *Journal of Applied Econometrics, 21*(2), 191–212.

Lobacher, P., & Jacob, C. (2020). Objectives & Key Results (OKR). *Das agile Betriebssystem für moderne Organisationen.* die. agilen GmbH.

Revella, A. (2015). *Buyer personas.* Wiley.

Shao, X., & Li, L. (2011). Data-driven multi-touch attribution models. In *Proceedings of the 17th ACM SIGKDD international conference on knowledge discovery and data mining* (pp. 258–264).

Shewhart, W. (1939). *Statistical method from the viewpoint of quality control.* Courier Corporation.

Sterman, J. D. (2000). *Business dynamics: Systems thinking and modeling for a complex world.* McGraw-Hill.

The Importance of a Focused and Standardized Operating Model in Managing Digital Customer Engagement

Lukas Trautner

1 The Importance to Think Beyond Strategy

"[. . .] according to recent estimates 66% to 84% of digital transformation projects fail" (Correani et al., 2020). Additionally, digital transformation is on top of CEOs' minds at the moment while the same CEOs report 70% of digital transformation projects do not lead to success. This is not only valid for digital transformation projects in general but also in the area of digital customer engagement.

1.1 From Strategy to Execution: A Gap to Be Closed by Operating Models

The key reason behind the high number of failing digital transformation projects is lesser the lack of a strategy but rather the complexity in implementing the strategy accordingly (Bollard et al., 2017) as well as the disruptive character of digital transformation projects on capabilities, processes, and others (Davenport & Westerman, 2018).

This problem has been described several times by multiple researchers. Matt et al. (2015) see in implementing digital transformation a transformation of processes, operations, structures, and management concepts. Beyond, it is important to focus on the organization of resources, developing a blueprint for the organization and in the end building a digital operating model (Blenko & Root, 2015).

Bollard et al. (2017) state clearly that most organizations have a plan and strategy in place, however on top they need to focus on the operating model, including processes, digital technologies, capabilities, and integration. In sum, they suggest to

L. Trautner (✉)
Infineon Technologies AG, Neubiberg, Germany
e-mail: Lukas.Trautner@infineon.com

U. Schneider, J. Hoika (eds.), *Digital Marketing in the Automotive Electronics Industry*, Management for Professionals,
https://doi.org/10.1007/978-3-031-30720-1_6

focus on two major value drivers: (1) an integrated operational improvement program aimed at connecting the dots, bridging silos and organized around customer journeys, and (2) taking a holistic approach to adopt several levers of the operating model at once, again with an integrated agenda. Dobru et al. (2021) mention that the focus needs to go beyond organizational charts, boxes, and lines.

Garton (2017) summarizes this dilemma indicating the importance of an operating model as the "bridge between strategy and execution," and Correani et al. (2020) once again make the importance of the issue clear when seeing strategy implementation more critical to success compared to a good strategy formulation.

It is however very important to understand that the impact of the operating model goes far beyond internal processes and structures, but focuses on the customer, business model, and value creation. Hence, Berman (2012) puts the customer in the focus and shows the importance of optimizing the operating model in order to drive value for the customer through the entire organization. Reijnen et al. (2018) and Bounfour (2016) argue in a similar fashion and indicate the impact of digital transformation on business models and subsequently the focus on the operating model.

1.2 The Value of a Sound Operating Model in Digital Transformation

The good news is that by now many executives have seen the massive importance of an operating model. A recent study found that 87% of CEOs that have digital transformations in place also expect a change in their operating model in the near future (Deloitte., 2020). A lot of research is by now focusing on the value of defining and implementing an operating model, while also pointing out common issues, in case the operating model is not defined and implemented properly.

de la Boutetière et al. (2018) verified that beyond other elements the operating procedures, capabilities, and culture have a very strong positive influence on the success of digital transformations, increasing the likelihood of success by a factor of 3. On top it was found that an improved operating model leads to a shorter time to market (Correani et al., 2020). Murphy et al. (2016) see the benefit of developing an operating model in an improved business performance, better connection with stakeholders, an increased process integration, improved coordination and decision-making, better ability to grow and scale quickly, as well as an improved risk management. On the other hand, there are clear disadvantages in having no operating model in place, such as operational inefficiencies, unclear accountabilities, low interaction and integration, and higher operating risks. Mankins (2017) points out that an "average company loses more than 20% of its productive capacity" because of inadequate structures and processes showing the tremendous value slight improvements to the operating model could have on the top and bottom line of the balance sheet.

In summary, when analyzing reasons that digital transformations fail, it becomes very clear that the focus is not just on defining the right strategy but on top, significant effort needs to be placed on the implementation of the strategy via a sound operating model. With that companies can increase the likelihood for success of their digital transformation up to a factor of three, while ensuring their teams run at high productivity. The experience described actually in many research articles also very much reflects my personal view on the implementation of digital customer engagement in the context of a large German semiconductor player. Having a good strategy in place, one that is aligned with customer needs as well as with company goals, is key, but the real work only starts once the implementation begins, as it means that in most cases many different teams need to be brought to the table, focusing on one goal, defining clear processes to scale, and then executing along these. The make or break point in several of these instances that I witnessed was clearly when strategies were scaled across the entire organization, as exactly in those cases a fully functioning operating model is key for success.

Throughout this chapter I will provide an overview over various definitions and elements of operating models in the existing literature, while providing, at the same time, an explanation of key steps in developing an operating model in the context of digital customer engagement. Closing the gap between theory and practice, two specific case studies on operating models in the B2B electronics industry for campaign management and content production are presented, while the chapter will close with an outlook on future elements and focus areas in an operating model.

2 Operating Model

An operating model can be defined in several different ways. There is not yet a common understanding and definition in place in literature. On top the term "operating model" itself is a rather new one, which gets more recognition since the early 2000s, and is still mostly used in consultancy and only in recent years found its way into scientific research. Depending on the type of business model, industry and size of an organization operating models can become complex. Hence, the goal of this chapter is to provide an overview of various definitions as well as concluding on highly necessary elements in the area of digital customer engagement.

As mentioned before, an operating model serves as a bridge between strategy and execution (Garton, 2017; Murphy et al., 2016). In literature the following elements are identified with an operating model:

- According to Campbell et al. (2017), an operating model includes (1) processes, (2) organization, (3) information, (4) locations, (5) suppliers, and (6) management systems.
- According to Galbraith and Kates (2010) and the STAR Model, one needs to investigate (1) processes, (2) people, (3) rewards, and (4) structure.
- According to Murphy et al. (2016), an operating model entails (1) governance, (2) culture and values, and (3) processes.
- According to Garton (2017) there is a need to focus on (1) accountabilities, (2) governance structures, (3) leadership model, (4) management of career

paths, (5) ways of working, (6) behavior, (7) people, (8) processes, (9) technology, and (10) tools.

- Imran et al. (2021) focus on (1) leadership, (2) structure, and (3) culture.
- Dobru et al. (2021) identified 12 elements clustered in 3 buckets: (1) processes, (2) people, and (3) structure:
  - Processes include process design and decisions, performance management, systems and technology, as well as linkages.
  - People include informal networks, culture, talent and skills, as well as workforce planning.
  - Structure includes governance, boundaries and location, "boxes" and "lines," as well as roles and responsibilities.

An overview of these definitions can be found in Table 1.

Based on these studies and the more detailed definitions of the various elements of an operating model described in literature, the following key clusters are identified and will be used throughout this chapter:

- *Processes*: Highlighted as a key element in all the studies reviewed, actively managing processes is an integral part of an operating model and serves as an input to several subsequent activities such as definition of roles and responsibilities as well as the required tools.
- *People and culture*: Several elements around people are discussed in literature, such as culture, values, capabilities, and roles and responsibilities. The implementation of a strategy requires the right people and on top also the right leadership.
- *Structure*: Too often the topic of organization and structures still gets the highest attention when operating models are discussed. Indeed, it is an important part of an organization to discuss "boxes" and "lines," as especially in hierarchical companies this still tends to lead to massive friction.
- *Governance*: A key factor in defining an operating model is the governance, even though there is no common understanding what it entails. In this study, we are clustering reward systems, accountabilities, management systems, and decision-making into this bucket.
- *Tools and technology*: Especially around digital transformation in general or digital customer engagement specifically, tools and technologies are highly important. While we will not focus on recommending single tools as part of this chapter, it is important that most elements of digital customer engagement require a set of tools and technology to help automatize and scale.

An overview of all relevant elements of an operating model in the light of digital customer engagement can be seen in Fig. 1 which are described in more detail in the next chapters.

Table 1 Elements of an operating model in literature

Core elements	Sub-elements	Campbell et al. (2017)	Galbraith and Kates (2010)	Murphy et al. (2016)	Garton (2017)	Imran et al. (2021)	Dobru et al. (2021)
Process	Process design	x	x	x	x	x	x
	Suppliers	x					
	Performance management						x
People	Leadership				x	x	
	Culture			x		x	x
	Value and behavior			x	x		
	Capabilities		x		x		x
	Workforce planning				x		x
	Roles and responsibilities		x				x
Structure	Locations	x					x
	"Boxes" and "lines"	x	x		x	x	x
Governance	Reward system		x				
	Accountabilities				x		
	Management systems	x		x	x		x
	Decision making			x	x		x
Tools and technology	Information flow	x					
	Tools and IT systems	x			x		x

Processes	People & Culture	Structure	Governance	Tools & Technology
•Process Design •Performance Management	•Culture •Values & behavior •Capabilities •Workforce planning •Roles & responsibilities •Leadership	•"Boxes" and "Lines" •Locations	•Reward system •Accountabilities •Management systems •Decision making	•Information flow •Tools & IT Systems

Fig. 1 Relevant elements of an operating model

2.1 Processes

As outlined before, processes are mentioned as a key enabler for digital transformation and in general in the operating model literature as one key element. The reason behind is the tremendous value it brings to the organization to define the workflow in detail.

De la Boutetière et al. (2018) could show that success rate for digital transformations increases by the factor 2.2× and 1.8×, respectively, in cases business processes are adapted and standard operating procedures are using digital technologies. Münstermann and Weitzel (2008) see a tremendous value in process standardization via, e.g., reduced end to end time, cost, and improved quality. Schäfermeyer et al. (2012) mention efficiency gains, decreasing risks, and higher quality.

In recent years and especially in digital transformation, more focus lies on agile processes, moving away from waterfall approaches, due to the insecurity, which is seen through technological advancements or external factors (Imran et al., 2021).

As part of the process cluster, it is important to optimize process design and performance management. It is key to understand that processes will have a strong impact on the definition of roles and responsibilities, tools and IT systems, as well as decision-making. One could say, based on the impact of process design, it is at the heart of an operating model and basically "how the organization creates [. . .] the value proposition" (Campbell et al., 2017).

2.2 People and Culture

People and culture are closely intertwined. Without the right people and a common culture, most companies will fail to deliver their products or services to the customer. Several elements pay into this cluster, such as culture, values, behavior, capabilities, workforce planning, roles and responsibilities, as well as leadership. Based on the breadth of this cluster, the value of it is of course significant.

De la Boutetière et al. (2018) mention a broad number of activities of companies that successfully implement digital transformations, such as leadership development, identifying needed skills, setting hiring goals, capability mapping, learning programs, etc. For each of those activities, the study showed that the success rate of delivering digital transformation increased between 1.6× and 2.1×. Dobru et al. (2021) found that both culture and workforce planning are particularly impactful elements that need to be included in the definition of an operating model. Tabrizi et al. (2019) see a tremendous value in focusing on the right mindset, while Angevine et al. (2021) focus especially on developing and upskilling talent, digital learning programs, and again on mindset change. Imran et al. (2021) focuses in his study on leadership with a focus on communication, leading by example, adaptability, mindset, vision, as well as agility, customer centricity, and collaboration. When focusing on culture, it becomes clear that values and beliefs play a very important role. Digital transformation has a disruptive effect on the organizational culture, and success of digital transformation depends on a cultural shift towards risk taking, collaboration, and customer centricity (Dobru et al., 2021; Imran et al., 2021).

In sum, it is key to focus on people and culture as part of digital transformations. Without taking staff along the journey, digital customer engagement cannot succeed. It is important to focus on bringing the right talent and leadership into the organization, investing into upskilling existing employees, while at the same time taking a cultural shift towards agility, collaboration, and customer centricity.

2.3 Structure

Once discussions about an operating model are starting, often immediately politics will start discussing organizational structures, hierarchies, reporting lines, and much more. Of course, these discussions also are justified, noting the importance of structures on the success of an operating model. Especially in this area, however, there is a clear recommendation to go back to the original design principles and map various options against them, to bring a few clear criteria to the table and avoid political games. We will discuss this topic in more detail as part of the next chapter.

Organizational structure was reviewed by many researchers focusing on operating models in digital transformation. Campbell et al. (2017) suggest differentiating between (1) operating work structured along value chain, different products and segments or along a matrix setup, and (2) support work with roles and responsibilities for policy (sets governance and processes), champion (sells ideas, but has no decision-making power), shared services, and core resources (acts as partner to the operating units).

Angevine et al. (2021) are focusing on principle structures for teams focusing on digital transformation, building digitalization units directly reporting to the CEO with a focus on driving high impact projects along the customer journey.

Tabrizi et al. (2019) share a case study with a clear argumentation towards flat hierarchies and cross-functional and cross-regional teams reporting directly into the CEO, which brought the clear benefit to generate and test ideas based on a multitude of different perspectives which then also supported a smoother roll-out to the entire organization.

Imran et al. (2021) see structure as one key lever for high performance in digital transformations and suggest focusing especially on two major goals: (1) becoming more agile and (2) becoming customer centric. In order to get there, he proposes investigating three key areas: hierarchy (e.g., less layers), formalization (e.g., goal-oriented approach), and integration (e.g., cross-functional collaboration).

Dürr et al. (2017) focus on their research as well as on the ambition to become more agile and enabling the organization towards open innovation. The research group saw a tremendous value in creating cross-functional teams.

In general, there is no right or wrong in defining organizational structures. It is key to make sure that the structure fits the strategy, and on top to ensure it fits to overall processes. In the case of digital transformation many companies seek for similar goals: (1) agility, (2) customer centricity, and (3) collaboration. All of that requires flat hierarchies, a direct reporting line to top management, if not the CEO and a shift of mindset coming with it.

2.4 Governance

While there is little research on governance in digital transformation existing, the importance of it cannot be denied. Code (1992) defined corporate governance as "[. . .] the system by which companies are directed and controlled." Based on this definition it becomes clear that as part of a review of the operating model, the governance plays a major role, which is also supported by a recent study from Dobru et al. (2021) that found governance to be one key element in successful operating model transformations. When looking into governance, they were focusing on "structure, authority, and membership of bodies that make critical decisions." Campbell et al. (2017) also focus on governance in their research, noting especially the importance of decision-making processes and decision bodies.

On the topic of governance there is definitely a lot of room for further research, understanding the real value an optimization can have on digital customer engagement. However, noting the transformational character, it becomes clear that deriving and updating decision-making processes, accountabilities, and transparent management systems is of utmost importance.

2.5 Tools and Technology

Tools and Technology shall not be the focus of this chapter. Since there are simply too many tools and technologies available to support various processes in digital customer engagement, the goal is rather to ensure the importance of defining and implementing the right tool landscape is understood.

De la Boutetière et al. (2018) identified in their study the impact of digital tools for the success of digital transformations. They could show that, for example, tools leveraged for analysis of complex information increased the success rate by a factor of 2.6×, while tools to make information available impacted the success rate positively by a factor of 2.1×. Additionally, companies that modified standard operating procedures, including digital tools, were 1.8× more likely achieving success.

Campbell et al. (2017) are sharing a similar perspective. They are especially looking into IT applications to support process execution as well as tools that are focusing on information and data. There is a clear suggestion to define an IT blueprint based on the value chain and key processes.

Tools and Technologies play an important role in implementing digital transformation strategies within companies. For digital customer engagement the focus needs to be specifically on marketing technologies, such as CRM, marketing automation, content management system, analytics systems, customer data platform, and many more. The key factor here is to ensure that the implementation of tools follows a holistic architecture as well as building it on a clear strategy and process landscape.

3 Approach to Define and Implement a Shared Operating Model

"Structure follows strategy" (Chandler, 1969) is a saying that by now made its way into many papers, books, and board offices. Even though it was first written down 60 years ago, it is still valid today and valid for the definition and implementation of any operating model.

It is clear and all research points to the fact that "form follows function," and before defining the various elements of an operating model, a strategy needs to be in place to ensure there is a high fit between what a company wants to achieve and how it is going to achieve it (Tabrizi et al., 2019). However, there are slight differences in the exact approaches that are recommended by literature, and we want to point them out with two examples:

- According to Campbell et al. (2017) on high level the whole process includes (1) strategy definition, (2) operating model definition, (3) transformation and implementation, as well as (4) execution in the new operating model. In more detail they recommend starting with a problem statement before understanding the strategy and current operating model. Afterwards they recommend developing clear design principles, developing various options, and evaluating them against design principles, before planning and implementing the changes.
- Murphy et al. (2016) recommend to (1) assess the status quo, (2) evaluate the need for change, (3) including the right team members, (4) define design principles, (5) shape the future state, (6) plan the change, and (7) implement the change.

Based on these approaches, one can summarize the process to define and implement an operating model as shown in Fig. 2: starting with (1) strategy definition, followed by the definition of clear (2) design principles, before (3) developing options for the operating model, leading to an (4) evaluation and decision and then focusing on (5) change management and implementation.

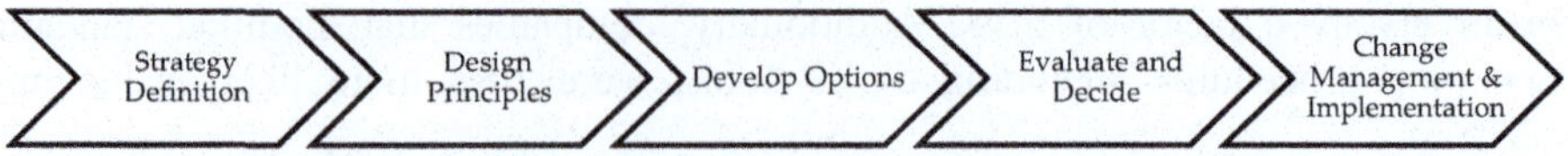

Fig. 2 Approach to define and implement an operating model

Throughout the entire process it is key to understand the status quo, while at the same time not losing the target state and vision out of sight. As part of this chapter, we want to focus especially on two important aspects: the definition of design principles as well as change management, as both of them are key to a successful implementation of an operating model that fits to the strategy.

3.1 Design Principles

Design principles "Translate[s] the strategy into a set of defining how the organization should operate" (Murphy et al., 2016). This is also the reason why they are tremendously important for a redesign of an operating model, as they reduce the complexity of several inputs, such as the status quo, the strategy, vision, key priorities, and many more into a couple of simple principles that can be used for definition as well as for the evaluation of an operating model.

Blenko and Root (2015) suggest to base design principles both on the strategic priorities and on the organizational assessment. As strategic priorities they are looking into ambition, key focus areas, and several specific elements such as target customers, capabilities, key decisions, targets, and growth sources. For the organization assessment they recommend focusing on organizational and cultural strengths and weaknesses, heritage and values effectiveness of critical decisions, and gaps in key capabilities. Garton (2017) suggests concentrating on selected principles only with a clear focus on what matters most to deliver the strategy. Campbell et al. (2017) provide a similar perspective, stating each design principle should be linking to a strategic objective and a design principle is representing a design dilemma.

In literature one can find several best practices and pitfalls when it comes to defining design principles. Among them you can often find (1) a focus on few selected design principles that (2) stay brief and allow for management to (3) make trade-offs. On top, it is important that design principles are (4) based on facts and that they go (5) beyond organizational structure and maybe most important of all that they are (6) aligned between key decision-makers (Blenko & Root, 2015; Campbell et al., 2017; Garton, 2017).

3.2 Change Management

"The real work starts once the operating model is defined." This sentence by a top manager in a big organization reflects on the importance of planning the implementation of an updated operating model carefully. The roll-out of how an organization or team should operate is a key step in the whole process and should not be taken lightly. Latest since Kotter (2012) defined his version of the change model, it became clear that focusing on the individuals that need to go through the change and especially focusing on their change curve is of utmost importance. Correani et al. (2020) identified the lack of proper change management as one of the key reasons why digital transformation efforts fail.

Based on various different change models as well as field research, Bellantuono et al. (2021) recommend to focus change management activities on (1) defining a strong leadership, (2) generating awareness on the need for change, (3) defining a clear change vision and strategy, (4) communicating said vision and strategy, (5) defining a change management team, (6) identifying short-term goals and pilot projects, (7) managing resistance to change, (8) training people, (9) collecting and analyzing feedbacks and monitor change, as well as (10) celebrating successes.

To do all that, especially with a focus on digital transformation and digital customer engagement, Campbell et al. (2017) suggest starting with a stakeholder map to understand the target audience for the change much better. Tabrizi et al. (2019) and Imran et al. (2021) focus with their research on culture, mindset, and leadership and propose setting a clear focus on those areas, when it comes to changes through digital.

All things considered, change management is an elementary step in the journey, one that should have a high dedication not just in the first instance of implementing a new operating model, but really through the entire process until the change arrived at the working level. Following through with the change effort is most likely the toughest and longest part of the entire process, but only when this is done right, the effects of an improved operating model can and will be seen.

3.3 Best Practices

When it comes to defining an operating model for digital customer engagement, digital transformation or in general, there are a couple of highly relevant and important best practices. Those tips can be clustered along the elements of an operating model and the approach to define it. A summary of the most important best practices can be found in Fig. 3.

Based on these best practices, one can derive a few common denominators. It remains key throughout the process to focus on (1) people, involving the right stakeholders and leaders, putting high focus on individuals and getting the right team to manage the transformation. As mentioned previously, there needs to be a continuous dedication on (2) change management, being clear on the problem statement and rational to change, aligning everyone on a single vision and including the right stakeholders. Beyond that management needs to keep an eye on (3) goal and target setting as well as the need to adapt the (4) culture of the organization to the change that is wished for (Campbell et al., 2017; Deloitte., 2020; Garton, 2017).

Strategy & Approach	Approach & Change	Processes	People & Culture	Governance
• Align organization to a singular vision • Make sure to have a sponsor • There is no right answer	• Agree on a few selected principles • Involve important stakeholders and leaders early on • Be clear on the rational to change • Get the right team	• Define good processes to share information across silos	• Put high focus on individuals and teams • Keep the need for cultural change in mind • Define clear R&Rs	• Focus on constructive conflict • Create complementary goals to optimize resource allocation • Support independent decision-making

Fig. 3 Best practices for an optimized operating model based on (Campbell et al., 2017; Deloitte., 2020; Garton, 2017)

4 Case Studies

Based on the definition of an operating model, relevant elements and sub-elements of its two case studies related to digital customer engagement will be presented: the first case study will focus on content marketing while the second will focus on campaign management. Due to the specific situation the case studies were derived from, it is important to note that not all elements of an operating model were treated equally, but the state as well as the design principles led to emphasize selected parts only. Both case studies are taken out of the consumer and industrial semiconductor market of a large player in the industry.

4.1 Case Study 1: Content Marketing

Situation faced: The multinational company was putting a significant focus on implementing an end-to-end digital customer engagement strategy to drive revenue and profit via digital channels for their business. Based on customer research and competitor analysis, a focus was set on improving the content strategy and the related operating model, with a focus on decreasing the complexity for the customer, serving the right content assets and information throughout the customer journey, and ensuring a setup and process that allows to scale effective content production across various organizations in the company. As part of this effort the teams started to define a content architecture in line with customers' expectations, including content definitions, customer journey mapping, and description of efficient content production processes. Moreover, a competitor analysis in the B2B technology and electronics industry showed a few significant differences, e.g., in culture, process, skills, as well as the supporting tool landscape.

Design Principles: Based on both the content architecture and the learnings from competitor analysis, a few highly relevant design principles were defined in order to ensure there was clear guidance for the definition of an operating model:

- Design Principle 1 (DP1): Put the customer first.
- Design Principle 2 (DP2): Ensure maximum reuse of content assets and information to scale.
- Design Principle 3 (DP3): Clear ownership for content in expert teams.
- Design Principle 4 (DP4): Provide operational support for content producers.
- Design Principle 5 (DP5): Focus on the 80% of standard cases.

Process: Especially based on DP1, DP2, and DP5, it was clear that the content production processes needed a refresh. The processes so far were not defined and supported via tools well enough to ensure content could be scaled in the customer's and company's best interest. Hence, it was decided to focus with the processes especially on two major pieces: (1) high-quality production of base content assets and (2) low effort processes to repurpose those content assets for various target audiences, channels, and formats.

For (1), there was a clear decision to create this content decentralized in the respective technical expert teams that are closest to the business and the relevant products, however providing them with support when it came to quality checks, translation, proof reading, and many further aspects. For (2) a different approach was taken: as much as possible the base content assets were standardized so that centralized marketing and content teams could create derivatives based on the relevant information, such as creating a short "How-to-Video" based on an application note or writing a blog article based on a whitepaper. To ensure the fit of this intent to the organization and strategy, the proposed process was validated in form of pilots.

Beyond focusing on the creation processes, the company also worked on content lifecycle management, as this was clearly a pain point, especially out of customer perspective. So far the organization did not establish a sustainable process that would allow to review documents at scale which led to several workload heavy cleanup projects throughout the years. As part of this process description, it however became once again clear that a full enablement could only happen with the right tools – especially a Digital Asset Management system – could be achieved. More details on this can be found in the section Tools and Technology. In the end the company defined a process that led to a mandatory review of content assets by the defined content owners on a yearly/bi-yearly basis supported by the right tools and target setting.

People: Especially based on DP2, DP3, and DP4, it became clear soon that an important part of the operating model was skills, roles, and responsibilities as well as strategic workforce planning. In general, it was clear that the right skills existed in the company; however a clear focus was to sharpen the R&Rs especially of the technical marketing teams to ensure the importance of content marketing and content production was highlighted in their job profiles.

Additionally, due to DP4 it was important to provide necessary support to make the job of a content producer easier. Hence it was decided to build up in-house agencies to scale especially the content repurposing and on top build up central technical content teams that provided regular reviews of technical content assets, made proposals for improvements, and implemented updated formats.

In order to do that, part of the whole initiative was a focus on workforce planning, ensuring the right and enough resources were planned and implemented to ensure that customer needs are fulfilled and that content production could scale.

Culture: A very important part of the operating model was the culture. Early in the project and especially due to detailed competitor analysis, it became clear that from a cultural perspective a change was necessary. DP1, DP2, and DP5 had a significant influence on it. A focus had to be put particularly on three key elements: (1) writing content for the customer, (2) building on what was already there, and (3) standardization is more important than individualization.

For (1) the key challenge was not that the teams didn't have the best interest in mind when they previously created content, but to ensure all teams truly understood the customer journey and the key questions of an engineer throughout the process. Hence, education on this was and still is necessary.

For (2) especially the limitation of a clear process and guidelines was taking its toll, but in the end led to higher productivity and higher clarity.

For (3) a focus was once again set on the customer. In the past the freedom to create individualized content assets led to the fact that customers that wanted to purchase products from different product families were confused by differentiating content assets and availability of it. Standardization therefore had two major effects: content production was becoming more efficient and the customer could find related information much quicker.

Tools and Technology: The company so far only had very limited tools supporting content production that led to two big problems: lack of efficiency (e.g., in process execution, or content reuse) and lack of enforced guidelines.

The key tools that were established to ensure process adherence and efficiency gains were a Digital Asset Management System (DAM) and a Content Management System (CMS) as website interface. Both tools allowed the teams to streamline content production, ensure content reuse, and provided standardization across organizational silos. While this already was a huge improvement, especially also for a proper lifecycle management and for the interaction with regional teams, there are still further improvements possible:

As part of the whole content marketing project, it became clear that marketing and content needs to be deeply embedded in the product development process. Hence, there is a clear need to include content production in the overall process, and with that also in related product lifecycle management (PLM) tools.

4.2 Campaign Management

Situation faced: The organization started investing more into digital communication in order to ensure key messages for existing and new products are placed in the market. As part of this activity the company recognized that so far there was no clear process nor strategy for campaigns in place. The teams were mostly working along individually defined processes in a setup that was hard to understand from the outside and from key interfaces. On top, campaign management for digital channels was based on yearly planning in a waterfall approach, even though there was a lot of change happening throughout the year, due to ever changing product launch calendars.

Based on leveraging best practices especially out of B2C a bigger project was defined for adapting the communication and campaign strategy and the operating model behind.

An important factor for the initiative was also to include the business units in the entire change, as there the relevance of digital customer engagement was not yet understood and valued.

Design Principles: Based on the concrete problem situation, being relatively inexperienced, with unclear processes and roles, a lot of manual effort and no option to scale, the project team and management defined a few key principles:

- Design Principle 1 (DP1): Embed the communication team very closely with business.
- Design Principle 2 (DP2): Scale campaign management via standardized processes and roles.
- Design Principle 3 (DP3): Allow for flexibility and agility to adapt campaigns easily.
- Design Principle 4 (DP4): Build and develop a team of campaign experts.

Process: Based especially on DP2 and DP3, three key processes were defined that in sum were adding up to an end-to-end process for campaign management:

- *Process 1: Communication Strategy Process*: with the clear goal to derive campaign focus topics and rough timelines for the campaigns on a yearly basis based on the business strategy which was also reviewed and updated on a yearly basis.
- *Process 2: Campaign Scoping*: Once a campaign launch date was coming closer, the goal of this process was the definition of a detailed campaign briefing including elements such as campaign strategy, key messages, key call to actions, key campaign activities (e.g., Search Engine Marketing, etc.), key campaign objectives, budget and KPIs, and several more.
- *Process 3: Campaign Execution*: Based on the detailed campaign scope, the teams then started the execution in close collaboration between business units, marketing communication, and digital marketing teams.

Once those new processes were implemented, they were reviewed and updated on a regular basis; especially process 3 was over time becoming more and more agile, working with a "Scrumban" approach, regular Sprints, and clear plans that everyone was aware about.

People: Considering the updated processes and on top especially DP1 and DP4, a clear need existed to streamline and update roles and responsibilities and focus beyond that on building additional capabilities in the team.

In general, four key roles were defined:

- *Campaign Strategy*: For each business unit one campaign strategist was responsible to define the communication strategy based on the business strategy, derive campaign calendars, and maintain the portfolio of campaigns for the respective business area. Additionally, the responsibility of the campaign strategist was the planning and maintenance of the budget. The key intent of this role was to build one person deeply embedded into the business unit that on top has an overview of all campaign and communication-related activities.
- *Campaign and Content Manager*: For each business unit a team of campaign and content managers existed that were responsible to plan and execute the campaigns, work with in-house and external agencies to develop the content, and closely collaborate with key interfaces in the business units to receive inputs. Campaign and content managers were the responsible individuals for Process 2 and Process 3 as described above. With this role, there was a clear and single interface existing for each campaign.
- *Omnichannel Marketing Manager*: This role was responsible to scale the key messages and CTAs as well as all produced content assets into a multitude of digital channels, such as Search Engine Marketing, social media, third parties, Email, and several more. The omnichannel marketing manager helped to build the bridge to internal and external channel owners, was an expert in digital marketing activities, and held important responsibilities in measuring the effectiveness of campaign activities to optimize them continuously.
- *Channel Owner*: the key responsibility of this team was the execution and optimization of channel activities in their respective channel. For each important channel at least one person was driving the digital activities, building strong expertise in the respective field and ensuring consistency across all campaign teams.

Beyond the roles described other teams and responsibilities were defined as a support across teams, such as analytics, content producer, and process designer.

Especially in the beginning and short after the change, the key focus was the improvement of capabilities, with the help of a few selected external experts, several pilot projects that provided on-the-job training, and on top of that more structured training format.

Culture: As always, also this change was coming with a necessary shift in mindset and culture, impacted mostly by DP1, DP2, and DP3. While the teams were coming from a past were everyone held responsibility for end-to-end processes, they now needed to move into a clear and strict division of labor to allow for scalability.

Beyond that, especially coming closer to the business units led to a cultural shift both within the marketing communication and digital marketing as well as on the business unit side. For the digital marketing team, the change was driven by the new focus on business goals and by acting as a consultant, expert, and service provider, while for the business unit teams the change was rather a switch in strategy from pure personal interaction to and added digital element.

Another change the teams were confronted with was the development of agile working methods. While few team members were happy about this change and implemented with high motivation, others were overwhelmed with the rigidity of agile methods on the one side, while lacking the 12-month plan on the other side.

The cultural and mindset change took several months and was once again highlighting the importance of a proper change management toolbox in such cases, to ensure the defined processes and roles are going beyond pure descriptions on a piece of paper.

Structure: As part of this change in processes and roles also the structure was adapted with two key goals in mind: (1) foster expert capabilities and (2) structure along value stream.

To achieve those objectives, the restructuring can be summarized as follows:

- Based on DP1, installation of one campaign team per business unit including the campaign strategist as well as the campaign and content managers.
- Based on DP4, installation of one channel marketing team, where individuals could be mapped to the business units to ensure single interfaces, but on top allow for the development of additional capabilities and expertise.
- Split campaign and content management team from the team of content producers as those require a different skill set.
- While keeping the team of channel owners separate, as before.

The structural changes helped the teams to understand and foster their new roles, while via relevant team meetings the overall value stream was kept in mind.

Governance: Especially based on DP1 and DP4 it was key to define clear targets in line with business goals to ensure the value of the new campaign strategy and operating model could be measured and the positive impact would be made transparent especially also to the business functions were an in principle change towards digital was long overdue.

As part of this objective, it was decided to map communication and campaign KPIs to business KPIs, along the entire sales funnel to ensure the impact of digital campaign activities can be mapped to additional revenue. Similar to many companies also in this case a step-by-step approach needed to be taken, as not all data was coming out of the same system and could be combined easily but starting with selected leading indicators in the beginning and adding others later helped significantly in the entire change process as the value could be clearly seen in the improved KPIs.

5 The Future of Operating Models: Agile and Based on Customer Journeys

Talking about operating models for digital customer engagement, this of course bears the question about future trends and innovative ideas. In general, those can be summarized in two sections: (1) Agile Operating Models and (2) Operating Models along the customer journey.

Agile is of course not just a trend for the future, but has been discussed widely; however adaptation especially at large players in various industries is still very much at the beginning, mostly focusing on smaller teams. The key value in agile operating models – at least when setup right – lies in faster decision-making, cross-functional collaboration, customer focus, and many more (Pardasani et al., 2019). In order to get there, again various elements of the operating model need to be touched, such as structure, people, tools, and processes, and once again it should be based on a clear strategy (Brosseau et al., 2019). Recent research also shows analysis on changing an entire company operating model towards agile, or on the other hand how agile can be implemented also in top management (Comella-Dorda et al., 2016; Garton & Noble, 2017).

On the other hand, an operating model based on the customer journey is still a rather new idea, where at the core it is about moving the entire organization closer to the customer, bridging siloes and start capturing more value out of existing capabilities (Bollard et al., 2017). On top, aligning the organization and in that regard more the processes, tools, data flow as well as roles and responsibilities to customer experience and the customer journey will significantly improve experience scores, as various different measures that play into a single customer journey are optimized at once (Chheda et al., 2017). Also, Garton (2017) argues with a clear ownership of any relevant customer journey, to ensure the customer is heard within an organization. The key question that remains open at this point is: how far it makes sense to implement the customer journey in internal structures. Is it just a matter of processes, information flow, and bringing together the right people, or is it also something that needs to be reflected in the organizational setup?

Out of digital customer engagement perspective, the importance of an optimized and aligned operating model towards the strategy is clear. Without touching how a company operates, real change will not happen. In doing so, there are many different aspects to consider and there is certainly no one-size-fits-all solution available, as an operating model heavily depends on the status of an organization as much as on the exact strategy defined. And only if both aspects are considered, a true value will be achieved.

References

Angevine, C., Keomany, J., Thomsen, J., & Zemmel, R. (2021). *Implementing a digital transformation at industrial companies*. McKinsey & Company.

Bellantuono, N., Nuzzi, A., Pontrandolfo, P., & Scozzi, B. (2021). Digital transformation models for the I4. 0 transition: Lessons from the change management literature. *Sustainability, 13*(23), 12941.

Berman, S. J. (2012). Digital transformation: Opportunities to create new business models. *Strategy & Leadership, 40*, 16.

Blenko, M., & Root, J. (2015). *Design principles for a robust operating model*. Bain Brief, Bain & Company.

Bollard, A., Larrea, E., Singla, A., & Sood, R. (2017). *The next-generation operating model for the digital world* (pp. 1–8). Digital McKinsey.

Bounfour, A. (2016). Digital futures, digital transformation. In *Progress in IS* (Vol. 10, pp. 978–973). Springer International Publishing.

de la Boutetière, H., Montagner, A., & Reich, A. (2018). *Unlocking success in digital transformations* (p. 29). McKinsey & Company.

Brosseau, D., Ebrahim, S., Handscomb, C., & Thaker, S. (2019, May 10). *The journey to an agile organization*. McKinsey & Company.

Campbell, A., Gutierrez, M., & Lancelott, M. (2017). *Operating model canvas*. Van Haren Publishing.

Chandler, A. D., Jr. (1969). *Strategy and structure: Chapters in the history of the American industrial enterprise* (Vol. 120). MIT press.

Chheda, S., Duncan, E., & Roggenhofer, S. (2017). *Putting customer experience at the heart of next-generation operating models*. Digital McKinsey.

Code, C. (1992). *The financial aspects of corporate governance*. The Committee on the Financial Aspects of Corporate Governance and Gee and Co. Ltd..

Comella-Dorda, S., Lohiya, S., & Speksnijder, G. (2016). *An operating model for company-wide agile development*. McKinsey Digital.

Correani, A., De Massis, A., Frattini, F., Petruzzelli, A. M., & Natalicchio, A. (2020). Implementing a digital strategy: Learning from the experience of three digital transformation projects. *California Management Review, 62*(4), 37–56.

Davenport, T. H., & Westerman, G. (2018). Why so many high-profile digital transformations fail. *Harvard Business Review, 9*, 15.

Deloitte. (2020). *If you want your digital transformation to succeed, align your operating model to your strategy*. Harvard Business Review.

Dobru, D. F., Hewes, C., Simon, P., & Welchman, T. (2021). Operating model transformations: Not all elements are created equal. *McKinsey & Company*. https://www.mckinsey.com/capabilities/people-and-organizational-performance/our-insights/the-organization-blog/operating-model-transformations-not-all-elements-are-created-equal

Dürr, S., Wagner, H.-T., Weitzel, T., & Beimborn, D. (2017). *Navigating digital innovation—The complementary effect of organizational and knowledge recombination*.

Galbraith, J. R., & Kates, A. (2010). *Designing your organization: Using the STAR model to solve 5 critical design challenges*. Wiley.

Garton, E. (2017, November 22). Is your company actually set up to support your strategy? *Harvard Business Review*. https://hbr.org/2017/11/is-your-company-actually-set-up-to-support-your-strategy

Garton, E., & Noble, A. (2017). How to make agile work for the C-suite. *Harvard Business Review, 19*, 2017.

Imran, F., Shahzad, K., Butt, A., & Kantola, J. (2021). Digital transformation of industrial organizations: Toward an integrated framework. *Journal of Change Management, 21*(4), 451–479.

Kotter, J. P. (2012). *Leading change*. Harvard business press.

Mankins, M. (2017). Great companies obsess over productivity, not efficiency. *Harvard Business Review*, 3.

Matt, C., Hess, T., & Benlian, A. (2015). Digital transformation strategies. *Business & Information Systems Engineering, 57*(5), 339–343.

Münstermann, B., & Weitzel, T. (2008). *What is process standardization?* (p. 64).
Murphy, A., Kirwin, J., & Razak, K. A. (2016). *Operating model: Delivering on strategy and optimizing processes*. Ernst & Young.
Pardasani, N., Danoesastro, M., Alfrink, K., Stutts, L., Schotkamp, T., & Hilbers, P. (2019). Taking agile transformations beyond the tipping point.
Reijnen, C., Overbeek, S., Wijers, G. M., Sprokholt, A., Haijenga, F., & Brinkkemper, S. (2018). A shared vision for digital transformation: Codification of the operating model canvas approach.
Schäfermeyer, M., Rosenkranz, C., & Holten, R. (2012). The impact of business process complexity on business process standardization. *Business & Information Systems Engineering, 4*(5), 261–270.
Tabrizi, B., Lam, E., Girard, K., & Irvin, V. (2019). Digital transformation is not about technology. *Harvard Business Review, 13*(March), 1–6.

A Framework for Orchestrating Higher-Level Processes for Successful Digital Customer Engagement: A Plaidoyer for a Digital Marketing Cortex

Uli Schneider, Lore Darcos, and Robin Schneider

1 Introduction

In past years, the success of semiconductor companies like Infineon often depended on investments in and exploitation of R&D, resilient supply chains, and manufacturing capabilities (Burkacky et al., 2021). Therefore, it is obvious that such a company tends to have a focus on product technology and process innovation, which has proven to be key success factors over many years, rather than differentiating through scalable marketing or customer engagement approaches. That also makes sense because the decision-makers within the customer base consist largely of engineers and electronics experts who are driven by a technical or technological mindset. Yet, we see a shift in mindset where marketing, and particularly digital marketing, as a practice and its value are more widely recognized, as the quantity of digital presence is instrumental in determining whether customers perceive the quality and the innovative extent of a product. Digital marketing is believed to be a practice that opens new markets and new routes into the market (Bauer et al., 2020). However, evaluating the value of digital marketing, also within our company, is often based on personal experience and instances where a promotional activity such as a video or banner has shaped the own perception and resulted in a personal impact. Often times, these experiences feed the narrative that marketing, and digital marketing in particular, is some kind of skill or art where creativity is the most important ingredient (Crader & Zaichkowsky, 2007; Fillis & Rentschler, 2005; Slater et al., 2010; Wadden, 2011).

U. Schneider (✉) · L. Darcos
Infineon Technologies AG, Neubiberg, Germany
e-mail: Uli.Schneider@infineon.com; Lore.Darcos@Infineon.com

R. Schneider
Rheinzabern, Germany

U. Schneider, J. Hoika (eds.), *Digital Marketing in the Automotive Electronics Industry*, Management for Professionals,
https://doi.org/10.1007/978-3-031-30720-1_7

Although such widespread anecdotal evidence contains a kernel of truth that isolated marketing activities can have a tremendous effect on a customer, this perception does not match the differentiation required in this area. Digital marketing is not less system oriented, and thus complex, compared to other corporate disciplines in everyday business: It requires the definition of goals, strives for real-time monitoring, carries out simulations, and identifies correlations and causalities and therefore needs to be embedded in the overall business context of a company so as to provide a competitive contribution. For that reason, the digital marketing discipline is better thought as an area which requires a cerebral cortex,[1] where higher processes are defined and orchestrated through the interlinkage of areas such as strategy, content marketing, sales, and many others. This analogy within the anatomy does also not fall short of considering the importance of the aforementioned creativity or considering the relevance of system thinking in digital marketing. As stated before in marketing practice and theory, creativity is often considered a marketing capability that is required to become competitive. By contrast, in the cerebral cortex as interconnected system, creativity becomes a result that is created in an area of cortex and results from the integration of different types of information according to a task's goal (De Souza et al., 2014).

Against this backdrop and under consideration of common taxonomy of models[2] (Hill et al., 1981; Homburg, 2000), the following chapter presents the reader with an integrated framework in which all relevant elements (descriptive model) and interactions at interfaces (features of an explanatory model) of our successful digital customer engagement approach in the automotive electronics industry are mapped. Accordingly, the framework serves the reader as a practical blueprint of a cerebral cortex, an overarching control system of digital marketing.

The model and its elements can be divided into three interdependent areas:

1. Association area: The strategic sphere of the model relates the marketing specific elements of the framework to a strategic intent
2. Sensory area: The customers' sphere represents the customer centricity and customer perspective within the framework
3. Motor area: The engagement sphere of the framework represents the tactical elements that are required for implementing digital marketing measures

These areas are held together by performance measurement based on data and metrics which ensure the right configuration of all areas. A configuration is the design and alignment of the different elements within one area to ensure the areas fit best and ultimately serve customer requirements.

[1]The cerebral cortex is the outermost layer of the brain that is involved in higher-level functions, such as language, perception, decision-making, and planning (Cadwell et al., 2019).

[2]The authors (Hill et al., 1981; Homburg, 2000) refer to four different types of models, namely, reference models, explanatory models, predictive models, and decision models, which represent business reality in a simplified framework depending on the purpose of the model.

It is clear that the elements (e.g., media channel) of the framework are not only usable in the automotive electronics industry, yet specifics apply to the use of the elements in the automotive context. Therefore, it is worth describing the elements in detail and based on the application in our Infineon Automotive context. In contrast, the design of the elements (e.g., how to design a specific campaign with a specific persona in a specific strategy field) cannot be described in detail. Due to the complexity caused by the multitude of configuration combinations (e.g., of target persona, market, media channel), an all-encompassing guide for different model configurations is not the goal of the following considerations.

2 Associate Area

The associate area addresses the strategic and content elements of the integrated marketing framework. These elements form the basis for connecting the marketing-specific elements of the framework with the broader business context at Infineon and ensuring that all digital marketing activities contribute to the company's business objectives. The elements included build on each other and are not a mere copy of the business strategy. The associate area aims to translate relevant parts of the automotive strategy, where digital marketing can support strategy execution, into marketing focus topics supported with relevant content.

2.1 Business Strategy

The business strategy, which is reviewed at regular intervals in any company, contains a wealth of information and decisions that focus on attaining a competitive edge. For a company of a significant size, however, it also contains the most relevant input and a boundary condition for the digital marketing discipline (Slater et al., 2011) such as focus markets, differentiation aspects, or topics for the upcoming strategy implementation cycle. Without going into detail about the strategy, this is no different at Infineon Automotive. The strategy defines the operational focus for the next years in terms of products or solutions in a broader sense as well as the differentiators for focus markets and regions from the areas of electromobility, automated driving, or automotive cybersecurity. Digital marketing activities must now be orchestrated to contribute to the strategic elements. This sounds obvious, but adherence to this strategy regularly proves difficult when, for example, product launches are delayed and prioritization of marketing activities is only along the backlog and not the strategy. That is when the digital marketing strategy comes into play.

2.2 Digital Marketing Strategy

A digital marketing strategy for the upcoming implementation cycle takes more into account than just the key advertising themes that have been delivered from the business strategy. It is the set of decisions and efforts (Day, 1990) by which a business expects to attain its (digital) marketing objectives and meet its customers' requirements (Slater & Olson, 2001) along the customer journey. The digital marketing strategy contains therefore an overview of the most important focus topics, which are already filtered according to four constraints: First, only focus topics in the business strategy that can be efficiently addressed through digital campaigns should be considered. For example, an advertisement for battery management ICs in the zero emissions area that addresses a global audience (one-to-many) is more appropriate than digital advertising for a custom part developed for one customer (one-to-one). Second, when defining the annual marketing strategy, consistency of topics must be considered when setting priorities and timelines. Therefore, the specific solution, product, or application campaigns should preferably be laid out over a long period of time rather than just a few weeks or months. The development cycles in the automotive industry are long, so that a short campaign cannot fully enfold its potential. It is also advisable to make the digital marketing strategy consistent across cycles in order to implement an "always-on" approach and stay at the top of the target groups' minds. Third, the digital marketing strategy refers only to products and solutions that are marketable, i.e., can be purchased by the target audience, and for which all the necessary documentation and records required by customers are available. A campaign cannot compensate for a delayed market launch. Ever. The fourth and final constraint to consider is that internal (technical) support for the focus topics is in place. In addition to the focus topics, the digital marketing strategy also includes the objective and the goals to be achieved with the upcoming digital marketing measures. The digital marketing plan does not include the tactics of the different campaigns that address the focus topics within the execution period.

2.3 Marketing Content and Content Marketing

Once the strategy and marketing focus topics are defined, it is of utmost importance that the appropriate content is available for the digital marketing activities. According to Rowley (2008), content marketing is providing customer value along the customer journey. The author further defines content as "bit-based objects distributed through electronic channels," and we have adopted this definition because it nicely illustrates how widely the content definition can be interpreted as long as the content adds value in the marketplace.

This means that content creation at Infineon is by no means just a digital marketing task, but also an integral part of the product development and the go-to-market process of products and solutions. From a marketing perspective, we simply need to ensure that product promotion only takes place once the product development and go-to-market process has been successfully completed and a required basic set of content such as documents, tools, and other information (e.g., website, data sheets, samples, etc.) is available and the customer can work with our products. While this set is practical and can often be used to a great extent for marketing campaigns, this content is not targeted to a specific campaign purpose and is not optimized for specific channels. While a product data sheet is the most relevant content piece for a product purchasing decision, there is more appropriate content

that can be used in a lead generation campaign that will in turn help initiate that purchase decision later on. Therefore, when defining a campaign, we need to ensure that the technical support and digital marketing teams create content that is best suited for the media channel, purpose, and targeted buyer persona. This is a true collaborative effort that requires the expertise of all parties involved. To provide better guidance to non-digital marketing teams on meaningful combinations of media and content, we have developed a content guideline that considers purpose, effectiveness, and structural guidelines. This should also be embedded in a broader content strategy (Fig. 1).

3 Sensory Area: The Customers' Sphere

As suggested in marketing literature, we at Infineon Automotive follow an integrated marketing approach (Ibrahim & Rehman, 2011) that is deeply rooted in customer centricity. Especially in our industry, which is driven by demanding technical and quality requirements, long-term commitments, and a globally distributed value chain (Sturgeon et al., 2009), we need to point out that our customers differ significantly from customers in other industries, not to mention the B2C context. Therefore, we started with the question of what drives the use of solutions and how customers actually use the electronics solution in which context. To do this, we defined both the most relevant target persona and the (digital) interaction context, namely, the customer journey.

3.1 Buyer Persona

The goal of a successful marketing approach is to create a unique and individual customer experience tailored to the individual customer's needs. However, given the sheer volume of different customers and the even higher number of individuals within the customer base that Infineon serves, we cannot derive several hundred of thousand possible customer profiles to create this unique experience. With this in mind, it makes sense to modularize our digital marketing offering to create this very unique customer experience. For this modularization, however, it is necessary to derive a set of customer information (such as interests, needs, and pain points) that is valid for a variety of profiles, regardless of which company they belong to. In theory, these archetypes of customers are called buyer personas (Revella, 2015), and they guide decisions about offering, the solutions' value proposition, omnichannel interactions, and the customer's journey towards purchase (Cruz & Karatzas, 2020).

In the beginning, we tried to keep complexity in check and considered it sufficient to focus and develop only personas of the key decision-makers in order to establish digital marketing process baselines and frameworks. These two decision-makers for buying automotive electronics are the development engineer who develop systems like body, safety or powertrain solutions as well as the purchaser who ensures compliance with commercial requirements. In reality, there are many more relevant buyer personas, such as the Pricing Manager or the Logistics Manager, but they do not play the most prominent role in the buying decision-making process.

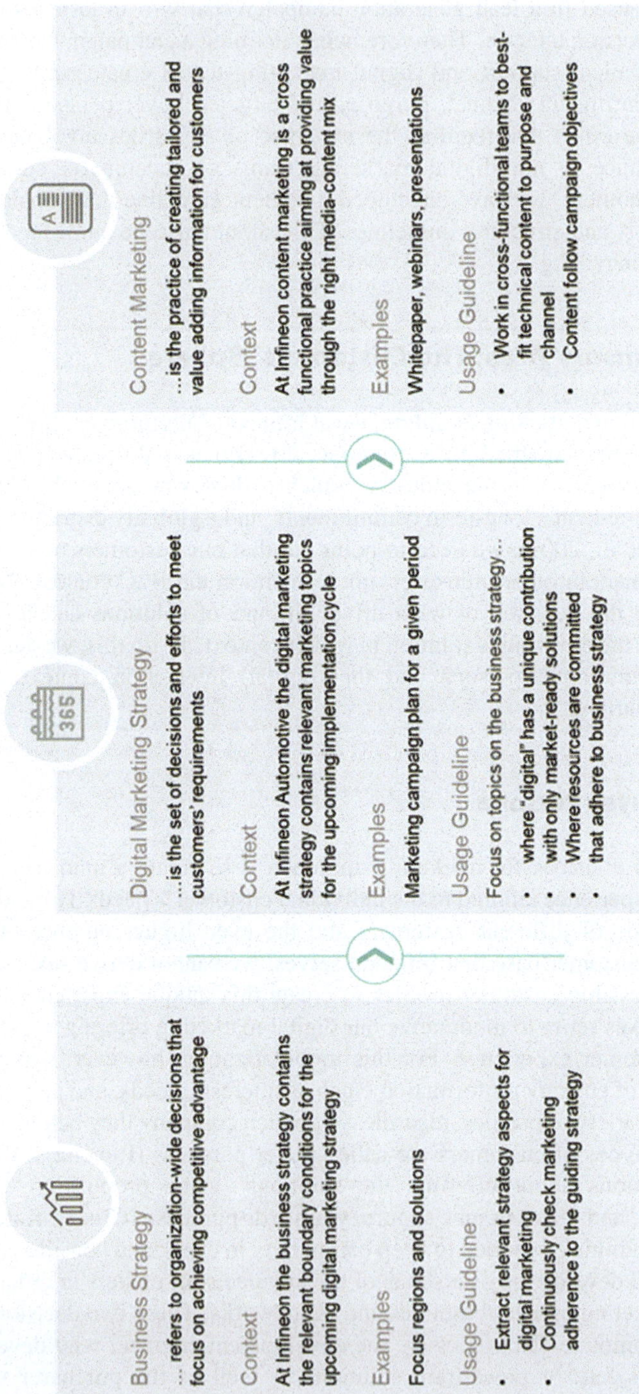

Fig. 1 Overview of associate area framework elements

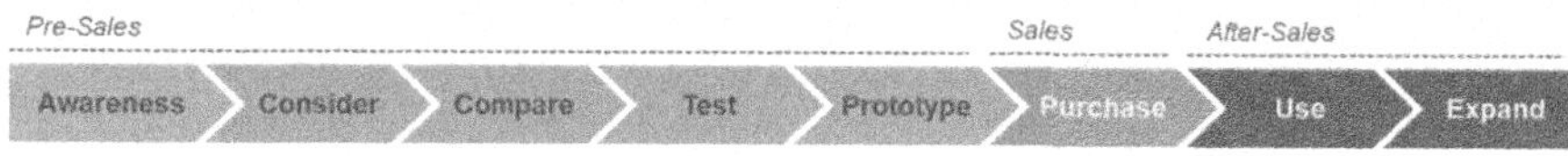

Fig. 2 Infineon's representation of a customer journey

3.2 Customer Journey

The aim of (digital) marketing campaigns and digital customer engagement is to guide the customer through their buying journey as efficiently as possible, and as stated above, another element that is important to create a tailored and unique customer experience is the customer journey (Lemon & Verhoef, 2016). According to Følstad and Kvale (2018), the customer journey addresses processual as well as experiential aspects of service processes as seen from the customer's perspective and describes reoccurring interactions between a solution provider and the customer. In simple terms a customer journey is a "walk in the customer's shoes" (Blomkvist & Holmlid, 2010).

The customer journey at Infineon aims to provide a seamless service offering and extends from awareness in the pre-sales phase to the usage expansion in the after-sales phase (Fig. 2). It has been developed and tested over several years with a variety of internal and external stakeholders and has undergone adjustments and minor changes over time.

Since we as a company largely use the same technical infrastructure, tools, and marketing channels for marketing purposes to serve our customers and meet their needs, the customer journey framework at Infineon Automotive is not unique to automotive customers. It makes sense to use the same customer journey framework as other business units besides automotive, but to suit the target audience, it is required that we configure the phases of the customer journey, namely the touching points, for automotive customers differently than other business units serving other industries. For example, the development cycles for automotive platforms differ significantly from those of other industries, so the customer journey is correspondingly slower. The two focal buyer personas also suggest that the customer journey is very different for both and usually proceed in a non-linear manner. The ultimate goal is that we can create a highly personalized customer journey with relevant touching points for each individual customer (user), tailored to their individual needs, if the tools and infrastructure allow for it.

With the definition of the model for the customer journey and the persona, it was for us possible to build up on these concepts and define specific objective for marketing campaigns and concert the campaign towards a common goal such as awareness, lead generation, and engagement (Fig. 3).

4 Motor Area: Digital Customer Engagement Sphere

After having laid out the associate and sensory elements of the framework, we devote the focus on the model's core of the tactical elements. The configuration of these tactical elements into a set of orchestrated activities across different channels is also known in the literature as digital marketing campaigns of an integrated

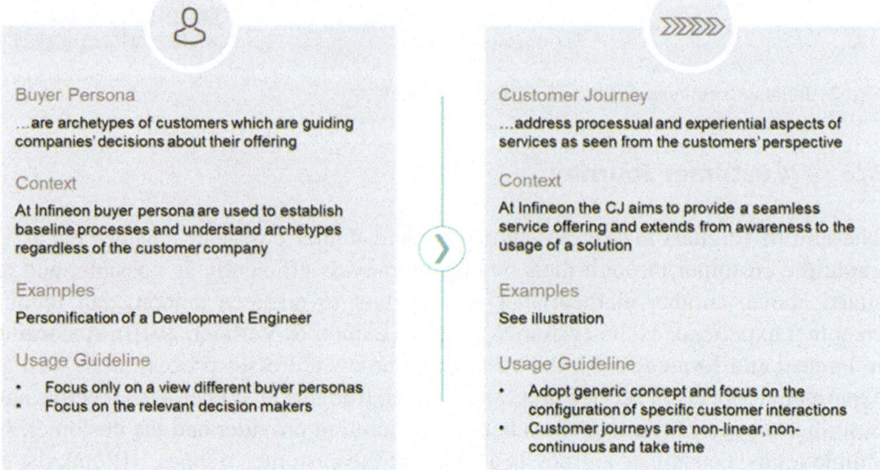

Fig. 3 Overview of sensory area framework elements

marketing approach (Leppäniemi & Karjaluoto, 2008) and represents the motor of the digital marketing practice. These elements answer the question of how to achieve digital customer engagement in an integrated marketing approach by the right selection of media channels in line with its associate and sensory elements and thus guaranteeing the promotional success (Ibrahim & Rehman, 2011).

In the framework (and as part of our integrated marketing campaign approach), we include paid, owned, as well as earned media elements in accordance with a commonly used taxonomy of both practitioners and researchers (Lovett & Staelin, 2016; Mattke et al., 2019; Srinivasan et al., 2016). An integrated marketing approach requires not only a comprehensive approach that considers all media elements, but also a synchronized approach of the media types where all media types are used and work in an orchestrated fashion. Therefore, it is important to acknowledge that each media type has specific benefits that are to be matched with the goals of a campaign so as to ultimately be able to contribute to our business strategy. In the following a detailed description of these benefits in the context of our firm and in our industry will follow.

4.1 Owned Media

Owned media refer to channels that are controlled by a company (Vieira et al., 2019). At Infineon these include our websites, forums, blogs, and social accounts such as Twitter and Facebook, where we know that as an Automotive division, we can possibly reach a critical number and quality of potential users in our target audience with whom we can communicate directly and indirectly. Accordingly, the purpose is to target possible customers who already know us, follow us, have engaged with us before, actively search for our solutions or associate our offering relevant for their system solutions.

4.1.1 Website

The website is our company's digital storefront which allows the presentation of both comprehensive and in-depth information. Particularly the product and application pages are key to present technical content such as product trainings, data sheets, and user manuals that our customers need to make any decision for a selection for their automotive system.

To be an effective enabler of the customer journey, the website has to provide an outstanding user experience and user interface design (UX/UI). User experience encompasses more than just the user interface and includes the experiences that result from the overall function and usability of the website, which become particularly relevant in the later stages of the customer journey. There, customers rely on many of the important digital services through online tools required for the entire automotive customer journey. Sometimes these services are gated and the prospective customer provides information so as to use tools, digital assistants, or download simulations. Nevertheless, there are other services such as product and solution finder that he or she can use, without providing contact information.

The gating strategy of assets and marketing collateral plays an important role to provide customers with added value in their search for solutions. That is, a gating strategy that places media content behind a lead capture form or in an area where a user must provide personal information to collect customer data, must ultimately serve the customer's long-term user experience for his or her journey. For example, we would not gate content that makes the customer journey unnecessarily cumbersome (e.g., by gating a datasheet) or unless we are certain that we can provide customers who are interested in the very gated content with related and meaningful information and services. To provide more clarity on what content should be gated, A/B testing, also known as split testing, can provide a customer perspective on the acceptance of gated and ungated content.

Even though many aspects of the website and its content are within one's own design freedom, the performance of the website depends significantly on the indexing of search engines (Google, Bing, Baidu), where search engine crawlers store and categorize information and content they find on websites so that it can be displayed in the results. Certainly, the UI/UX aspects and gating measures mentioned above also have an impact, but following the search engine optimization (SEO) guidelines of the major search engines makes all the difference when it comes to search engine ranking results.

In general, three types of SEO measures are relevant: First, on-site SEO, where we make sure that the content on the pages is relevant to the target audience, especially the development engineer. To do so, the usage of the right keywords, titles, and meta tags as well as the links to relevant product and application pages is important. When reviewing keywords, it's important to keep an open mind because often our company's internal terminology doesn't necessarily match that of our customers and the marketplace. The second SEO aspect, technical SEO, relates mainly to infrastructural and IT related matters, and from the perspective of a business unit, there is only little we can do. However, we ensure that only the needed and not outdated content is on the website to keep the loading times at a good level. In the third SEO aspect, the off-page SEO, we ensure that the link building and social media activities are synchronized with the focus and advertising campaign activities.

4.1.2 Blogs

Running a blog also helps improve SEO performance and thus influences search rankings through signaling to the search engine that our website content provides relevant answers to our customers' questions. However, the main reason for setting up and running a blog is user-centric: The Infineon blog builds trust with users and potential customers interested in using our technologies, services, or products by providing in-depth technical discussions about the practical application of these very solutions. The published contents can also easily be tied into a digital marketing campaign without the drawbacks of more formalized formats such as white papers. A publication in a blog offers one of our target buyer personas, the development engineer, the chance to read in-depth technical content. It is usually shorter, supports website traffic,[3] does not have to meet the format requirements, and is accessible for unregistered users. This allows Infineon to use the blog as a channel to fan out quickly information of company knowledge with experts who cover current topics without a cumbersome whitepaper creation. To reap these benefits of a blog, content must be relevant, varied, and consistent, and therefore, it is recommended to create an editorial plan which also includes committed technical resources for the content creation. The disadvantage is that customer information (e.g., lead or engagement information) is lost through gateless access.

4.1.3 Forums and Community

The blog is an integral part of the Infineon developer community, which provides a variety of information in other community formats such as forums, knowledge-based articles, or resource libraries. In order to be able to use the advantageous basic principles such as speed of information dissemination, scalability, and self-service of these formats for a strategic digital customer loyalty approach, the formats must be embedded in the respective campaigns and their focus topics. Similar to blogs, the unformalized publication process allows internal experts to disseminate in-depth information quickly to a large audience. But in contrast to blogs, other community formats (particularly forums) also allow users and customers to bring problems of all kinds to our attention and expect quick response times without having to route a complaint or request through an organization until the right information owner is found. This helps both the user and Infineon in several ways. For example, a user who tests and debugs microcontroller-based designs and encounters problems will find support quickly in the developer community. This is because, first of all, the traditional support structure at Infineon depends on the customer and project characteristics. A small customer (or even a mass-market customer), without an assigned internal contact, would at best get limited focus and a quick reference to

[3] The contents of a blog will be indexed by search engines.

standard support material, as attention in the automotive sector is often dictated by the multi-million-euro designs of key players in the industry. In contrast, finding an answer (regardless of the size of the customer opportunity) in the community requires only that at least two experts be brought together on the platform, and is typically a matter of hours, often faster than traditional support structures. Additional help is provided by the inherent characteristics of liking and amplifying problems and solutions in a community. As a solved or unsolved problem can be voted on, the importance, occurrence, and urgency of the solved or unsolved problem is signaled to all members of the community. The fact that the solution provider does not have to be an Infineon employee enables not only speed, but also scalability of the amount and number of solutions. This is particularly evident in Infineon's emerging areas, where the growing number of resources is initially more concerned with gathering requirements, solutions, and business development than with comprehensive customer support. If the self-service infrastructure, the network of existing problem solvers, dedicated champions, and the growing number of members within the community are well organized, this will help to ease the burden on Infineon resources in the medium term. However, as mentioned at the beginning, in order to unleash the full potential of a community for strategic customer engagement, it is of utmost importance to synchronize the structure of community support with the strategic focus of marketing campaigns and therefore advisable to consider procedural and ownership aspects when defining the community support set-up.

4.1.4 Owned Social Media

Unlike community, blogs, and forums, our social media accounts are not suited for providing technical information and support, but rather for promoting events and collateral as well as making the customer aware of the mere existence of emerging trends and its matching Infineon solutions. Social media marketing activities therefore require little efforts and, apart from the provision of suitable digital marketing content and an editorial plan, do not require a complex support structure from the business unit. Typically, the users in our target audience who engage with Infineon's automotive social media content are at the early stages of their customer journey, and our content, which consists mainly of videos, animations, and pictures, is focused on either our individual portfolio products (including software), an interoperable portfolio chip set, or other offerings such as tools or differentiators (e.g., functional safety support).

4.1.5 Mailings

In contrast to social media, the e-mail channel can provide relevant content for a wide range of different phases of the customer journey. On the one hand, mailings can be used to generate awareness for solutions by sending a generic newsletter with a variety of product launches or a one-shot on a specific topic to a tailored target group. On the other hand, mailings can also be highly customized and tailored to the specific customer needs at each stage of the customer journey. In this case, a multi-stage nurture mailing guides the customer successively through the customer journey, while we recommend our solutions and tools along the way. Either way, to be successful with e-mail marketing, it is important to define a suitable email marketing

Table 1 Overview of Infineon Automotive's used owned media channels

Owned Media	Purpose for Infineon Automotive	Media Characteristics	Main Influencing Factors
Website	Digital storefront of our company products and solutions	• One-sided dissemination of information • Allows presentation of in-depth content • Allows presentation of comprehensive content	• SEO (on-page, off-page, technical) • Continuously optimize gating strategy • Continuously optimize UX/UI • A/B testing
Blog	Self-hosted website journal to showcase technical content and its noteworthy features	• One-sided dissemination of information • Allows presentation of in-depth content • Enable trust-building through discussion of in-depth content • Attracts qualified website traffic • Improves website's search ranks	• Compelling in-depth technical content • Editorial plan with assigned experts • On-page SEO
Forum and community	Self-hosted platform connecting users around a common automotive electronics interest to ease retention and loyalty	• Bilateral communication channel • Allows presentation of in-depth content • Supports scalability through information self-service • Allows fast access to company experts	• Editorial plan for comm. posts • Access to experts (internal) • Assigned and responsive community managers
Owned Social Media Channels	Communication channel for our latest offering to an existing broad user base	• One-sided dissemination of information • Allows presentation of high-level content	• Compelling high-level content • Editorial plan for posts
e-Mailings	Communication channel for a tailored promotion to a selected existing user base	• One-sided dissemination of information • Allows presentation of high-level content (newsletter) • Allows presentation of technical content (nurture) • Suitable for lead nurturing	• Compelling suitable content • Optimized marketing automation approach (calendar, triggers) • Thorough email campaign approach (newsletter, nurture, drip, blast) • Email UI/UX

automation approach, which includes workflows (with triggers and delays), which segments the subscribed recipients and is continuously improved by UX/UI and testing efforts. The disadvantage of email marketing is that it is a one-way communication and recipients cannot effectively or easily respond to the content they have received. The lack of direct communication with subject matter experts, sales reps, or application engineers limits email marketing as a preferred channel when it gets too technical.

Table 1 shows a summary of our owned media channels and highlights that the entire customer journey can be covered via these channels. Whether it's developing new target groups via social media channels or providing important information during the design-in process via automated mails, depending on the objective, the use of owned media channels can guide users either through individual stages, multiple stages, or the entire customer journey. What the overview in Table 1 does not show, however, is that the full potential can only be exploited if all customer data is used effectively and ultimately only serves the customer's journey. Additionally, if the owned media mix is not aligned with itself, with the use of paid media, or with the focus topics such as applications, products, and other solutions, there is a risk that the use will not be focused and the effort required to build, maintain, and execute marketing activities will be diluted.

4.2 Paid Media

Paid media contrasts with owned media, which Infineon uses to promote its products and solutions for the automotive industry, because, as the name suggests, they have to be paid for (Vieira et al., 2019). The range of paid media is broad, from search engine and social media ads to more traditional options such as print ads in trade media, billboards, and television commercials. However, when promoting products and solutions, it is vital to target the appropriate audience. Since the target group in the automotive electronics industry is very specific and probably smaller compared to consumer target groups, it is of utmost importance to opt for a paid media mix that reaches exactly this target group. Infineon Automotive's paid media mix, for example, deliberately excludes television advertising and billboard advertising in order to avoid promotional wastage that we still pay for. Only the most relevant media channels are presented below. Besides, it should also be mentioned that the paid media landscape is changing rapidly and a complete list would therefore quickly become outdated.

4.2.1 Paid Social Media

Compared to the company's owned social media channels, where we promote our (product) solutions alongside other posts and news, the paid social media activities are used to promote automotive solutions to a specific target audience who is not necessarily following the company's social media accounts. So, one of the main purposes of using social media is to reach new potential customers and users of the relevant target groups and make them aware of the company's offer, instead of continuing an already started customer journey in the final stages. Therefore, content suitable for this purpose tends to be more general in nature and includes videos, training, or explanatory animations instead of a technical data sheet with detailed facts or simulation models. Content or unique campaign-specific advertising activities are shared on popular social media platforms such as Twitter, Facebook, LinkedIn, or YouTube. Since only the relevant target groups are to be reached, platforms that enable professional targeting based on their position with specific companies in specific locations are preferred for marketing purposes.

The immediate results of using paid social media in terms of impressions and views are substantial, but there are two points to consider when using paid social media activities for automotive marketing: First, the conversion of social media views into relevant user traffic on owned media such as the firm's website is vanishingly small. While social media are the platform of choice for branding purposes, depending on the marketing purpose, other media are better suited. Second, social media activities create a perception bias among relevant non-digital marketer stakeholders. While social media is highly visible within the (company's own) social media bubble, the same is not necessarily true for the relevant target groups outside the company. In a high-tech environment like the semiconductor industry, where marketing content is created by and with technical experts, their support often depends on the visibility of the result, not necessarily on the effectiveness of the digital marketing activities. Therefore, it is important to also transparently communicate the results about the effectiveness of the use of social media.

4.2.2 Search Engine Advertisement

The opposite is true for search engine advertising (SEA), and its popularity suffers from perception bias: search engine advertising is very effective for external audiences who use search engines to find information about solutions to their specific tasks. On the other hand, its effectiveness is not very visible to internal stakeholders who are needed to provide technical information and support to set up an effective SEA campaign with providing and reviewing the right keywords and up-to-date content on websites.

SEA is paid advertising displayed prominently alongside organic search results on search engines such as Google, Baidu, or Bing. Every time a user enters a search query, an auction begins in the background of the search engine for the best spot on the search engine results page (SERP) for relevant ads. In this live auction, the highest bid is assigned the highest position in the search results. The right choice of keywords therefore plays an important role in SEA and the bidding for the auctions. Again, it is important to distinguish between internal and external terminology to the company. The wording used by the company for certain solutions may not match the terms commonly used in the market. For this reason, it is important to use specific tools and perform keyword analysis. In conclusion, SEA is one of the most effective means among paid activities to generate user traffic on the company's owned channels. Although SEA can compensate for certain SEO weaknesses in the short term, in the long term both SEO and SEA must be used correctly to place content in a sustainable and return on investment-oriented manner.

4.2.3 Display Ads

While search engine ads appear in the SERP for potential customers as soon as they start searching in search engines, display ads appear while people are visiting non-vendor websites on the Internet. The disadvantage of display ads is that you may not reach engineers who are actively searching for semiconductors right in the moment with display ads. This means that display ads can be used effectively to raise awareness or retarget and engage users, presenting our solutions to audiences that have previously interacted with our online product offering. However, to effectively use display ads for marketing solutions to automotive systems engineers, it is important to choose the right ad type and select relevant pages for automotive audiences. Traditional display ads consist mainly of images and some text which are placed on relevant websites. In contrast, a discovery ad, which is often mobile-friendly, adapts to placement (native), and thus aims to show users content related to their electronic areas of interest, is suitable for more specific product-related content in later stages of the customer journey. Thereby, discovery campaigns leverage search engines' understanding of user intent to present more relevant and engaging ads to target audiences (Table 2).

Using the right paid media mix in marketing in the context of the automotive semiconductor industry is particularly suitable for guiding potential customers through the phases of the customer journey, such as awareness and consideration, by promoting new solutions or promoting more technical benefits to highly targeted audiences, where you leverage customer data acquired from owned channels and the

Table 2 Overview of Infineon Automotive's used paid media channels

Paid Media	Purpose for Infineon Automotive	Media Characteristics	Main Influencing Factors
Paid Social Media	Communication channel for tailored promotions to a selected new or existing user base	• One-sided dissemination of information • Allows presentation of high-level content • Suitable for videos and pictures	• Suitable content for social media • Targeting (differentiated, concentrated, micro-targeting)
Search Engine Ads	Promotional channel for tailored promotions to a selected new or existing user group which is actively searching	• One-sided dissemination of information • Allows presentation of high-level content • Suitable for texts and pictures • Recipients' high willingness to engage	• People re-targeting (demographics, audience) • Contextual targeting (keywords, topics)
Display ads	Promotional channel for a tailored promotion to a selected new or existing user group with an affinity to the solution	• One-sided dissemination of information • Allows presentation of high-level content • Suitable for texts and pictures	• Suitable content that matches goal • Template use • People re-targeting (demographics, audience) • Contextual targeting (keywords, topics, placements) • Platforms specification requirements •

algorithms of search engines. However, as mentioned earlier, synchronizing owned media processes with paid strategic focus also enables us to move forward in later stages of the customer journey. By definition, paid media incurs a budget and therefore a cost, but when synchronized with focus processes established for the owned channel, no dedicated technical campaign support is required.

4.3 Earned Media

In general, earned media refers to media activity primarily on social media such as coverage, comments, shared content, or snippets of conversation about a company's brand and solutions that originate from third parties on non-proprietary channels without the company having paid for the promotion. Vieira et al. (2019) define earned media activity as the sum of likes, shares, and comments on social media platforms such as Facebook and YouTube. Poynter et al. (2014) also include favoring discussions from forums and bulletin boards when referring to their definition of earned media. The advantage of earned media, besides the low costs, is the authenticity and thus trustworthiness of independent reviews and mentions of Infineon solutions. Similar to paid media, only a selective but particularly relevant list is presented in the following, rather than claiming to be exhaustive.

4.3.1 Forums and Community (Owned and Third Party)

As mentioned above, Infineon operates its own forum and community, in which third parties or customers also provide solutions and reviews of Infineon solutions. In addition to the fast response times to inquiries, the contributions of other customers signal trustworthiness to the users of the aforementioned platforms by sharing their experiences. For marketing purposes, in addition to our own communities and forums, Infineon Automotive also relies on third-party platforms that offer similar opportunities to address immediate feedback and signal correct responses. The discussions in communities and forums help potential customers in later stages of their journey to find support for their development ideas, challenges, and projects. As a vendor, we welcome the creation of any platform that helps our customers with our solutions. However, since we cannot guarantee every discussion and its accuracy, we need to transparently signal to our customers on our owned platforms which solutions are ours.

4.3.2 Collaboration with Influencer

Another way to use earned media is to have influencers discuss or publish your content. Creating engaging and relevant content is one of the best ways to promote Infineon solutions. However, the challenge with influencer marketing is finding a personality that fits the automotive industry, goals, and target audience. This is also the challenge of using influencer marketing in the automotive electronics sector: electronics influencers or makers come from a DIY culture that overlaps with hardware and hacker culture (Nascimento & Pólvora, 2018), and would not typically work on large platforms that meet automotive industry standards. The purpose of influencer marketing is therefore not to support customers in the prototyping phase, but rather to develop technical target groups and increase awareness among students or hobbyists who will come back to Infineon later in their careers (Table 3).

In digital marketing the effect of earned media on conversions is usually very high at almost no cost. Earned media help to build trust between potential customers and the solution they are looking for, without them having to trust the vendor, but rather independent third parties like other customers. At the same time, this is also the challenge for Infineon Automotive to take advantage of earned media activities. First, in a B2B environment, potential customers working on systems in a competitive environment might not be willing to share too much prototyping information online. Second, influencers who share their experiences create awareness to a target group of hobbyists and students who, in the best case, will only pay off in the long term when they become decision-makers for major system designs of Tier 1 suppliers or OEMs in a few years' time. Fig. 4 summarizes the owned, paid, earned media approach of Infineon.

Table 3 Overview of Infineon Automotive's used earned media channels

Earned Media	Purpose for Infineon Automotive	Media Characteristics	Main Influencing Factors
Forums and Communities	Third-party platforms which allow an unbiased discussion	• Multilateral communication between unbiased users and experts • Trustworthy	• Responsive, neutral, and supportive engagement
Collaboration with Influencers	Using independent users as ambassadors	• Unbiased third-party communication • Trustworthy • Underrepresented in the automotive electronics industry	• Joined promotions • Free samples and boards

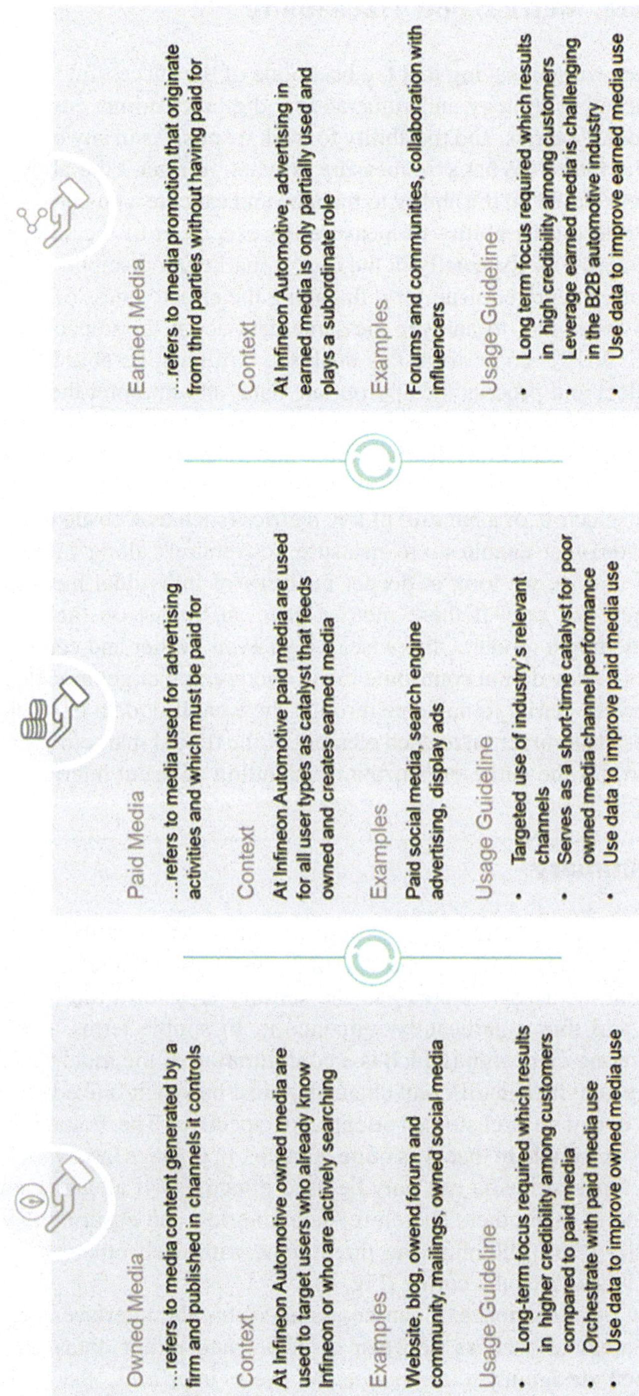

Fig. 4 Overview of motor area framework elements

5 Data, Metrics, and Traceability

It almost goes without saying that the backbone of the successful implementation of a digital marketing strategy and value-adding digital customer engagement practice is based on data, metrics, and the ability to track results. As in any other function, and following the motto "What you measure is what you get," the ability to influence performance is based on the ability to manage and execute a business strategy, which in turn is based on the ability to measure the execution of the strategy (Kaplan & Norton, 1992, p. 71). Especially in the digital marketing discipline, where there is a wealth of data, the prerequisite for influencing the effectiveness of digital marketing strategies is the ability to analyze the same data about the impact of the strategies (Saura et al., 2017). To perform this analysis, you must be able to define the right metrics, collect and process the appropriate data, and interpret the underlying data. Particularly important is the order in which the metrics and proxies are defined first, followed by data collection, interpretation, and visualization of the results.

Our digital marketing target model at Infineon Automotive deliberately focuses on a limited selection of a handful of key metrics (such as website users, downloads, qualified leads) that enable us to measure conversions along the entire customer journey. Of course, we look at deeper analyses of individual measures with additional metrics, but only if these metrics have an impact on the few higher-level metrics of the target model. Otherwise, we go even further and cease entire marketing activities if they do not contribute to the overarching target model. This cascaded approach creates clarity to navigate through the wealth of data in strategy execution and provides clear direction to each element of the digital marketing framework and, by extension, for the entire organization, including adjacent interfaces (Fig. 5).

6 Summary

The explanations of the previous sections are summarized in the Digital Marketing Cortex Framework in Fig. 6. The diagram shows the interaction of all areas and illustrates that the associate area and the sensory area form the framework for the motor area and thus significantly influence it. In simple terms, this means that a digital marketing campaign (which is a configuration of the motor area with the use of marketing activities in different channels) must be synchronized with the strategic component and with a customer-oriented perspective. The framework shows that what sounds so simple in theory is quite complex in practice, as a variety of activities in different types of media can only be used effectively if all areas are coordinated with and among each other. Therefore, data, metrics, and ensuring their traceability play a crucial role in aligning the three areas with each other and thus form the framework brackets of the cortex (Fig. 6).

Based on our experience, it can be assumed that the interfaces between sensory and motor areas as well as between associate and motor areas are of particular interest when designing a campaign. At these interfaces, the strategy and the customer perspective meet the operational elements of the digital marketing

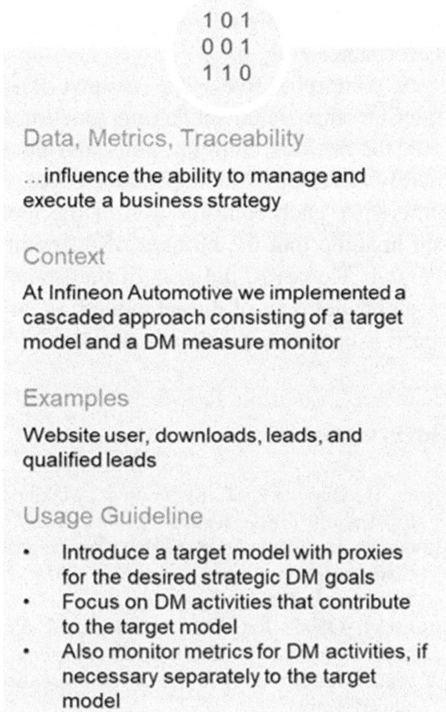

Fig. 5 Summary of the data, metrics, and traceability framework element

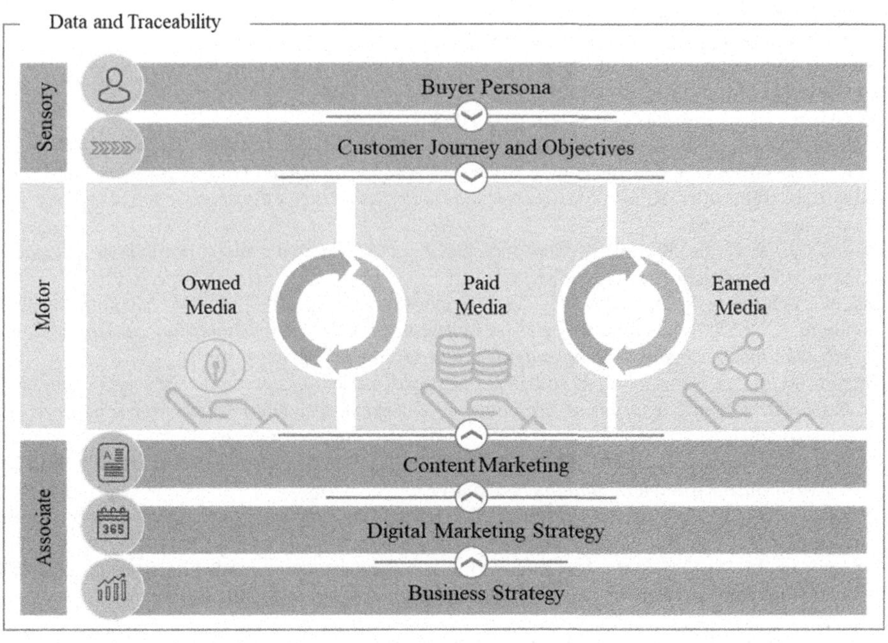

Fig. 6 The cortex framework of digital marketing

framework, and the configuration and alignment of these elements determines the success of the digital marketing campaigns and its contribution to the business performance (Fig. 6).

As comprehensive as the framework is, it also has its limitations. While the model describes the digital marketing function in a comprehensive way, it does not help with the various configurations and characteristics within the individual areas. It merely describes the dependencies of the areas within and among each other. Otherwise, each configuration of the model would have to be explained, and one can imagine that the number of different campaign configurations would be innumerable. However, the goal of the framework is to present the comprehensive and essential elements of digital marketing, as well as to highlight the interdependencies, and it is not intended to be a decision model and thus accomplish this task.

References

Bauer, H., Burkacky, O., Kenevan, P., Mahindroo, A., & Patel, M. (2020, April). *Coronavirus: Implications for the semiconductor industry*. McKinsey & Company.

Blomkvist, J., & Holmlid, S. (2010). Service prototyping according to service design practitioners. *Conference proceedings, ServDes. 2010, exchanging knowledge, Linköping, Sweden, 1–-3 December 2010*, 2, pp. 1–11.

Burkacky, O., de Jong, M., Mittal, A., & Verma, N. (2021). *Value creation: How can the semiconductor industry keep outperforming?* https://www.mckinsey.de/industries/semiconductors/our-insights/value-creation-how-can-the-semiconductor-industry-keep-outperforming

Cadwell, C. R., Bhaduri, A., Mostajo-Radji, M. A., Keefe, M. G., & Nowakowski, T. J. (2019). Development and arealization of the cerebral cortex. *Neuron, 103*(6), 980–1004.

Crader, S., & Zaichkowsky, J. L. (2007). The art of marketing. In *Brick & mortar shopping in the 21st century* (pp. 107–126). Psychology Press.

Cruz, A., & Karatzas, S. (2020). Understanding your buyer persona. In *Digital and social media marketing* (pp. 69–97). Routledge.

Day, G. S. (1990). *Market-Driven Strategy*. The Free Press.

De Souza, L. C., Guimarães, H. C., Teixeira, A. L., Caramelli, P., Levy, R., Dubois, B., & Volle, E. (2014). Frontal lobe neurology and the creative mind. *Frontiers in Psychology, 5*, 761.

Fillis, I., & Rentschler, R. (2005). *Creative marketing: An extended metaphor for marketing in a new age*. Springer.

Følstad, A., & Kvale, K. (2018). Customer journeys: A systematic literature review. *Journal of Service Theory and Practice, 28*, 196.

Hill, W., Fehlbaum, R., & Ulrich, P. (1981). Organisationslehre. Bd. 1 und Bd. 2.3. Aufl. In *Bern*.

Homburg, C. (2000). *Quantitative Betriebswirtschaftslehre: Entscheidungsunterstützung durch Modelle; mit Beispielen, Übungsaufgaben und Lösungen*. Springer-Verlag.

Ibrahim, M. S., & Rehman, S. U. (2011). Integrated marketing communication and promotion. *Researchers World, Journal of Arts, Science & Commerce, International Refereed Research Journal, 2*(4).

Kaplan, R. S., & Norton, D. P. (1992). The balanced scorecard: Measures that drive performance. *Harvard Business Review, January*. February.

Lemon, K. N., & Verhoef, P. C. (2016). Understanding customer experience throughout the customer journey. *Journal of Marketing, 80*(6), 69–96.

Leppäniemi, M., & Karjaluoto, H. (2008). Mobile marketing: From marketing strategy to mobile marketing campaign implementation. *International Journal of Mobile Marketing, 3*(1).

Lovett, M. J., & Staelin, R. (2016). The role of paid, earned, and owned media in building entertainment brands: Reminding, informing, and enhancing enjoyment. *Marketing Science, 35*(1), 142–157.

Mattke, J., Müller, L., & Maier, C. (2019). Paid, owned and earned media: A qualitative comparative analysis revealing attributes influencing consumer's brand attitude in social media. *Proceedings of the 52nd Hawaii international conference on system sciences*, p. 10.

Nascimento, S., & Pólvora, A. (2018). Maker cultures and the prospects for technological action. *Science and Engineering Ethics, 24*(3), 927–946.

Poynter, R., Cassidy, F., & Duckworth, S. (2014). Measuring not counting. *Evaluating social marketing communications.*

Revella, A. (2015). *Buyer personas: How to gain insight into your customer's expectations, align your marketing strategies, and win more business.* Wiley.

Rowley, J. (2008). Understanding digital content marketing. *Journal of Marketing Management, 24*(5–6), 517–540.

Saura, J. R., Palos-Sánchez, P., & Cerdá Suárez, L. M. (2017). Understanding the digital marketing environment with KPIs and web analytics. *Future Internet, 9*(4), 76.

Slater, S. F., Hult, G. T. M., & Olson, E. M. (2010). Factors influencing the relative importance of marketing strategy creativity and marketing strategy implementation effectiveness. *Industrial Marketing Management, 39*(4), 551–559.

Slater, S. F., & Olson, E. M. (2001). Marketing's contribution to the implementation of business strategy: An empirical analysis. *Strategic Management Journal, 22*(11), 1055–1067.

Slater, S. F., Olson, E. M., & Finnegan, C. (2011). Business strategy, marketing organization culture, and performance. *Marketing Letters, 22*(3), 227–242.

Srinivasan, S., Rutz, O. J., & Pauwels, K. (2016). Paths to and off purchase: Quantifying the impact of traditional marketing and online consumer activity. *Journal of the Academy of Marketing Science, 44*(4), 440–453.

Sturgeon, T., Memedovic, O., Van Biesebroeck, J., & Gereffi, G. (2009). Globalisation of the automotive industry: Main features and trends. *International Journal of Technological Learning, Innovation and Development, 1*(1), 7–23.

Vieira, V. A., de Almeida, M. I. S., Agnihotri, R., da Silva, N. S. D. A. C., & Arunachalam, S. (2019). In pursuit of an effective B2B digital marketing strategy in an emerging market. *Journal of the Academy of Marketing Science, 47*(6), 1085–1108.

Wadden, J. D. (2011). Marketing creativity: The influence of personal and proximal work factors on creative activity. *Marketing Management Journal, 21*(2), 70–80.

Part III

Configuring Campaigns and Optimizing Digital Customer Engagement as Well as Insights from Academia and Other Industries

Designing Campaigns and Optimizing Campaign Performance: The Ingredients of Campaign Excellence

Kati Zieger, Uli Schneider, and Lore Darcos

1 Modern Digital Campaigning and Communication at Infineon Automotive

Large tech companies, managed by people with an engineering background, often focus primarily on the latest product innovation and product technologies, and invest their main resources into developing them. Therefore, it's not surprising that companies in this sector and generally in the Business-to-Business automotive sector tended not to allocate sufficient resources when setting up comprehensive digital marketing processes and use digital marketing as an important tool to market its products to the right audience. However, the business environment in the semiconductor sector has changed over the years.

As Infineon experienced substantial growth, partially driven by an expanding customer base, it became evident that there were significant ramifications that necessitated a strong focus on digital and scalable communication activities. This realization stemmed from the understanding that as Infineon's customer base grew, the company needed to adapt. By developing a comprehensive go-to-market process, we at Infineon Automotive have set an important milestone on the way to better marketing of new products and services. This includes the development of strategic marketing packages addressing the broad market rather than specific needs of a direct customer such as customer presentations and technical trainings for Sales and Product Management. The new digitization initiatives have helped Infineon Automotive to develop an effective campaign strategy that underlines the power of a comprehensive and integrated strategy. Fostering digital initiatives coupled with creating a comprehensive digital marketing strategy, a company can exploit potential, such as identifying key trends in the automotive industry, analyzing customer

K. Zieger (✉) · U. Schneider · L. Darcos
Infineon Technologies AG, Neubiberg, Germany
e-mail: Kati.Zieger@infineon.com; Uli.Schneider@infineon.com; Lore.Darcos@Infineon.com

U. Schneider, J. Hoika (eds.), *Digital Marketing in the Automotive Electronics Industry*, Management for Professionals,
https://doi.org/10.1007/978-3-031-30720-1_8

behavior, measuring the performance of activities, helping with continuous improvement, and most important increasing overall customer satisfaction.

In the past at Infineon Automotive, marketing campaigns had been largely seen as a means to temporary raise the attention of a customer to a certain new trend or a product, rather than a strategic tool to support reaching overall business goals. Marketing campaigns had therefore been largely driven by single ad-hoc activities aiming to temporary push higher revenues for a single product. The general perception prevailed that single or isolated activities such as creating a promotional video or sending a single mailing can be directly linked to an increased sales volume. Even though this could be true in theory, the approach of utilizing a customer journey and the strategy of reach and convert are contrary to this assumption. These models suggest the implementation of a certain chronological sequence of campaign activities. This is to attract visitors and get them to perform predefined valuable activities for the benefit of our business, such as filling out a contact form or eventually making a first purchase.

Guiding a consumer through a predefined customer journey by creating personalized content, focusing on a specific customer segment (buyer personas), and achieving predefined goals are important key elements when it comes to effectively planning and implementing campaign activities. Further cornerstones of strategic campaign planning include having a solid marketing plan orchestrating all marketing activities throughout the year, containing goals and allocating budgets and priorities for all team members involved. The following chapters describe key elements of a customer-centric campaign strategy and show the transformation of single marketing activities that had been turned into an annual marketing plan aligned with multiple stakeholders within a multinational company. It will also highlight how to effectively plan and execute each single campaign based on the usage of the Plan-Do-Check-Act-cycle (PDCA-cycle) method. In addition, several practical examples will demonstrate how Infineon Automotive's strategic campaign planning has been transformed focusing on data and metrics to achieve digital marketing objectives in line with an overall business strategy and influence the decision-making.

1.1 Digital Marketing Plan Based on Strategy Alignment

Building a campaign strategy as part of the company's business strategy

Consistency with an Infineon wide story

Before we start planning marketing campaigns for each business unit, we ensure that all campaign topics are consistent with and support Infineon Automotive's business strategy. Consistent messaging to our customers at corporate and business unit level creates strong brand integrity. The current Infineon story focuses on digitalization and decarbonization, which serves as a guiding principle for the division's overall communication and digital marketing strategy. The so-called Automotive's divisional "Core Beliefs" (e.g., zero emissions become real) underlines our convictions about the future development, which we want to shape.

Within each core belief, the growth drivers and how the technology will help to achieve them are described as well as how to differentiate ourselves in the market place.

For example, a specific campaign theme that supports this principle would be an automotive battery management campaign that enables the development of more efficient, durable, and reliable battery-powered applications for electric vehicles. As electric cars help to reduce overall CO_2 emissions, this could be an appropriate application theme for a campaign. Furthermore, focus areas are based on megatrends and growing market segments.

1.1.1 Staying Abreast of Technology: Including Latest Trends into a Business Strategy

Sweeping changes in the automotive industry and the pace at which, for example, the electrification of the car is progressing form the basis for annual marketing planning by defining focus products and applications. Each year, the focus applications are updated, with Infineon always keeping an eye on upcoming market and technology trends in order to respond with targeted campaign measures. This conceptual framework forms the basis for further marketing planning and the selection of campaign focus areas, products, and – in Infineon's case – focus applications.

1.1.2 Digital Marketing Planning Aims at Continuity

Before the introduction of an annual campaign planning phase involving all relevant stakeholders, the digital marketing team responded to individual product line requests and carried out isolated activities that were not based on a customer journey concept or an overarching strategy aimed at growing in a specific segment or responding to specific trends. Without a company-wide focus, resources in the form of staff and budget are not allocated to the right activities to expand a business.

Today, the digital marketing plan aims at continuous planning, meaning we follow the same internal process every year to plan focus topics, translate them into campaigns, and share them with all responsible stakeholders. This gives us the opportunity to set common goals and make them transparent to all key functions, and the same annual process creates planning certainty. Every year, the marketing plan is evaluated in comparison to the previous year in order to pursue the strategy of continuous improvement.

1.2 Annual Marketing Planning Process

The roadmap from an overall marketing strategy to individual promotional activities

The annual planning aims to clarify the following principles with the different departments within an organization:

(i) Relevance to a broad market segments/mass market
With the increasing focus on the more customers in recent years, the focus of DM activities has also shifted. One of the major targets of the annual campaign

planning is to identify topics of relevance/ applications of relevance to our customer based upon trends. All topics need to be relevant for a broader market segment to become a campaign topic. The most important question to ask is whether the focus topics are relevant to all our stakeholders in terms of feasibility and market potential, and whether they serve a broad market segment.

(ii) Resource allocation across all company functions
The annual planning ensures that free resources are available and used in the most efficient way, and aims to accommodate all stakeholders. Each business function, from channel management to product management, can then start to set their individual schedule and plan resources for the whole year. Especially when it comes to allocating resources for multiple campaigns, a solid annual plan is essential for a company.

(iii) Marketability of products
Functional alignments with product management help to learn about the product roadmap and future planning of each business line. At Infineon Automotive, a separate plan covering all new product launches forms the basis for the focus topics and campaigns that underline Infineon Automotive's system understanding competence.

1.3 Annual Campaign Planning Phases and Stakeholder Alignment

The following chapter describes the process of creating an annual plan involving the company's key stakeholders. This serves as an example of what the creation of an annual plan might look like in an international company. It also outlines the principles and scope of an annual marketing planning at Infineon Automotive. After the planning phase, a compelling marketing plan will be created that combines the specific business objectives with a set of prioritized topics and turns them into a solid plan that is executed throughout the entire year. The planning follows every year a distinct multi-stage procedure and includes various alignment meetings and workshops with different departments in the organization.

One of the first and most important steps is the synchronization within each department itself. This already involves a handful of teams, from business units, divisional central functions, regions as well as management. The goal of this alignment is to prioritize and create an overview and schedule of campaign activities for each focus topic. It requires that the key focus areas and solutions for the year have already been identified by the business units for the year and agreed and prioritized by the various levels of management throughout the organization.

The following steps in the annual stakeholder process require preliminary cross-divisional coordination to identify first potential interfaces and create cross-divisional synergies between the digital marketing teams. Identifying cross-divisional focus areas that can be combined into an overarching campaign can lead to a collaboration between different divisions. During this coordination between all departments, the focus topics for the coming year were presented. Each department shares the results of their previous department-specific campaign planning, focus applications, and products for potential cross-departmental campaign opportunities.

The following workshop builds on the preliminary coordination between the relevant digital marketing stakeholder including the channel responsible. Against this backdrop, each of the stakeholder groups present their prioritized topics and campaign activities regarding products and applications. There is as well a final accordance towards cross-divisional interfaces. Based upon the communication plan of each digital marketing team, the required resources for owned and paid marketing channels like social media, email marketing, or search engine advertisement (SEA) are compared with the existing resources.

The review meeting also includes the alignment of focus topics, as well as the agreement on product campaigns based upon which products will be launched in the upcoming fiscal year. After this meeting between various internal stakeholder groups, the annual plan will be consolidated and detailed into the agreed topics and resources as well as in a budget planning. Once the plan is finalized, it is finally communicated to all regions, internal and external departmental stakeholders and all levels of management.

All in all, the annual marketing plan serves as a roadmap and is essential to putting a marketing strategy into action and successfully achieving a company's business goals, resulting in revenue growth. Second, a marketing plan provides a clear path for the coming year by outlining how your individual promotional efforts will support your overall plan. Organizational coordination and open discussions among all teams involved in the campaign process are critical to efficiently plan resources (staff and budget) and obtain relevant information about upcoming trends, new products, new trends based on market forecasts, etc. An overall plan also creates additional planning certainty for all stakeholders involved.

The annual stakeholder alignment is a time-intensive but powerful communication tool for generating synergy effects at corporate level, giving employees ownership, involving them at an early stage, and creating a high level of transparency about the Infineon strategy process. In addition, a clear product roadmap, for all business lines gives us – the campaign management team – the opportunity to integrate new products into all promotional activities.

2 Campaign Preparation

From overall planning to individual campaign planning

After defining and agreeing with all stakeholders, a comprehensive annual campaign plan can be tackled. Before we start planning each single campaign, we will have a look at the strategic basics that can be applied to all campaigns, such as (1) creating a buyer persona for better targeting, (2) translating each campaign into a strategy of reach and convert, and (3) incorporating a target-driven campaign approach.

2.1 Modern Campaign Ingredients I: Target Groups and Buyer Persona

A target group is a cluster of consumers who either have the same interest, e.g., all customers who are interested in a certain product like microcontroller, or who have the same demographic characteristics such as age, gender, or country (Hannig, 2017).

The model for creating a buyer persona goes one step further. It suggests to focus on a specific idea of a fictional customer within this segment and giving it a face and a name, and most importantly, describing this customer's pain points (Thompson et al., 2017). Infineon Automotive primarily worked with the model of a target group before introducing the buyer persona profiles. For example, for a mailing campaign, a specific segment in the customer base was selected that had shown interest in a particular product or application or was selected based on its web behavior. As part of a project to design the buyer persona, two buyer personas were described in detail and researched: the engineer and the purchasing department. In addition, the following information was collected and summarized:

(a) Profile: Personal characteristics like age or study field, working environment, tasks and activities, goals and pain points, etc.
(b) Channels: Which channels are used to gather information, e.g., forums, social media channels
(c) Collaterals: Which formats are used by the Buyer Persona, e.g., datasheets, application notes, or video tutorials

The clearer the picture and background information (see Fig. 1) we gather about a buyer persona; the better marketing teams can develop personalized marketing materials and promote them on the right channels a potential customer uses to seek information.

Having created a profile of the desired customer, we can now build a picture of a particular person and not only (1) create content that solves that person's problems, (2) place the "right" content at the "right" stage of the customer journey, but ideally (3) also place the content at the preferred channels of the customer. The content we create is therefore more personalized, addresses the specific needs of a customer, and has a greater impact as we aim to create the most fitting content.

Buyer Persona Profile

Background • Age • College Degree • Professional experience	**Working Environment** • Company Size • Team Role	**Tasks & Activities** • Daily tasks & decision making process	**Goals** • List few major goals	**Challenges** • List few major challenges
Decision Making • Responsible to make final decision? • Decision criteria: Price, Lead time, technical specs etc.	**Gain Points** • This makes me happy	**Pain points** • This gives me a headache	**Key Information Sources** • Experiences • Contacts • Platforms	**Collaterals** • Document types

Fig. 1 Example of creating a buyer persona based upon different criteria

In addition, visualizing a specific person facilitates the process of creating the most effective selling points and unique selling propositions in the first place. By taking a customer-centric approach and focusing our activities on the customer, we can now create specific messages that are integrated into our campaigns and address the personal needs of our customer. This method can be applied to all activities planned for a campaign.

Creating a buyer persona profile can be a time-consuming process. This development can involve multiple stakeholders in a company who are in direct contact with the customer and can best describe their working environment, daily tasks, and challenges. Moreover, there are numerous possibilities to research customer behavior by, for example, conducting a consumer study if there are no public studies available. Moreover, companies might run the risk of making general assumptions rather than focusing on a customer's actual pain points.

2.1.1 Customer Centricity and Simplicity: Persona and User Journey thinking

When it comes to targeting, the key point can best be summed up by the common saying, "Marketing to everyone is marketing to no one." Therefore, based on our experience in the digital marketing team, we believe that having a fictional person representing our target audience helps us better understand our customers and facilitates the creation of more problem-focused content.

Generic content that doesn't solve customers' problems can lead to unnecessary investments that eat up financial and human resources and are eventually less effective. By knowing our target audience well and finding out what turns them into customers increases the chance to stand out from your competition. Including more than one Buyer Persona into a campaign and creating multiple messages can add complexity for marketers. Therefore, it is not important to create many buyer personas, but those that really matter to you, namely, those who make the decisions in a company (Revella, 2015).

Firstly, selecting a specific target audience for each campaign is a good start to connect with potential customers and to bring out a general segmentation. The second step is to evaluate this selection against metrics. Google Analytics can provide clarity and information about region, gender, age, and customer behavior. Thirdly, we suggest to research your Personas and integrate them into your campaigns by creating tailored digital marketing content.

2.2 Modern Campaign Ingredients II: Strategy of Reach and Convert

2.2.1 From Strangers to Visitors, from Contacts to Buying (Satisfied) Customer

Different models such as the PRACE or the RACE (Chaffey & Smith, 2017) model suggest how to build the entire customer lifecycle by creating a marketing funnel that goes from reaching out to potential customers, interact at different channels across all touchpoints to converting potential customer.

For the sake of simplicity, we have decided to reduce the complexity and focus first on two components: "Reach and Convert" and the development of marketing activities that fit this strategy. The following chapter describes the Reach and Convert model, how it can be applied to marketing activities, and how its success is measured using specific metrics.

Strategy of "Reach"

At the stage of reaching our target audience, we aim to promote our brand, products, and services. By publishing and promoting content using a mix of different digital activities like paid, owned, and purchased marketing activities, we aim to attract potential customers to our website to maximize the traffic. Examples of reaching our preferred audience could be a paid social media post asking to download a document (e.g., an e-book) that includes a link to our website, or clicking on a link in an email to get more information by reviewing the technical parameters of a newly launched product.

There are a number of metrics that can be used to evaluate the web performance of "reach" activities. One important indicator is measuring the number of "unique visitors" that came to the websites, landing pages, or advertising pages. This number can be used to measure all activities, including campaign activities, but also organic traffic. At Infineon Automotive, this metric is embedded in the targeted operating model and is one of the key performance indicators called #Suspects. Another important metric to see if campaign activities lead to more traffic is the number of clicks or the click-through rate. For example, to place a banner on an external platform such as an online trade magazine and use this platform as an advertising hub to attract the interest of your target audiences and direct them to your website (Fig 2). Another measure you can use to target potential customers is to look at your website bounce rates. For example, a high bounce rate may indicate that the advertising message and the linked content to your website may not match, or that the content is simply not interesting to our target audience.

Therefore, as part of a reach strategy, it is advisable to (1) clearly define the target group of the promotional activities, (2) meet this target group on their preferred channels, and (3) assess whether the content offer/message entices a customer to click for more information.

Fig. 2 Example of reach activity: banner placement at an external platform "All about Circuits"

Strategy of "Convert"

Conversion in the marketing context means that a visitor comes to your website and performs a desired action or task from which a company benefits. A conversion therefore requires that we have first successfully reached our customers. Conversion rate is the measure of conversion and reflects the percentage of customers who visit the website compared to the user who actually perform one of the predefined conversions. It can be calculated with a simple formula and is expressed as a percentage. Conversion rate = number of actions performed /((number of all visitors)*100) (Ayanso & Yoogalingam, 2009). Some examples of conversions include a visitor signing up for a newsletter, clicking a buy button and purchasing a product, downloading a fact sheet, or registering for a simulation tool, to name a few. When focusing on this phase of the marketing funnel, the marketer must not only define the action(s) a customer should take, but also manage and direct them with various measurements:

(a) Define clear conversions and measure their conversion rate.
Every conversion we track should support our marketing goals. We can distinguish between "hard and soft" conversions. This means that hard conversions are closer to the purchase decision and a visitor often comes to the website with a specific intention. In contrast, we can define numerous soft conversions, where we see that a customer has shown interest, but it is less concrete, so the visitor is not yet ready to place an order. This means that we need to "push" the visitor further along the customer journey by offering additional compelling and value-adding information.
(b) Derive measurements based upon defined conversions.
Based on the Digital Marketing Team's findings, we summarize the following key actions to translate the previously defined requirements into concrete website improvements:

1. First and foremost, an attractive web design can increase the chances of conversions and forms the basis of our marketing activities. This includes, above all, an intuitive navigation (additionally using breadcrumbs), a memorable image, short loading times, etc., so that a customer stays on a website and engages with the content placed on it.
2. Clear and eye-catching call-to-actions positioned prominently on the website, preferably with colored buttons and "above the fold" – meaning that the most important content (according to your conversion targets) can be found at the top of the website without scrolling further down. See the example of Infineon, where the "Download Datasheet" button is also defined as a conversion in combination with highlighting certain content to distinguish it from other, less important content.
3. High-conversion websites tell their visitors directly what is unique about their products and why they should buy them. Therefore, including unique selling propositions (USPs) at the top of the page can help achieve the conversion goal of

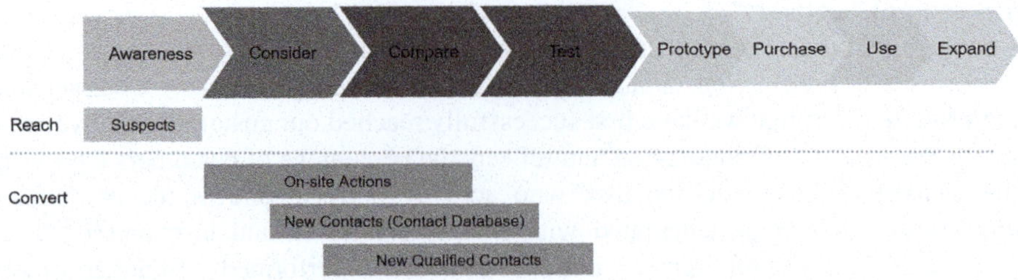

Fig. 3 Reach & Convert strategy along the customer journey linked to KPIs

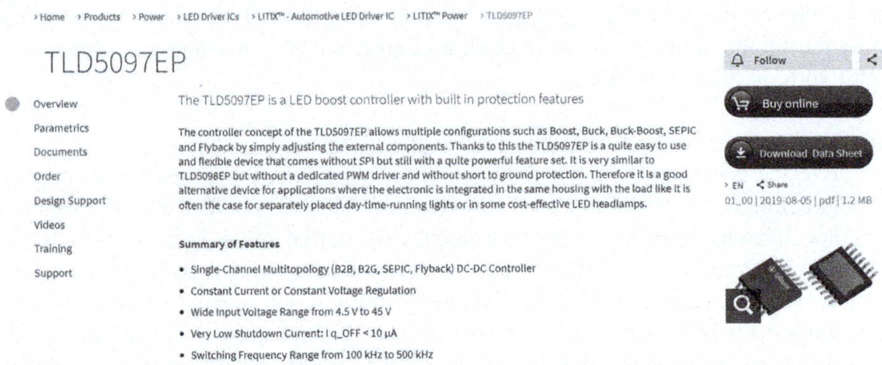

Fig. 4 Clear call to actions (two buttons in different colors red & blue) to convert visitors (example product TLD5097EP)

purchase clicks. This includes designing landing pages for specific content you want to highlight that aligns with your conversion strategy.

4. The user experience (UX design) is one critical factor and helps us seeing a website through the eyes of our customer.

Implementation of "Reach and Convert Strategy" at Infineon

Our "Reach and Convert" strategy is reflected in the goals we have set for our digital marketing activities. Some KPIs focus on reaching customers (at Infineon we measure suspects). Other KPIs focus on converting customers, meaning we want them to take on-site actions or leave their contact information to become a new contact (e.g., register for a webinar) and eventually convert them into a qualified contact. The last goal requires a customer to perform multiple actions, which are defined using a clear schema for a lead management process (Fig 3).

1. At Infineon Automotive, we consider datasheets as an important decision criterion for our engineers in the consideration and comparison phase, as they contain specific technical information about a product. Therefore, we have created a

Fig. 5 Example of banner highlighting "converting content" using Power PROFET products as example

conversion called "On-Site Actions: Download Datasheet." By integrating a button below the existing "Buy Online" button, this objective is prominently placed and additionally highlighted on the website. Previously, the datasheet was integrated in the left navigation under "Documents" and not highlighted separately (Fig. 4). With this change, Infineon was able to significantly increase the number of downloaded datasheets by simply highlighting the desired conversion. In addition, several campaign activities, such as an email campaign, specifically reference this button with CTAs such as "Download Datasheet" or "For more product information, please click here."

2. Infineon Automotive provides its potential customers with a comprehensive package of documents such as product presentations, application notes, articles, technical presentations, and so on. This could be counterproductive in terms of a conversion rate if there is no clear indication for the customer which documents to select or download. However, by including banners we can either highlight the latest documents/training/products, etc., but also point out what the customer should do on our website. In this case, it's about registering and downloading a whitepaper and signing up to use online simulation tools to provide design support (Fig. 5). This is in line with the conversion goal that we offer content that creates "#new contacts."
3. Redesigned landing pages for specific content, such as downloading a white paper or attending a webinar, increase the likelihood of a customer registering by showing what's inside for the customer and providing a clear call to action (see button "Download here" – Fig. 6). Previously, documents were integrated into the documents section, but the benefits of downloading a document and leaving contact details were not visible to a website visitor.

Without a combination of a strategy to first reach your potential customers and a concrete focus with predefined conversions, a company runs the risk of spending its marketing budget on advertising campaigns without having a concrete goal in mind.

Fig. 6 Whitepaper landingpage: High voltage automotive Battery management systems

Therefore, creating comprehensive conversion roadmaps (along the customer journey) that can be measured regularly helps to create a unique user experience that convinces potential customers based on call-to-actions. This includes designing a website or landing page from the ground up to be conversion-oriented. A UX designer can help here to improve the design of a website according to the conversion strategy. A "reach and convert" strategy is a good start to focus on what is important to a company. Further steps (see the PRACE or RACE theory) could entail engaging with the customer to build a long-term relationship allowing companies to take their business to the next level and secure future business at the same time. Furthermore, there are more possibilities to personalize the content to each individual user by using, for example, "dynamic content." The company HubSpot suggests using web data to "create different versions of your website to display to each individual visitor" for targeted campaigns (4 Data-Driven Ways to Create More Targeted Ad Campaigns, n.d.).

2.3 Modern Campaign Ingredients III: Measurement Framework

The shift towards a target-driven campaign focus

In recent years, campaigns have been conducted without clear numerical targets for a campaign being set beforehand. However, the campaigns were measured afterwards, and the campaign results were summarized in a summary sheet. The goals were set more general, such as increasing market share in a certain segment, rather than following the SMART method (Doran, 1981), which also suggests setting specific and measurable qualitative objectives. At the end of each campaign, the responsible campaign manager produced a report based on their own measurement criteria, such as click-through rates or total number of emails opened. This led to the major problem that the evaluation of the campaigns was not consistent, so that it was difficult to compare the campaigns with each other. What it boiled down to was that the main question of whether a campaign was successful could not be answered clearly in some cases. Eventually, this changed fundamentally with the introduction of a unification of campaign goals in conjunction with quantitative KPIs that contributed to overall business objectives. The shift to a new mindset for the digital marketing team and supporting departments combined with a goal-oriented model in the form of a dashboard also gave us the ability to constantly monitor campaigns and respond with appropriate action when it was foreseeable that we would not meet campaign goals.

2.3.1 Target-Driven Campaign Approach

The introduction of a goal-oriented framework, where the overarching objectives are visible and communicated from the beginning, was a crucial turning point that brought a number of benefits. All campaign activities are now aligned based on how they contribute to the overall goals. The objectives determine the activities, not the other way around. One of the main key drivers of setting up this new approach is the importance of and access to valuable data on insightful customer behavior, as well as the introduction of an overarching objective for digital activities for the entire automotive division. Measuring the impact of marketing campaigns against previously defined objectives, interpreting the outcomes, and defining and driving actions based on data have become the main focus and one of the core competencies of the digital marketing team at Infineon Automotive in recent years.

Other advantages of a goal-oriented mindset:

(a) Shared understanding of goals among all stakeholders, resulting in the whole team working towards the same goal(s).
(b) Data-driven decision-making: no arbitrary selection of activities according to the personal preferences of the stakeholders. All activities are planned based solely on the objectives.
(c) Monitoring ad performance in real time allows us to take countermeasures (e.g., stop an activity that is not performing and invest the budget in a more promising activity). This leads to best-in-class activities, where insights are used already during a campaign, not only afterwards.

2.3.2 Target-Operating Model

Measuring and analyzing the effectiveness of digital activities

Before implementing a system focused on measuring defined KPIs, the entire digital marketing team had to manually pull their campaign results from various data sources such as Google Analytics or from a marketing automation tool and an Excel report based on information from the customer database. This data was not easily accessible, nor were all KPIs displayed in a clear dashboard. The link between the activities performed in a given campaign and their direct impact on the four measurement points could either not be assessed at all or only partially. Second, continuous (at least monthly) status queries or reports were not possible, as this was a very tedious and time-consuming process. In addition, there was no information on the overall results of all campaigns in total. Because of these hurdles, the decision was made to create a "single point of truth" to measure the effectiveness of our activities in guiding customers through the customer journey.

For this project, one of the main goals was to create an easily accessible dashboard, but it was also of utmost importance to make sure everyone understood the goals equally. When creating a framework, we selected a few measurement points to assess growth, progress, and to see conversions along the customer journey. We also made sure that everyone involved in achieving these goals knew their exact meaning, and introduced a clear definition for each KPI. The approach here was to start with a handful of goals (see Fig. 7), rather than overwhelming the user by measuring literally everything. After defining the project scope and requirements, the focus was on merging data from multiple sources into a complete but streamlined solution. We then rolled out each dashboard for each KPI to selected stakeholders over a full year. To realize the full potential of the data, we combined several purposes of the framework into one dashboard. The results can be described as follows:

I. Quantitative measures of the campaign: Comparison of the figures to previous years.
II. Qualitative criteria: Usage of filters to assess why promotional activities did or did not go well (lessons learned).
III. Full transparency: Creating a "single source of truth" that serves as an evaluation framework for an entire department.

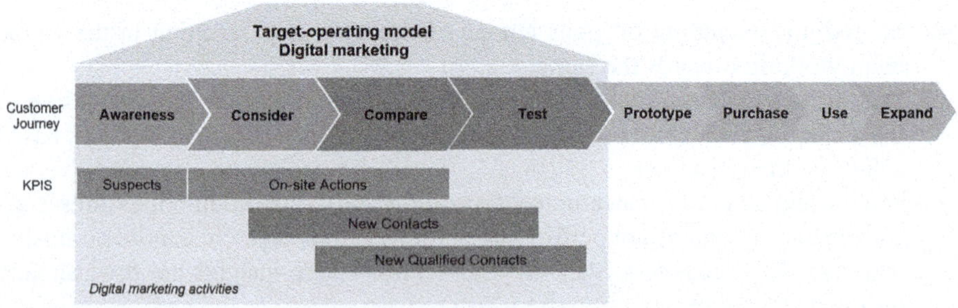

Fig. 7 Target definition – selected measurement points (KPIs) along the customer journey

IV. Digitalize departmental KPIs: Quick real-time results by combining data from multiple sources (analytics and customer base/automation platform) into one tool.

Within the digital marketing activities, the first and major goal is to create traffic to the site in the form of visitors to the promotion pages, application pages, and product pages. Secondly, we want the user to engage with the content of the website and perform certain actions on the website. The main focus is to get these visitors to consume certain content/assets, such as training videos or downloading datasheets. As part of the conversion strategy, we promote not only the downloading of important content, but also the idea that an unknown visitor becomes a new contact. By providing gated assets, such as registering for a live webinar or downloading software tools, we obtain the contact information of an interested visitor. This allows us to contact the user and send them promotional materials based on their interest. If we email a contact after a webinar and send them more in-depth documents about the products presented in the training, a contact in the database may become a "qualified contact."

After establishing the measurement framework and a comprehensive set of objectives, we were able to break down the overall goals into specific campaign objectives. Figure 8 shows how to derive specific activities for each campaign to achieve the overall objective of each of the four KPIs.

2.3.3 Plan I: Target Setting

As mentioned earlier, every campaign should start with a clear idea of the purpose of the campaign – whether it is to gain more leads, increase brand awareness, or generate interest in a newly launched product. Based on the purpose of a campaign, the objectives for it are derived. When we introduced goal setting in advance of each campaign, we did so by creating a pilot campaign project to get a feel for setting numeric goals, since we had little or no previous data available. First, we summarized various parameters that influence the goal setting for the selected campaign: (1) reference of past campaigns if available; (2) industry standards like click-through rates; (3) market-related, e.g., the market size, new or established market; (4) predefined campaign size and the budget connected to it; and (5) campaign focus (awareness, lead generation, customer retention, etc.). Despite the different aspects, there are a variety of methods for goal setting in theory such as OKR (Objectives and Key Results) described by Jacob and Lobacher (2020) or setting backward targets. However, one of the most common methods for describing goals is the SMART method, which serves as a common basis for a goal-oriented mindset.

We defined the setting up of campaign's objectives as the first step in the PDCA-cycle (Shewhart, 2012), making it an essential part of the "plan" phase (see Fig. 9). Using the PDCA-cycle for campaigns helped our team to update and optimize the campaign process to support the idea of continuous improvement in digital marketing.

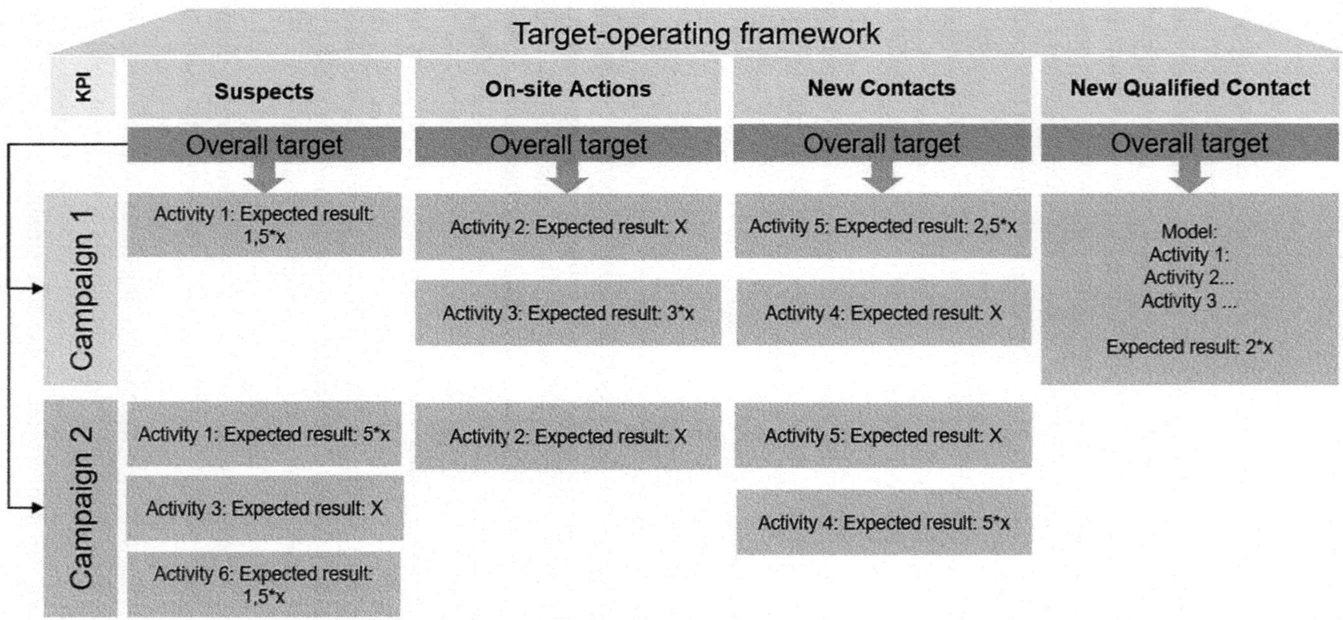

Fig. 8 Breaking down overall targets into single campaign activities

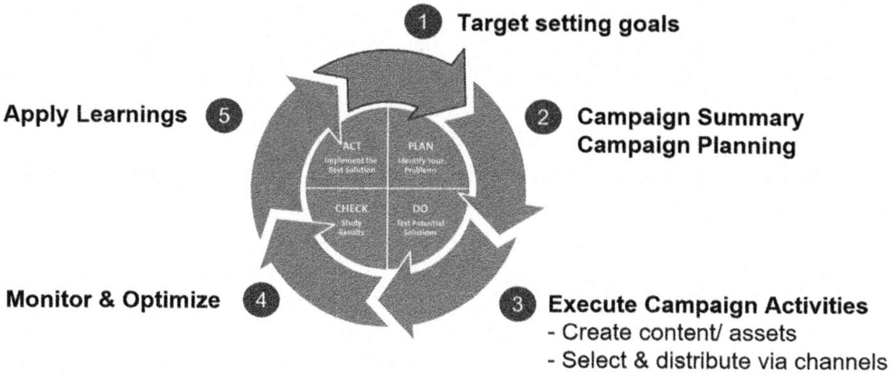

Fig. 9 PDCA-cycle showing all campaign lifecycle activities

2.3.4 Plan II: Campaign Summary and Scope

A campaign is defined as a grouping of multiple activities to capture current trends, promote focus applications, or highlight newly launched products. Setting up a campaign and executing valuable promotional activities can be a complex undertaking. Therefore, when planning a marketing campaign, it can be helpful to summarize the key objectives in a brief overview. This campaign summary should also answer important questions about your target audience, the products you want to promote, and your positioning in the market relative to your competition. By introducing a one-pager template that summarizes a campaign, the following aspects should be covered:

- Current market challenges and how we respond to them with our offering (positioning)
- Target groups and regional focus
- Listing of highlight products and application(s) being part of promotional activities
- Initial ideas summarizing the most important activities in an overview
- KPIs based on campaign objectives/main focus (e.g., awareness or lead generation or a mix)

In a campaign kick-off meeting, this summary is presented to the application managers so that they can collectively agree on the main purpose of a campaign and fill in the missing information. It also serves as a guide for the digital team roles (campaign and content management) to better understand the topic itself and the market requirements in order to execute a successful campaign. This campaign summary is then shared regularly with all stakeholders, such as senior management, to provide a quick overview of focus applications, key campaign objectives and activities, and should provide a current status.

As part of Infineon Automotive's overall process for launching a new application, standardized campaign processes and templates are necessary to ensure that the asset list is complete and all necessary actions are performed during the campaign. The checklist suggests different deliverables depending on the scope of a campaign, such as the creation of a customer presentation, a website, and the establishment of a "Campaign Messaging guide" as an integral part of any promotion. The method helps to translate the desired market positioning into significant marketing messages supported by a list of proof points. The messaging template is another standardized method to help develop clear, compelling, and brand-compliant product or system marketing messages to support and strengthen consistent market communication inside a campaign. The final step in the planning phase is to translate the action points from the checklist into a timely communication plan that serves as a project plan for each campaign. A key point here is to plan individual campaign assets/ content to match the right stage of the customer journey and create a seamless user experience starting with the "reach phase" and moving on to convert potential customers.

3 Marketing Roles and Responsibilities

Throughout the lifecycle of each campaign, the responsibilities of the various functions at Infineon Automotive are clearly defined. The overall campaign planning is driven by the responsible for the divisional marketing communication strategy and its controlling in coordination with the Application and Product Managers. The design and content creation phase of each campaign, as well as the campaign execution phase, the Campaign, Content, and Product/Application Managers work hand-in-hand to drive activities. This chapter highlights the individual roles and associated key responsibilities in the digital campaign process. Second, we show how the RACI matrix is applied to represent the overall collaboration in a multinational company with a large group of heterogeneous stakeholders using Infineon as an example.

3.1 Marketing Communications Strategy and Controlling

This function is responsible for translating business unit plans into a comprehensive communications strategy. This includes defining and communicating objectives and managing budgets accordingly. Marketing Communication Strategy and Controlling performs a gap analysis to derive insights and improvements for the upcoming communication strategy.

3.2 Content Manager

The Content Manager works hand-in-hand with Campaign Management to agree a communications plan that lists all promotional campaigns. His or her primary responsibilities include developing and executing communications activities in the form of designing, refining and writing campaign materials, such as creating a social media ad or drafting an email advertisement. By using insights such as metrics and statistics about target customer demographics and preferences (see Buyer Persona), the content manager is able to create content that leads to conversion.

3.3 Campaign Manager

Working closely with the application and the content manager, a campaign manager defines goals and numerical targets based on the campaign objective, which are summarized in a campaign one-pager. This includes defining the scope of the campaign and a detailed communication plan. The campaign manager runs the campaign and uses web analytics to monitor the success of a campaign, but also intervenes when it is foreseeable that campaign goals cannot be met.

3.4 Regional Digital Marketing Manager

At Infineon Automotive, there is a regional counterpart for all global marketing functions. A global role has worldwide responsibility. In contrast to this, a regional role takes responsibility for a specific geographic area, such as China or Japan. For example, while the global role focuses on creating all marketing materials, a regional strategy proposes to adapt these global promotional materials to a specific region in terms of translations, topic selection based on market assessments, and the choice of regional channel marketing, e.g., using "WeChat" and external digital platforms such as dianyuan.com in China.

3.5 Channel Manager

The Channel manager is responsible for a variety of channels, including email, social media, and search engine advertisingand acts as a channel expert advising campaign managers and content managers on how best to integrate their digital marketing activities across these channels by pursuing an omni channel strategy – meaning all channels are aligned.

3.6 Supporting Roles

3.6.1 Application Manager

Most of Infineon Automotive's campaigns are defined as application campaigns that target a specific function or systems in cars, such as a battery management system or an on-board charger for electric vehicles. These campaigns focus on all relevant components from power supplies to microcontrollers to sensor components and show a complete product portfolio in a block diagram. The application manager plays a key role in creating campaign assets and works closely with business units and their product management and technical marketing to put together all the go-to-market contents for a specific application (e.g., application notes or promotional videos).

3.6.2 Product Management

The tasks of the product management role vary depending on the size of the company. At Infineon, product management leads marketing activities at the product level and is responsible for capturing product requirements for new products, provides market insight and ensure business and design wins in various channels. In the context of a campaign, product management is involved in the initial phase of a campaign and presents its product roadmap to decide on the integration of its products into the campaign planning.

RACI Model to Set Up Clear Responsibilities

Using a RACI scheme (Bartlow & Harris, 2021), a company can easily define collaboration in a multinational company where multiple stakeholders are involved in a project, or in our case, a digital marketing campaign. The "RACI model" or scheme stands for accountable, responsible, consulted, and informed. The model proposes to list all stakeholders of, for example, an advertising campaign and define their level of involvement in a project or task based on the four RACI components.

Responsible: Performing and completing a task or activity
Accountable: Final approving authority that can be consulted as well
Consulted: Serving as consultant or counsel
Informed: Receives information about activity status

The following Table 1 is an example of how the marketing roles (top) and tasks (left) are integrated into the R-A-C-I matrix.

By defining different marketing roles and responsibilities within the organization, we have highlighted the need and focus for effective marketing of products and solutions. To make marketing a true core competency and achieve best-in-class marketing, we have created a scalable model with roles across the organization. The RACI model is an easy-to-understand overview that describes which team members are responsible for which tasks during a campaign. Each role is clear and collaboration is well defined. This can have a positive impact on accelerating processes because we have defined team members who are responsible for specific activities and prevent ambiguity from holding up or potentially hindering the process.

Table 1 Example of tasks and responsibilities per campaign listed in a RACI chart

RACI Example: Campaign Collaboration

Campaign Tasks	Marketing comm. strategy & controlling	Campaign Manager	Content Manager	Channel Manager	Application Manager	Product Manager	*Regional DM Manager*
Annual campaign planning & topic alignment	R	I	I	A	C	C	C
Plan • Target setting • Butget planning • Campaign summary • Communication plan	A	R	C	I	C	I	R (region)
Do • Content creation • Channel selection	I	C A	A C	I I	R I	C	I R (region)
Check • Status quo targets • Regular reportings	A	R R	C	C	I	I	I R (region)
Act • Create learnings	A	R	C	C	I	I	I R (region)

4 Campaign Lifecycle Activities

4.1 Do: Execute Single Campaign Activities

In the "DO-phase" following the PDCA cycle Fig. 9, the campaign activities from the previous campaign planning are carried out. In this stage, the content manager is responsible for creating the selected campaign assets in close collaboration with the technical experts, such as the application manager. The role of the content manager is to advise and guide the experts on how to create specific campaign assets, such as a whitepaper. His or her main task is to create converting content that addresses and ideally solves the customer's pain points previously described in the buyer persona.

When it comes to content/asset creation, it can be beneficial to first get an overview of the assets on a topic that (1) already exists, (2) needs to be updated, and (3) needs to be created from scratch. In addition to helping technical experts with content creation such as e-books, promotional videos, customer presentations, or trade show content, it is equally important to develop inspiring marketing ads to promote the content in the most compelling way possible. Banners, images, the main message, etc. that appeal to your target audience, as well as marketing slogans and converting ads that speak the language of our potential customers, have a great impact on the success of a marketing campaign.

In a second phase, this content must be distributed across multiple channels to increase media exposure as part of an omnichannel strategy. To promote the content created, we have several options. Either we use our own media platforms such as our social media channel Linkedin or email marketing to target specific customer segments and working closely with each channel manager. Or we select paid channels, such as booking external platforms/media space, for which the marketing campaign budget will be used. Ideally, the campaign manager follows a strategy that proposes a mix of both, using internal and external media to get the most out of the campaigns and achieve predefined goals. At this stage, the detailed campaign calendar helps to prepare, execute, and implement activities in a timely manner.

Moreover, content repurposing is key to effectively using the content you've already created and converting it to a different format for use on a another platform or channel. Customizations can include different graphic formats or adjusting the text length to fit a specific channel. It's not only important to know what content a potential customer is looking at, but also on which platforms and channels we're meeting our preferred audience. The reach and conversion strategy are the foundation of any content strategy, providing for both specific reach activities/assets and converting content along the customer journey.

The following example briefly describes the execution phase of a webinar including goals, planning, content creation, and the design of promotional activities such as the landing page and an email invitation.

Step 1: Targeting
: One of our main goals is to generate new leads and add them to our contact database for further qualification. We take the lead target and derive the most promising lead generation activity from it. Since we have determined that conducting a webinar should bring in new leads, the planning phase prior to the webinar includes creating a schedule of content creation as well as promotional planning.

Step 2: Asset creation
: In the next phase, the content – in this case the creation of a presentation, the preparation of questions and answers, and finally the recording of the webinar for a specific date – is created by the technical expert in close cooperation with the content team. Based on the definition of the desired target group, the right hosting platform for this segment must be evaluated and eventually booked.

Step 3: Promotion
: In the promotion preparation phase, all activities are created, such as a sign-up page that answers the question of who and why a potential customer should attend the webinar. Further activities include defining the key takeaways, creating email invitations, placing banners on social media channels, and other advertising for external platforms.

4.2 Check: Monitoring and Optimization of Promotional Activities

We conduct monitoring of each campaign to continously measure the targets and evaluate individual campaign activities. Having a powerful target-operating tool already in place has been a major upside during the entire digitalization process of the key performance indicator setting. Based on the experiences in our team, we recommend to regularly check upon your results and its progress which gives us the chance to readjust goals or activities even during a running campaign. These adjustments can include A/B testing, changing the subject line of an email, or adding another segment to the audience, to name a few.

To ensure regular reporting, we update a campaign summary every month and compare goals to current results, which is one of the main tasks of the campaign manager in our digital team. This gives us the chance to always have a status quo with real-time results of our campaigns and check if we are on track to reach the objectives. When we look at the results of our webinar example, we noticed a high registration rate and a high number of participants. Unfortunately, the number of leads was relatively low because the email invitations were sent to contacts in our database who are already Infineon leads. Due to budget constraints, there was little external advertising, such as paid social media advertising.

4.3 Act: Applying Campaign Learnings

Digital Marketing has made it its mission to become the expert in translating business objectives into digital campaigns, recommending the right promotional activities, producing engaging content, and finding the best channel to match the target audience. By learning from previous years' experiences and identifying the best performing activities, we are now able to gain a deeper understanding of our customers, their journey and their preferences. This will enable us to focus exclusively on activities that met the defined objectives and eliminate other promotional activities that do not contribute to our business goals. The "act" phase can be seen as a learning phase, where we can draw conclusions from our campaign analysis and translate them into concrete actions for current and future campaigns. As we have the possibility of looking at real-time results, this phase goes hand in hand with the monitoring and optimization stage of each campaign activity.

However, in some cases, it is not obvious at first glance why one campaign was successful or, on the contrary, why another campaign performed poorly. Interpreting and questioning those campaign results is one of the main competencies offered by the digital marketing team.

Recommendations to collect and apply learnings:

1. Campaign result read-outs: sharing positive/negative results in your marketing team including challenges, learnings, key insights
2. Documentation and storage of outcomes/key insights as well as best practices within your team (collaboration tool/archives/wikis)
3. Detailed analysis: what worked well/ what didn't work, and why, e.g., what are the major lead magnets

We believe that setting clear goals for digital teams, measuring data, and evaluating activities will lead our company to best-in-class marketing and give us a competitive advantage. Although we focus on largely standardizing campaigns, our experience is that there is no such thing like a "one solution fits all" strategy. As a result, we see the need to evaluate each campaign individually against a number of different criteria. This can be seen as learning process towards campaign excellence. As we did not reach the defined new lead goal for the hosted webcast, we can look at other webinars that have achieved or even overperformed their goals and try to copy the promotional activities as best practice. Nonetheless, creating a webinar and promoting it consists of many steps and activities, from choosing the webinar topic to finding the right audience and hosting it on a platform. Therefore, each of these steps can also offer optimization potential. Especially when promotions do not perform as intended, it is recommended to evaluate each step by creating a user journey mapping to include a customer-centric perspective.

5 Chapter Summary

In almost every industry and discipline, we find that the data we collect about our customers is one of the most valuable assets of all time. The information contained in our customers' data gives us the ability to learn what content resonates best with our website visitors or what promotional efforts are the most effective. Many examples have shown that achieving campaign excellence is a question of the interplay between processes, planning, strategic goal setting, and optimization cycles.

We would like to emphasize that the previous chapters refer exclusively to the structures, company size, particulars of the semiconductor industry, stakeholder roles, and many other specifics at Infineon Technologies. However, Infineon Automotive's digital marketing approach is to some extent scalable to the size of any company in terms of stakeholder management, marketing budget size, number of campaign themes, goal setting, planning cycles, etc. The processes described can be applied to similar organizational structures, and the application of the PDCA-cycle can be easily transferred to different types of companies with different business objectives.

Our path to optimized campaign activities based on the annual marketing planning and a goal-oriented mindset can serve as a practical example for other large companies facing similar challenges, such as multiple interfaces and stakeholders that work hand-in-hand in a dynamic market. By integrating the models used in this chapter, illustrating different processes and examples of how strategies have been put into practice, the reader can benefit from our experience of building a digital framework and identify potential challenges in digital marketing as well as common pitfalls.

In this context, several learnings can be summarized, such as setting goals and ensuring that a tool/system is in place to measure them and obtain customer insights that will help to optimize your campaign strategy. Other prerequisites for best-in-class campaigns, referred to in this chapter as the most promising campaign ingredients, include the following recommendations: Get to know your customers (buyer persona), know their journey (create a customer journey for your business), and know where to meet and engage with them.

References

4 Data-Driven Ways to Create More Targeted Ad Campaigns. (n.d.). Retrieved December 14, 2022, from https://blog.hubspot.com/marketing/data-driven-targeted-ad-campaigns

Ayanso, A., & Yoogalingam, R. (2009). Profiling retail web site functionalities and conversion rates: A cluster analysis. *International Journal of Electronic Commerce, 14*(1), 79–113.

Bartlow, A., & Harris, T. B. (2021). Scaling for success: People priorities for high-growth organizations. *Columbia University Press*. https://www.jstor.org/stable/10.7312/bart19444

Chaffey, D., & Smith, P. R. (2017). *Digital marketing excellence: Planning, optimizing and integrating online marketing*. Taylor & Francis.

Doran, G. T. (1981). There's a SMART way to write management's goals and objectives. *Management Review, 70*(11), 35–36.

Hannig, U. (2017). *Marketing und sales automation: Grundlagen – tools – umsetzung. alles, was sie wissen müssen*. Springer-Verlag.

Jacob, C., & Lobacher, P. (2020). *Objectives & key results (OKR): The agile operating system for modern organizations*. Independently Published.

Revella, A. (2015). *Buyer personas: How to gain insight into your customer's expectations, align your marketing strategies, and win more business*. Wiley.

Shewhart, W. A. (2012). *Statistical method from the viewpoint of quality control*. Courier Corporation.

Thompson, S., Eva, N., & Shea, E. (2017). Watching the movie: Using personas as a library marketing tool. *Reference & User Services Quarterly, 57*(1), 17–19.

Meaningful Marketing Content for Automotive Customer: A Process Guide for Modular, Buyer Persona Centric, and Channel Optimized Content Creation

Anup Shukla, Alexander Schwertlein, and Uli Schneider

1 Introduction

The customer of today is evolving and so is the content marketing landscape! The formats of content that were not utilized a decade back are now influencing the purchasing decision of the customer, especially automotive customers who require semiconductor electronic solutions. With the change in the marketing mechanisms, new dimensions and opportunities are introduced in the market (Bauer et al., 2020). Hence, there is a need to learn, adapt, apply, and follow the cycle of changing content in the digital marketing era. In this chapter, we will outline how to develop a digital marketing content strategy for the automotive semiconductor industry encompassing:

- The relation to digital marketing strategy
- The selection of impactful content pieces
- The good practice for creating engaging content

We will cover the above strategy in the sections to follow. The first section talks about the fundamental automotive semiconductor business and how business and digital marketing strategies translate and trickle in the content strategy. We will also throw light on evolving trends in content marketing. In the second section, we dive deeper into the relevant content formats used across the customer journey and highlight important performance indicators. In the third section, with an exemplary content format, we describe the content management cycle and use it to derive content creation – good practices. With this outline, let the content journey begin.

A. Shukla (✉) · A. Schwertlein · U. Schneider
Infineon Technologies AG, Neubiberg, Germany
e-mail: Anup.Shukla@infineon.com; Alexander.Schwertlein@infineon.com; Uli.Schneider@infineon.com

U. Schneider, J. Hoika (eds.), *Digital Marketing in the Automotive Electronics Industry*, Management for Professionals,
https://doi.org/10.1007/978-3-031-30720-1_9

1.1 Content at the Core: Key Ingredients for B2B Digital Marketing Recipe

Before diving into the topic, let us set up a general understanding of how the automotive semiconductor industry functions and what are the important elements to be considered in the context of content marketing. Although we try to use less industry jargon, as and when the need arises, we will explain the terminologies widely used in the context of the automotive semiconductor industry.

Generally, the semiconductor industry classifies its customer base into a pyramid based on the business opportunity with customers. These business opportunities are measured in terms of revenue generated. Perry Marshall explains the 80/20 rule in his book where 80% of sales revenue is achieved by the 20% of the customers, and this holds true in the segmenting of the semiconductor customers (Marshall, 2013). Top of the pyramid are the Tier 1 and focus account customers which are approx. 80% of the business. At the bottom of the pyramid are the mass market customers. This customer base is very large and usually forms the 20% of the business revenue. This is also illustrated in Fig. 1. The contribution of this mass market cannot be ignored because there is a growth opportunity due to the entry of emerging customers. Here the content plays a significant role to cater this vast pool of customers.

Now that we have seen the customer pyramid, we will describe how digital marketing and business goals translate to content strategy. Often, business strategies are defined in terms of the following parameters:

- Avenues for revenue growth
- Broaden customer base
- New product introduction in the market
- Differentiate in market

Digital marketing strategies take into consideration the above parameters when implementing marketing initiatives. These initiatives are brought to practice by

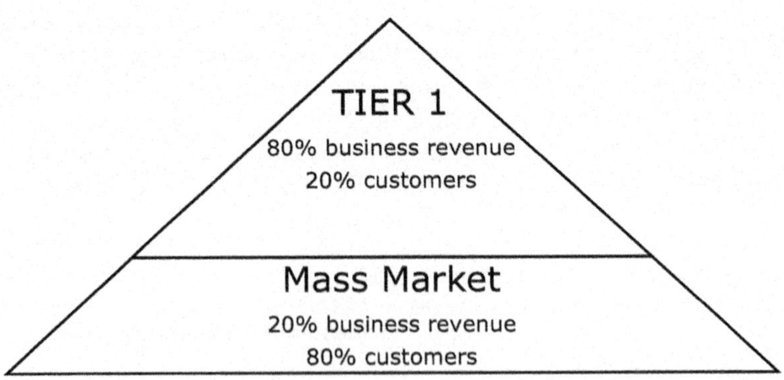

Fig. 1 Customer pyramid

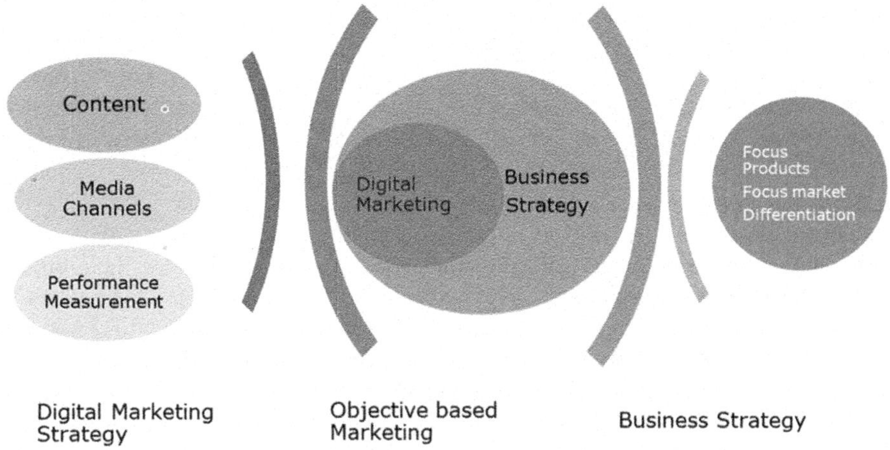

Fig. 2 Amalgamation of content, digital, and business strategy

placing content conducive to our digital marketing and eventually business strategies. For example, if a business goal is to introduce a new product, digital marketing requires creating collateral that guide users through their buying cycle. To make the non-expert audience aware of new products, we create content pieces like product briefs and videos. A product data sheet and user manual are needed to compare and evaluate the product at a later stage. Further, to engage with the interested target group, gated content like webinars or white papers are created. Gated content is the one where users have to register by providing contact details and consent before accessing the content. Figure 2 illustrates this translation.

Now that we have seen the categorization of customers and fitment of content strategy, let us see the evolution of content which has been a source of information and education to the customers. Over the decades, communication media and customer persona have evolved, and so have content marketing tactics. If one had to ask a semiconductor customer around two decades ago – how she or he get to know about the new semiconductor products or solutions, they would probably say through printed articles in tradeshows, press releases, electronic magazines, printed newsletter, or perhaps in conferences or through a salesperson. However, media has advanced by leaps and bounds since then and so has the content format and its promotion. From printed brochures and newsletters to webinar and digital newsletters, content has transitioned from analog to digital. This brings forth a question – why this change in the trend?

Let's start by answering the above question. The automotive market is not only growing but also transforming. The buzz words like electric mobility, connected cars, and autonomous driving, which were only concepts two decades ago, are now already a reality or on the verge of reality. Transfer of IT and consumer-electronic features to the automotive domain has transformed the car from a mode of transport to the experiential transport (Traub et al., 2017). And these trends call for new opportunities and hence the automotive industry sees growth in emerging players. Automotive manufacturers are growing in numbers. And the automotive suppliers in the supply chain for these manufacturers are growing exponentially. For a semiconductor industry like Infineon, catering to all these emerging players through physical sales and service team is not enough. A scalable solution to train the distributors, partners, internal sales force, and customers is needed. In the past, customers expected a visit by a sales executive to inform them about new products and solutions. However now, B2B customers proactively search for information on the Internet, and website's and content's perceived quality influences their buying decisions (Koch & Hartmann, 2022). Although a sales force is still needed to close the deals, digital content jump-starts customer engagement. So, it is important to refresh content regularly on websites and other media. From a content creator's perspective, it has become easy to scale and revise the content with digital channels. Moreover, content now caters to a broad customer base and regions. And most importantly, it is possible to measure the performance of the staged content. New automotive players and suppliers are emerging, and hence need scalable marketing tactics to include the new customers. Content in our industry serves two functions – enabling and embarking: enabling our internal sales force and distribution channel with the relevant training and presentations which they need to interact with customers and embarking the customer in their buying journey with relevant information on solutions and products and navigating them in the right direction.

While creating content is an art that involves a high degree of creativity, a defined process is still a prerequisite. Hence, equally important is the content management aspect. Various factors need to be considered, namely, the profile of the customer, channels, and desired outcome. In the next section, we describe how content guides a customer on the journey from the "Unknown" to the "Known."

1.2 Content Across the Customer Journey: From the Stranger to the Customer

While one-size-fits-all content piece would have been the best and most cost-effective solution for suppliers and customers, it is hardly feasible in practice. A person who is new to the product offerings in the semiconductor industry will need easy-to-understand, less technical, and visually engaging content to spark interest. Engineers who are well-versed in semiconductor products need technical information on the products and perhaps need more hands-on content. A person who needs to make a purchasing decision will need product differentiation information over the other products in the market. This is a challenge and also a window of opportunity to make an impression on the customer with be fitting content. Table 1 illustrates an extensive list of content formats used in the automotive semiconductor industry.

For our semiconductor customers, key content pieces during the initial stages of a product launch are a product data sheet, product roadmap, content on the website, tools or software, etc. Product data sheets provide product information and operating conditions. While the plethora of content pieces are available at different stages for

Table 1 Content formats

Content format	Content description and purpose	Customer journey relevance	How to measure performance (# – number)
Application or solution web page	This includes • Introduction about the application: technological context and brief introduction of the product highlights • Application diagram • Application notes • Application boards/ reference designs • Simulation models • Videos and trainings Target of the application pages is to drive sales and present Infineon's complete product offering for a dedicated application	Awareness, consideration, comparison, samples order, prototyping, purchase, after sales	#unique visitors #downloads #click through rate
Brochure	It is a classic marketing document with higher level information on products, application, and features. It is more visually engaging than the white paper and detailed than the product brief	Awareness, comparison	#downloads
Customer connector	It provides a product value proposition. It summarizes why a company should buy the product and comprises sales relevant information for distributors	Awareness, consideration, comparison	#downloads
Data sheet	Data sheet describes a product, its diagram, features, applications, and operating parameters	Comparison, consideration, evaluation	#downloads
Development tools and boards web page	This page contains information on boards and development tools to either facilitate the evaluation of a product or demonstrate the use of a product in a certain application	Consideration, comparison, samples order, prototyping	#unique visitors #downloads #buy button click
Go-wider-boards list	The go-wider-boards list can be considered as a board pricelist for distribution. It gives a recommendation which boards are suitable for mass market and should be stocked by the distribution partners	Consideration, comparison, samples order	#shipped boards

(continued)

Table 1 (continued)

Content format	Content description and purpose	Customer journey relevance	How to measure performance (# – number)
Multistage mailing	Contacts added to a multistage mailing automatically receive emails in a logical/story-telling sequence at least three times, for example: Intro stage (1 email): From thought leader (e.g., address market challenges, introduce technology breakthroughs, offer guidance through the latest solutions) Main content stage (2–3 emails): Through comprehensive portfolio (e.g., highlight product families, going through Infineon's portfolio, provide matching products, provide all relevant technical documents) Closing stage (1 email): To complete support (offer support, highlight evaluation boards, offer relevant software/tools/forums, ensure that the customer considers solutions) It is an action of lead qualification	Consideration, comparison, samples order	#downloads #click through rate #qualified leads
Newsletter	It is a monthly or quarterly product sheet covering information of the new product releases and provides a summary of available product information (general description, documentation, presentations, promotion content, commercial information, etc.)	Awareness, consideration, comparison, samples order, prototyping, purchase	#unique visitors #downloads #registrations #buy button click
Permanent one-shot mailings	This mailing concept is customer-centric. It addresses a narrow target group by sending mailings based on customer's interest. The purpose of this mailing is to qualify leads	Awareness, consideration, comparison, samples order, prototyping, purchase, after sales	#qualified leads

(continued)

Table 1 (continued)

Content format	Content description and purpose	Customer journey relevance	How to measure performance (# – number)
Podcast	Podcast in context of semiconductor industry, for the subject matter topic with the industry (What-Is-a-Podcast, n.d.)	Awareness, consideration	#unique visitors #leads generated
Product brief	This content is a 2-pager providing the details such as product specification, key applications, features, and benefits	Awareness, consideration	#download
Product web page	Central storage for all public and restricted information and self-service portal for all service provided around the product: • Product overview and search functions • Promotion materials • Technical documentation • Tools and software • Partners, training, support	Awareness, consideration, comparison, samples order, prototyping, purchase, after sales	#unique visitors #downloads #buy button click
Social media posts (organic and paid)	While the goal of social media posts is to build relationships and connections with target audiences, it is widely used by B2B industries for brand awareness, website traffic, product awareness, and engagement on social media platforms as Facebook and LinkedIn. Organic posts are visible on company's own social media page whereas paid ones are targeted based on the multitude of criteria	Awareness, consideration, comparison	#unique visitors # leads generated
Time sensitive – single shot mailing	• Event invitation • Webinar invitation • Special topics with truly time-sensitive information	Awareness, consideration, comparison	#downloads #click through rate #qualified leads
Trainings, online courses, eLearning	Trainings serve 2 purposes: • Enable internal and external sales forces • Provide customer right solution through digital learning catalog	Awareness, consideration, comparison	#leads generated #qualified leads

(continued)

Table 1 (continued)

Content format	Content description and purpose	Customer journey relevance	How to measure performance (# – number)
Webinar	A webinar is an engaging online event with interactive tools to talk about topics like market trends, product portfolio, solutions, and technical deep dives Attendees can typically watch webinars in real time or on-demand after the day of the live webinar	Awareness, consideration, comparison	#leads generated #qualified leads
White paper	It is informational and factual document talking about market trends, technological solutions, and subtly marketing the products. It is in-depth guide or write-up unlike product brochure	Awareness, consideration, comparison	#leads generated #qualified leads

educating customers, the ones stated above are the most needed by partners and customers to start working with our products. However, content creation has to be tailored to the the customer persona and our objective. For instance, if a customer doesn't have technical depth on the product, a video or the product brochure will provide basic information on the product or create interest. Or if the customer is already informed about the basic know-how, he might need further engagement through a product fact sheet, user manual, application guide, and a product selection guide. Hence providing tailored content based on the target persona, market, and desired outcome is needed.

1.3 Content Creation: Good Practices

As much as it is true that creating content involves creativity, the robust process of creating content is needed for consistency and efficiency. Scalable content creation is only possible if a standard practice is in place. With this one can ensure channeling creativity with consistency. In this section, we describe the content management cycle and use it to derive content creation: good practices. Here we use the webinar content format as an example.

Plan-Do-Check-Act Cycle to Arrive at Standard Practice for Content Creation Process

To arrive at the best practice for content creation, we follow the content management cycle. The cycle starts with the "Plan" phase where a selected content format is

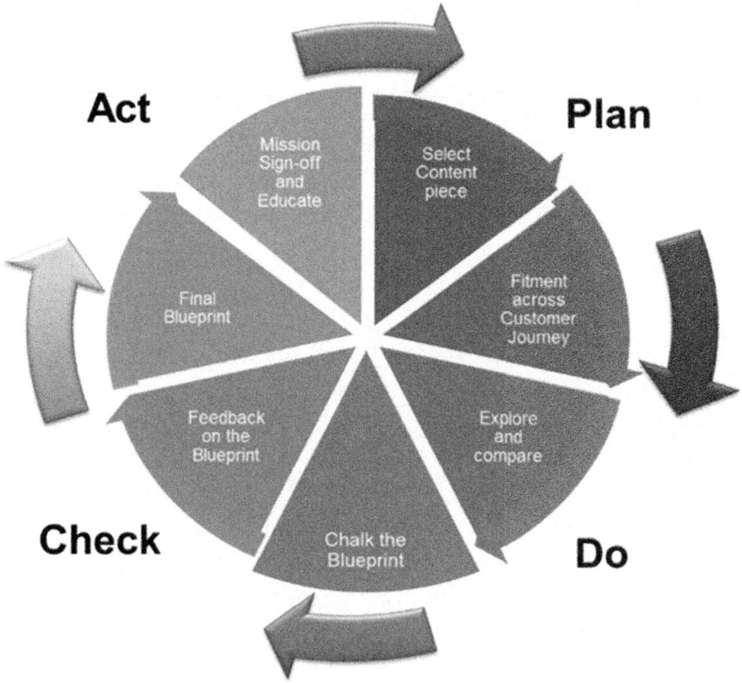

Fig. 3 Content management cycle

chosen and checked for its relevance across the customer journey. In the "Do" stage, we explore various content pieces and compare internally and also across the automotive semiconductor industry. We note the qualitative aspects of the content such as narration style (educative, expert, story or trend based, etc.), key message delivery, illustration style, and length of the content (pages, time duration, etc.). Once we have gone through sufficient content pieces of a particular format, we formulate a blueprint on how to create consistent content. We also define what are the basic building blocks of the content and how a high-quality content should resemble. The blueprint is then shared with the team for feedback and then we sign off the blueprint and share it with the stakeholders. Again, we continue the cycle and select the next content format. Should the blueprint again need refinement, we put it through a similar cycle and keep room for continuous improvement. The visual representation of the cycle is in Fig. 3. Now that we have glanced over the overview of the cycle, let us deep dive into each step until chalking the blueprint. Here we will use webinar as an exemplary content piece. However, we will also give the final outcome of white paper creation process.

1.3.1 Selecting the Content Piece

We discussed in Table 1 various content formats being consumed by the automotive semiconductor industry. Each content format caters to one or many stages of the

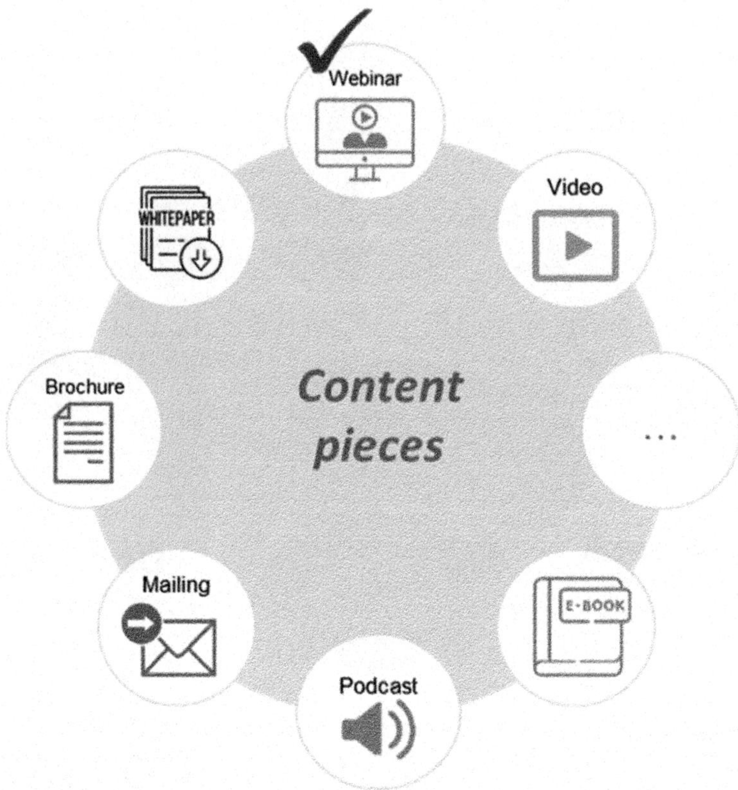

Fig. 4 Content formats

customer journey – from awareness to the usage of the product or solution. Among all the relevant formats, we have chosen a webinar to explain the content management cycle as shown in Fig. 4.

1.3.2 Fitment Across Customer Journey

In this step, we check the fitment of the content across the customer journey. The webinar is the widely used content format in the current scenario across many stages of the customer journey. However, it is mostly used until the comparison stage as illustrated in Fig. 5. In the awareness phase, webinar helps customer discover new products and solutions. During the consideration phase, the webinar educates the customer on the technical capabilities and usability of the products and solutions. In the next stage, the webinar guides the customer to compare various product offerings available in the market. Now that we are aware of the purpose webinar serves to our customers, we advance to the next step of exploration.

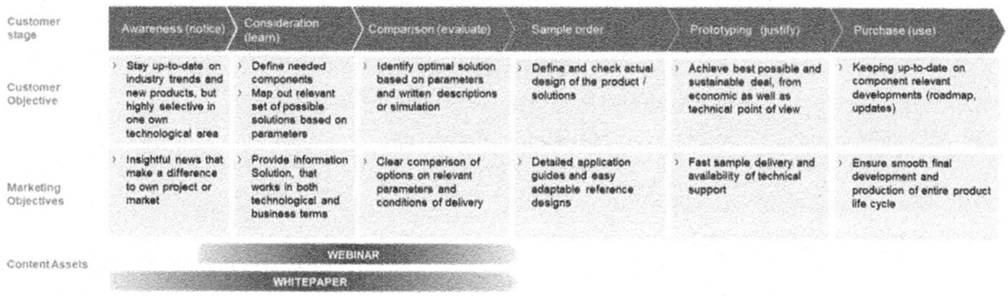

Fig. 5 Fitment across customer journey: webinar

1.3.3 Explore and Compare

In this step, we understand the concept of the webinar, followed practices, and peer-to-peer comparison of webinar examples. Let us start with an understanding of what is a webinar and its type. A webinar is an engaging presentation on topics such as market trends, new product introduction in the market, product or solution portfolio, and technical deep dive sessions. The experts or group of experts deliver a presentation to a large audience over the Internet. These are generally interactive sessions, with participants getting information, asking questions, and discussing in real time. Participants have options to follow webinars in real-time or recorded (on-demand). Webinars have become the established format for businesses in this digital age for lead generation.

Webinars can be grouped into different classification categories. Here, we classified them into three types. The first type is a live webinar with a real-time presentation with live Q&A. In this format, live interaction is possible between the speaker and the audience. In the second type which is hybrid mode, the presenter uploads the pre-recorded presentation on the host portal, and there is a live Q&A at the end of the presentation. In this format, the presenter has the flexibility to record the presentation until the desired quality of the recording is achieved. In this webinar, one gets rid of the technical issues associated with live streaming. In the third type, the entire presentation and Q&A are pre-recorded. Questions related to topics are gathered upfront before the recording and the speaker answers those questions during the recording session. This webinar type offers the most flexibility to the speaker to create high-quality content. From the audience's perspective, it is possible to attend at one's convenience, since it is already available on demand on the website. Figure 6 illustrates the difference among each webinar category.

In Sect. 1.3.2, we understood what purpose webinar serves across the customer journey for the customers. Now let us go through the desired outcome from the perspective of a content marketer. Webinars are established sources for high-quality sales leads. It is also an effective format to nurture and engage existing leads with new content. It is a cost-effective communication medium spanning across the globe. Through the webinar, a content marketer can reach out to the targeted audience. Webinar channels also enable the feedback mechanism where attendees can rate or

Fig. 6 Types of webinar

survey the webinar, which in turn helps content marketers to fine-tune their marketing activities.

After evaluating various webinars in the semiconductor industry, we deduced general guidance on webinar creation and promotion. In the next section, we will go through the blueprint of the webinar creation process.

1.3.4 Chalk the Blueprint: Webinar and White Paper

In the previous section, we explored various types of webinars and their purpose for content marketers and customers. Now we will go through the step-by-step guideline for webinar creation. In the first step, the marketing communication expert (MarCom) sets the kick-off call 7 weeks prior to the webinar date with the subject matter expert to align on the topic, format, storyline, target audience, and timeline. Based on this input, MarCom fills and gives the briefing template to the webinar hosting platform. In the next step, 5 weeks prior to the webinar, the webinar host creates the registration form. Meanwhile, the subject matter expert prepares the presentation on the topic. MarCom reviews and proofreads the presentation for content, design, and branding. Now this presentation will either be pre-recorded or directly presented on a live day depending on the type of webinar. If the format is pre-recorded or hybrid webinar, the subject matter expert will record the presentation in PowerPoint tool or MarCom will facilitate the studio recording of the presentation. The recording is to be delivered 14 days prior to the webinar date. One week prior to the webinar date, the hosting platform will guide the presenter or subject matter expert through the interactive tools of the platform. This step is valid for only live or hybrid webinar formats. On the day of a live webinar, there is a 30-minute preparatory call for technical checks and other questions. Once all the technical issues are sorted, webinar runs around 45 minutes, followed by up to 15 minutes of Q&A session. Figure 7 describes the above steps in the nutshell. On the similar lines we also show the blueprint of the white paper creation process in Fig. 8.

After the webinar is hosted, the next step is measuring and monitoring the performance of the content. In Table 1, we mentioned the relevant performance indicators (KPIs) to measure and evaluate the outcome of the content. For webinars, the key performance indicators are the number of new leads generated and how

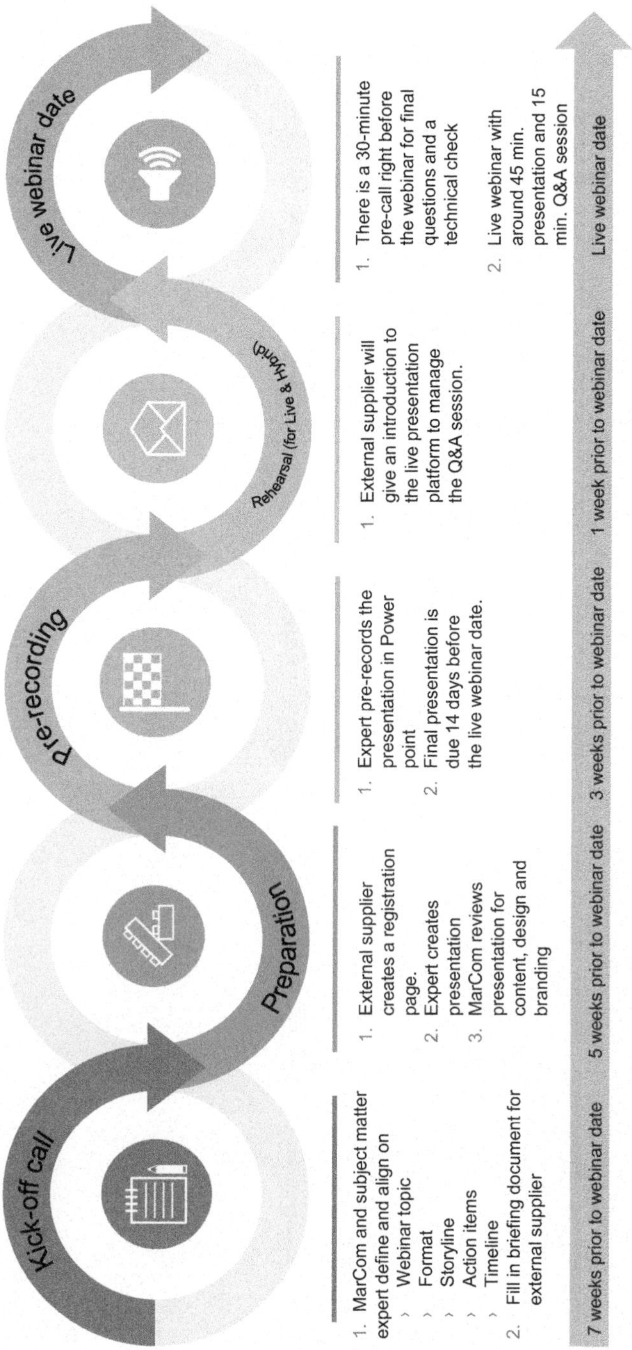

Fig. 7 Blueprint – webinar creation process

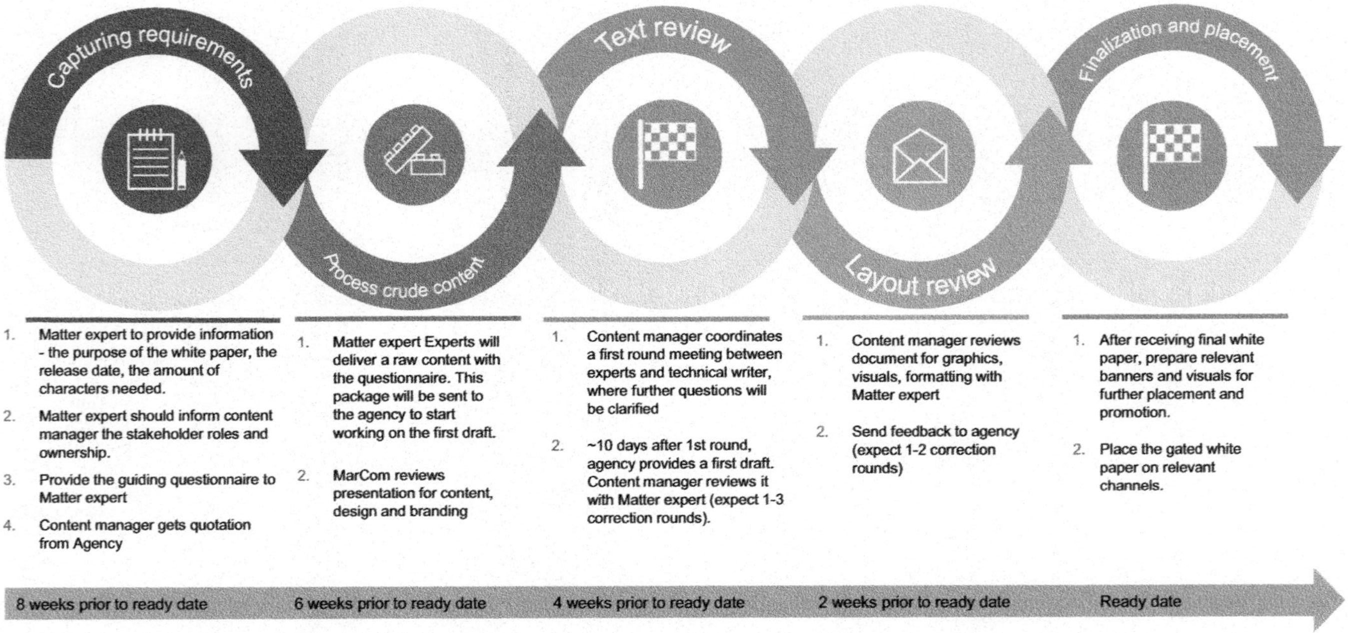

Fig. 8 Blueprint – white paper creation process

many existing leads are nurtured or engaged. These leads then attain status as market qualified leads which are pushed further through the sales funnel for nurturing.

Now that we know the relevant KPIs to measure the performance of the webinars, it is also important to compare it with the other content format at our disposal that yields same KPIs. For instance, if the objective of the marketer is to generate new leads, he could choose from the webinar, white paper, or any other gated content. Gated content could be premium downloadable content like brochures, software, etc. which needs prior registration. In order to decide on which format to choose, there are various factors to be considered, namely, cost, duration of content placement, and recurrence of usage. While live webinars provide more than five times more leads than white papers in the same duration, white papers have recurring benefit of promoting many times on different channels. The cost of creating a white paper and then promoting it on various channels need to be compared with the cost of hosting the webinar. There is also qualitative aspect for both the content pieces which cannot be compared. A white paper is well-known technical write-up in the semiconductor industry and provides a much deeper understanding of the topic, whereas webinars are more engaging and facilitate two-way communication between the presenter and the audience.

1.3.5 Review the Blueprint

Once the blueprint is ready, it must be reviewed by the two peer groups – one functional and the other cross-functional. In the functional round of review, the peer group consists of specialist content managers from the same or other business segments. This peer group does a detailed review of the blueprint. Here the blueprint is checked for its feasibility and loopholes. In case there is a loophole, the blueprint must be reworked. If there is a missing piece, it is also factored in. In the next round, we approach the cross-functional group consisting of campaign managers who would check the process from the promotion perspective. They would advise on the promotion channels and the objectives of the content pieces.

1.3.6 Blueprint Finalization and Mission Sign-off

After the review round with peer groups, we are ready with the final blueprint. In the next step, it is important to share the learnings and best practices with the stakeholders. In this step we also give more context to this blueprint by including the following aspects of the content piece:

- Customer touchpoints: Across which stages are the content piece relevant?
- Customer and marketing objectives: On one hand, what benefit does the content piece entail for the customers, and on other hand, what are the marketing goals of the content manager?
- Creation and promotion: Here we describe the format, structure, blueprint, and promotion channels.
- References or Best Practices: Here we provide reference to best performing content pieces

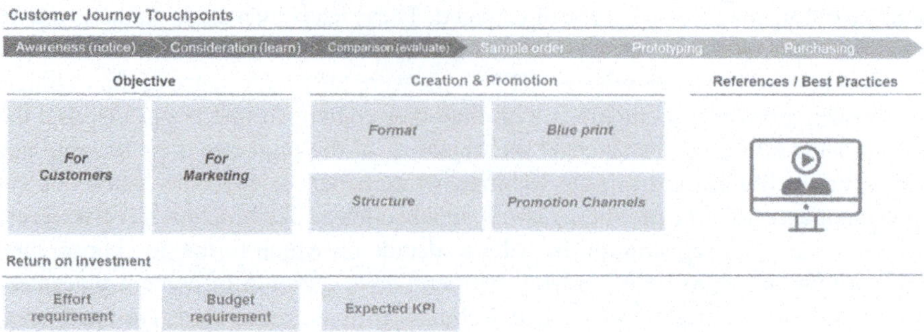

Fig. 9 Template for content sign-off

- Return on investment – this is an important part of the template covering effort, cost, and the expected results of the content pieces.

With all these details as a part of the package, the content piece is ready to be signed off. It is then shared with the stakeholders. The purpose of this template is to help stakeholders choose the right fit content piece to achieve their objective and reap a good return on their investment (Fig. 9).

2 Summary

We started the chapter with insights and the importance of content for marketing in the automotive semiconductor industry. We also covered the relevance of different content pieces across the customer journey. In the sections following that, we deep-dived into the content management process with an example and arrived at the content blueprint. We hope this chapter helps you in your content marketing initiatives and choose the right fit content for your objectives. Here we would also like to highlight that scope of our chapter was in the context of the automotive semiconductor industry and focused on the business-to-business (B2B) customers. The approach might differ for other types of industries or B2C customers, but the essence of persona-centric content still applies. In the roadmap of content standardization, we will create the blueprint for more assets.

In nutshell, choosing the right content format conducive to your marketing goal and customer preference may not be straightforward. However, if the goal is clear and guideline is in place, choosing the right content asset is not an uphill task.

References

Bauer, H., Burkacky, O., Kenevan, P., Mahindroo, A., & Patel, M. (2020, April). *Coronavirus: Implications for the semiconductor industry*. McKinsey & Company.

Koch, C., & Hartmann, M. (2022). The impact of a company website and its perceived quality on the buying intention in b2b-settings. In *Advances in digital marketing and eCommerce* (pp. 9–18). Springer.

Marshall, P. (2013). *80/20 Sales and marketing: The definitive guide to working less and making more*. Entrepreneur Press.

Traub, M., Maier, A., & Barbehön, K. L. (2017). Future automotive architecture and the impact of IT trends. *IEEE Software, 34*(3), 27–32.

What-is-a-podcast. (n.d.). Retrieved November 1, 2022, from https://www.podcastinsights.com/what-is-a-podcast/

In Pursuit of a Scalable Channel Optimization in B2B

Eric Siegel and Uli Schneider

Everyone wants to be a black belt, but no one wants to train like one.
Guy Mezger, American Mixed Martial Artist, founding UFC Member, 7th degree Blackbelt

1 Introduction

This quote from a famous mixed martial artist reverberates through our head when thinking about digital transformation and specifically the needs for a proper digital marketing architecture and landscape. Digital marketing is the newest disruptor to what has probably otherwise been a rather stodgy and innovative-less process for marketing and sales. 100 years ago, sales "eCommerce" was a catalog and by "snail" mail, supported by more traditional sales managers (e.g., direct, indirect, and internal external) and brick and mortar shops. It wasn't until the 1980s that real eCommerce came about, and even then, it was mainly for computer parts. It didn't take a recognizable shape until the mid-90s with Amazon and eBay coming into existence. Then the dot com era thrust digital everything into the main stream, creating

E. Siegel (✉)
Infineon Technologies AG, San Jose, USA
e-mail: Eric.Siegel@infineon.com

U. Schneider
Infineon Technologies AG, Neubiberg, Germany
e-mail: Uli.Schneider@infineon.com

U. Schneider, J. Hoika (eds.), *Digital Marketing in the Automotive Electronics Industry*, Management for Professionals,
https://doi.org/10.1007/978-3-031-30720-1_10

"internet marketing" which slowly became an all-encompassing, often misused pronoun for "digital marketing."

Sadly, with a high desire to be relevant many companies jumped on the bandwagon of "digital marketing" hoping to get in on this ever-present cyber gold rush of the modern era. Unfortunately, they didn't take the time to really reflect if they were ready, or fully understood what it means to make a "digital transformation" as the term is now coined. Digital transformations take massive effort and aren't as simple as mashing the like and subscribe button of your favorite creator on YouTube/TikTok. These rushing companies might be off put or fall victim to distractions like comments of "You got no NFT strategy (bro)?" or "We're all in on crypto, (bro)." (Note the "bro" added for extra frat boy effect.) These statements are meant to intimidate the meek and uneducated; don't fall for it. Any flavor of the moment, like the two aforementioned digital attributes (or insert your own preference depending on when this is published and you read it), is an example of how "digital" has its own encoding and subterfuge built in it. You need to handle it with care and prepare, look for what has been around, and see how you can systematically build up expertise, not rush in because you feel you are behind or will lose relevancy. These feelings are good motivators and can be very true statements (see Kodak Film and Blockbuster Video as tried and true examples of missed opportunities to transform), but it's better to ensure you have a good understanding of what it takes.

One really needs to make sure you are up for the challenge:

- Do you have the right stakeholders involved?
- Buy in from the top middle and/or bottom?
- What is your IT landscape and architecture looking like?
- Do you have a process to make changes and incorporate new vendors and/or technologies?
- Do business stakeholders have a voice; are you really being customer centric?

Are you nervous yet? There are a lot of traps on this perilous journey, however some can be overcome while underway, but managing expectations before departure will help minimize flare ups during what can be an all-consuming venture, that if not done properly could result in a minimal or no return on investment. This chapter is meant to help you home in on the needs for "digital marketing" or as I call it engagement marketing, one major aspect of the digital transformation you may be undertaking. It may not give you every detail you need, but it should at least give you some guiding principles to think about. It should also help you understand how you can build competencies in a crucial aspect of any transformation: How to fully tap into the new powers of digitalization and think beyond digitizing twentieth-century business processes with twenty-first-century technology to eradicate neglected customer experiences.

2 A Marketing Gravity Check in the Age of "Digital"

When setting out to market to your customers, you must decide some fundamental concepts of who you are as a company. What are your appropriate sales channels?

- Digital? (i.e., E-commerce/web or EDI?)
- Inside sales (people waiting by phones?)
- Direct sales (an account manager proactively hunting?)
- Indirect sales (another firm, who is selling your product, and potentially your competitors? An ecosystem partner perhaps?)
- Physical brick and mortar (a building with perhaps a collection of products on display?)

By first knowing these channels, you can then accurately ensure you effectively plan and coordinate any marketing activities that promote and sell your product or service, more traditionally called a "campaign" (but I like to call it: the marketing journey). There is no sense in creating awareness on any channel or progressing any part of the customer journey if there is no place to ultimately harness that nurtured curiosity and customer need and convert it into long-term profitable partnerships (notice how I didn't say "make a sale"). The mindset must truly transcend from vendor into partner, meaning mutually assured success. If you or your team are thinking only in short-term then you will not achieve sustainable long-term growth (which may be ok if that isn't your current goal). Once you know your end sales channels (or mix thereof), you can appropriately start to plan the marketing activity goals you wish to accomplish.

After mapping your sales channels, the next step is to really ask if your company is truly customer centric. It's very easy for a company or people therein to say they are, but as the old adage says "actions speak louder than words." Ask yourself:

- Under what conditions does my company ask for feedback from my customers?
- If (hopefully) yes, how do we incorporate that feedback into improvements (in our systems/processes/communications)?
- How do we reach out to our customers?
- What words do we use when we communicate with our customers?
- Do you know how customers interpret those communications?

One of us having been a part of few brand refreshes in my professional experience, I've witnessed one that transformed a self-centered, post-apocalyptic themed marketing voice to one that was humanistic and real; acknowledging that we may be a "Business to Business" enterprise, but it is still driven and moved along by people. Your content in your marketing materials is paramount. If you come across as a pretentious and bombastic high school jock you might engage with one customer but completely alienate another. This need to understand your customers and their personas highlights the danger of the easy, often over leveraged form of marketing: Broadcast Marketing.

Broadcast marketing is your traditional marketing from one to many people of whom you may or may not know who they are. Activities of this nature would be:

- Organic social media posts
- Publications and press releases
- Investor relations/quarterly statements
- Influencer-based marketing

All of these activities serve to push a message or content out into the world with no real directly known recipient. Broadcast marketing will always have its place and can be an essential form of marketing for any startup (next to earned organic content); primarily for social media, influencer marketing, distribution-based channels, but it is highly relevant for investor and public relations. The trap you do not want to fall into is blindly overlooking personas for tailored communications and needs. Even newsletters and distribution lists have choices of content and topics of interest, but in today's evolving dynamic world people have multiple projects, and again it's rather self-centered for you as a company to expect your customer or contact to stop and update you on what they are working on explicitly (unless perhaps that contact calls an account manager directly for consultation, due to a developed solid partnership mentality). As much as you should strive for that one to one bonded relationship, a competitor can always be one release away from undermining that connection. In the world of streaming tailored content why cling to broadcast strategies alone? You may be asking yourself, "Then, what else can I do? Where do I go?"; Allow me to answer, "This is the way: Engagement Marketing."

3 What Is Engagement Marketing?

When first hearing the term, it seemed so self-explanatory yet also redundant; shouldn't all marketing be engaging? Yes, it should, but as previously mentioned creating one email to subject everyone in your database to isn't using technology to the fullest.

Purely digitizing twentieth-century business practices with twenty-first-century technology will not yield the results you seek. Sadly over $1.7 trillion dollars in investment were spent in digitalization by the end of 2019 reaching over 6.8trillion by 2023 (Robuck, 2020) with only 84% of CEOs saying they have seen a high return on investment (Corish, 2022). This low return of value is because people are not leveraging the full power of new technology that they now access. They aren't thinking in terms of how they can get better, but merely adopting a myopic view of company centric incremental improvements vs adopting the highly dynamic customer centric and transformational mindset to focus on ***neglected customer experiences.*** To put it in perspective here are some numbers on release and refresh rates (see Table 1) for digital applications for various industries (Fitzpatrick & Strovink, 2021).

Table 1 Release and refresh rates for various industries

	Traditional	*Leading*	*World-class*	*Why it matters?*
Time to Market	1-2 years	2-6 months	8-12 weeks	to compete for consumers
Release Frequency	1-4 *per year*	1-4 *per month*	10-50 *per day*	to find what matters

Where do you find yourself? You may be saying, wait digital applications can be quite complicated to scope, build, and improve upon; they aren't the same as "marketing." But that is the point. Engagement marketing is more in tune with digital application mindset than the traditional broadcast marketing.

Broadcast marketing alone, though effective, will ultimately provide a neglected experience contrasted to a tailored engagement marketing oriented one. If you can observe behavior on your platform (website, device, any product that can report back user behavior), you can plan a tailored marketing strategy, product roadmap, and better anticipate your customer's needs.

"Great, but you didn't answer the question: What is Engagement Marketing?"

Engagement marketing is the ability to leverage all your customer data and insights to understand, even anticipate, your customer's needs and problems by providing content, material, solutions via a data-driven, always on, automated, marketing journey mindset.

Notice nowhere in that definition do we mention the word "campaign." A marketing campaign has a start and an end date; engagement marketing consists of marketing "flows," like an unending river of continuity, leading our customers on their journeys (again, theirs not ours!). Engagement marketing is best characterized into three types of communications:

- Time sensitive
- Trigger based
- Reactivation (or a lack of triggers)

Time-sensitive events can be an exception in terms of leveraging a campaign mindset. As these are usually time-bound events:

1. The bake sale is in one week.
2. The bake sale is in one day.
3. The bake sale has started!
4. The bake sale is about to end.
5. The bake sale ended, our next one will be. . . .

Campaign mindsets, even if using data to target, will neglect listening for cues that the customer is ready to engage (but admittedly can tap random unknown interest). That said, from our experience in the semiconductor industry very few customers *collaboratively* plan the specific 3–6 month windows where they will initiate new design cycles for their products, thereby only saying “speak to me about new releases of your product between March and August.” If they do and actually wait on you, congratulations you’ve cultivated the cult-like mentality and fanaticism that titans of industry dream of (but if you think those winners just lucked into it, think again).

A quick note: We do recognize that some highly consumer-focused companies have certain holidays they target product releases every year. This is a prime example of where the Account Manager can run point in leading the conversation, but it should not be any counterpoint to the need to listen to our customers for when they are ready to engage.

Back to our regularly scheduled chapter

The remaining two communication types, trigger based and reactivation require a bit more rigor to develop fruitful outcomes. Even in the time-sensitive bake sale example, you saw five stages of engagement that were clear, and regardless of the customer’s willingness, time was moving them from one stage to another. For the remaining two flows, you will need to listen to your customer and observe their behavior to understand and interpret their actions into understanding the next best action. We’ll get more into setting these up and what it takes in the following paragraphs.

Engagement marketing activities are rooted in automation and personalization. If broadcast is a generic push, then engagement marketing is a highly personalized reaction sent directly to a specific known contact. They are usually deployed after observing a series of key customer journey steps, to indicate where a person is in their own stage. Examples of engagement marketing-based journey segments:

- A customer, who has provided consent for tracking and marketing, goes to a webpage positioning a newly released product and spends 30–60 seconds on the page, but doesn’t convert.
- Engagement marketing activities that could take place:
  - A follow-up communication to them asking any number of subjects:
    - Do you need help finding the right product?
    - Did something go wrong?
    - How was your experience on the website?
  - That communication could be sent in a multitude of ways:
    - To their email
    - Direct communication via an app push notification or direct message of a known channel (WhatsApp, WeChat, Instagram, etc.)
    - A remarketing-based Display Ad (GDN, Social, or otherwise)
    - An SMS to their phone
    - A direct call from an inside sales or account manager

The list can go on and on, but in order to leverage all these channels properly one will need to ensure the MarTech Stack and ecosystem is harmonized.

4 Data Are the Pixels by Which We Paint the Picture of Our Personas

Once you know who your customer is and ideally have all your first party data at your disposal, you can then start to scientifically do the experiments (or data science analysis) to understand what channels are best to leverage to engage and respond to known customer needs and which ones can be leveraged as effective to get your message out there and draw the unknown customers into the light of the known. In order to do this a solid data architecture will be required (something similar to a Customer Data Platform, or in older setups a data lake, or something in between), a place where you can aggregate and analyze all data inputs into understanding and analyzing the customer's mindset and corresponding journey stage.

Engagement marketing is a by-product of this customer-centric mentality and consists of many things like end-of-end customer journeys (more on that term later) but having clarity on your data architecture and even more important the bandwidth to engineer your data together so you can analyze it. This allows you to unlock the insights of understanding who your customers are, i.e., your personas, to create tailored content to help explain the value proposition of the product or service you bring, and thus move any "partner" down the funnel for harvest in their preferential channel of choice.

In order to proceed there are some fundamentals we will assume you have:

- A valuable service offering
- A platform to collect **consented** customer data
- The digital infrastructure necessary to analyze, act, and attribute that data

From here you can start to accurately plan out your (end-to end) marketing journeys but know that not all actions have to start in the digital world. If you have a physical sales force, you should not neglect the wealth of information they may bring to the table. In fact they are a great way to bring special value and attention to key customers to get insights that can be otherwise misinterpreted. Regardless of how you get the information (physically, digitally, etc.), you need to map customer journeys and understand how they want to do something vs how you allow them to do so, and the corresponding feelings and pain points. Customer journey mapping via swim lanes is a great way to understand and give a face to the neglected experience you wish to solve. There are amazing software out there to enable customer journey mapping with ease, but simple ones can be managed with excel, white boarding software, or good ole' analog pen and paper.

In Fig. 1 you can see some basics at play. To keep it with something everyone can understand, it maps the need to get a morning beverage, and the preference is coffee. In order to map the journey properly, we have included the two-key player of the

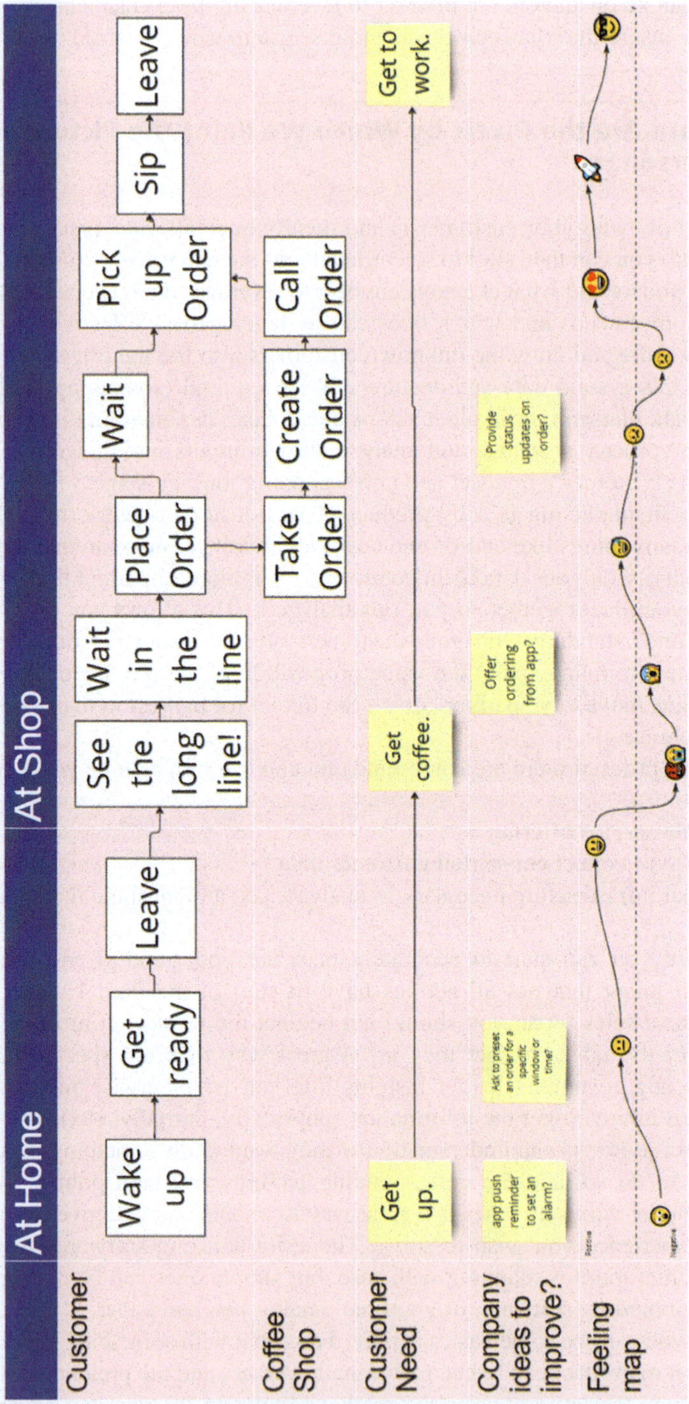

Fig. 1 Example of basic customer journey mapping

customer (row 1), and the coffee shop employees (row 2). You could of course sub-segment that latter group more (front of the house, back of the house, etc.), but for simplicity we kept it as two key players in the exchange. It shows the two environments and areas the experience takes place at: home (Column 2) and the coffee shop (Column3). You may wish to use customer journey stages instead of actual locations, purely your decision on the level of detail needed. Row 3 covers the customer needs, which should be collected through customer surveys, not internal assumptions. (Note: You can start with internal assumptions, but these should be clearly noted then vetted, but you run the risk of confirmation bias.) "Company Ideas," row 4, are a place to capture ways you can improve the experience shown above, there are no bad ideas right? Finally, Row 5 displays the Customer's feeling map, you could also include feeling maps for all players, but this will increase complexity. This map displays how the customer is feeling, happy, sad, angry, or positive and negative, and overall helps you map where to focus your efforts.

For this example, we have some common recurring themes, a customer who is in a hurry and hates waiting (maybe a persona, In-a-hurry-Henry!), as mapped via the customer feeling map against, needs, and actions. By looking at the order of operations and feelings, this company has identified four new product offerings or enhancements to their customer experience that should hopefully improve the overall experience. Hopefully you can see how a swim lane diagram such as the above is a great example of how to map your customers' feelings and needs and uncover the hidden neglected experience you can improve. This exercise can lead to a combination of improvements for your platform or product, a website or app, and ultimately your engagement marketing strategy.

To build off of the above example a swim lane can not only map your customer journey through the appropriate channels you'll need, you can add additional rows showing what content (or experience) will be required (wireframes of emails or UX!). Mapping a customer journey is one of the most pivotal activities to undertake, and should be done with as many customers as possible, with ideally as open a mind as possible (i.e., you may need a third party to help facilitate this to ensure the impartiality). It can be an intense and eye-opening exercise, dispelling perhaps some of the longest held beliefs about your customers (by your executives or even sales!). In the end it's about seeking to understand and provide truth. By understanding a customer's pain points, you can understand how digital or physical experiences can improve the whole process, and ideally the seamless integration of both physical and digital together, or "phygital," as we like to call it.

For B2B electronics direct sales environments, more often than not the path to a sale, or making a lifetime partner can be circuitous (pun intended), as there may be multiple personas within one company or customer that you need to navigate and engage with at different times. Creating content appropriate for each step of the customer journey is a crucial activity. This enhanced level of personalization is necessary to facilitate a pleasant customer experience (and ultimately allow you to hack the traffic lights for your sales team to be all greens). Understanding your personas and the journey allows you to understand what type of content and on what channel may be necessary or best.

5 Customer Centricity for Marketing Content and Journeys

Taking on such a task can be daunting, and even then, you may not get the journey 100% right. People are different; tastes and trends evolve. The important thing is to stop and think about what each potential problem your customers are facing is and how they try to solve them. By doing this you can hypothesize where to start and what will be needed. It all starts with a series of questions:

- What is my customer's problem?
  - What are the words they would use to describe this problem?
- What solutions exist on the market today to solve this problem?
  - How does my solution differentiate from those on the market?
  - What is your solution's Value Proposition?
- What content do I need to generate to explain current market conditions and tradeoffs?
  - Will I have something different in the future I can discuss?
  - How do the different personas care about this subject matter? What areas?
- What will someone do differently having engaged with any content I provide?
- What are the key behaviors and actions we can observe that would indicate where a customer is on their journey?

Asking yourself these questions allows you to zero in on the various needs for any campaign you'll develop. For instance, if your goal is thought leadership, then you can focus on the awareness and future orientation, whereas if you are doing a product launch, you will need to be much more concrete in terms of documentation and support.

- How do customers find your data sheet or product page?
- Is there a white paper that can lead them there?
- An article or video that guides them to the options in the market to solve their problem?

The steps a customer would take to indicate they have interest in a subject would be very different as a thought leadership-oriented campaign. It might be more targeted towards retaining brand equity and discuss at a higher level than say a product-specific pitch showing the virtues of one product in a specific application. Regardless of the goal, having a clear understanding of the words your customers use will ensure you are creating tailored content that will resonate with them.

A quick word on Keyword Research:

Keyword research is the underlying backbone of any marketing campaign. If you are not speaking your customer's language, then you will never be able to position your value to them or connect your offering to needy potential partners.

Once you understand your customer's pain points from a swim lane of a journey and their cares abouts via the persona definitions and what actions they have taken, now you have to convert your value proposition into specific reactionary journeys and the goals and KPIs to measure success and what content may be needed. To give a concrete example, let's attack the classic abandoned shopping cart. The goal should be checking out and completing the sale. By analyzing the user behavior, you may understand and know: what kind of customer is this? This will help you tailor the message.

- First time customer?
  - Do they know they didn't check out? Send an instructional follow-up.
- Frequent customer?
  - Perhaps they got distracted and need a simple reminder.
- Reactivating customer?
  - Do they need an incentive, i.e., 5%?

What channel(s) show effective engagement?

- Do they come to your app? Website? Respond to emails?
  - Understanding where they like to engage will allow you to ensure higher likelihood of conversion.

If you don't have enough data on a particular contact or customer, you can then turn to the dark arts of data science. Are there similar customers that share the same actions but show similar engagement on other or new channels you could investigate?

This will help you with creating the right mix of content and channel focus. Mapping the behaviors, you can observe into journey segments (the classical customer journey steps are awareness, consideration, decision, purchase, support/care); you can start to classify what behaviors would put a customer into those stages. With that you should be able to build out a rough end-to-end journey (or near end to end). So, in our pervious example, what lead the customer to put the item in the cart would be the predicating customer journey stages (awareness and consideration). Our advice is always to start from the right-most segment and move left. Most marketing teams tend to work left to right, which to me is like getting people to show up to the party when you are still setting up! By building and optimizing journeys from right to left, you will one reward those who have already put in the pain to move forward in your existing neglect experiences and further reward loyalty and bonding, as well as generally work with a smaller number to focus on wrinkling out any issues vs amplifying existing errors in the system.

6 The Marketing Journey Stages and Flow Creation

A good way to approach the end-to-end journey development is simply to create a chart where you list each journey stage in a column. Figure 2 shows an example of one:

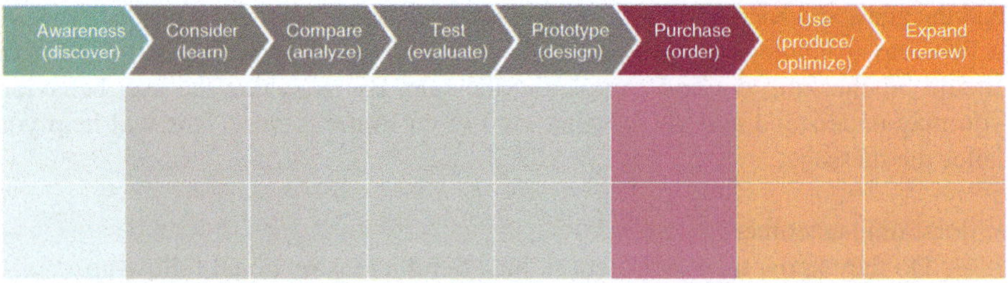

Fig. 2 End-to-end customer journey activity table

- What actions would indicate a customer is in which column?
- What actions would indicate they have advanced further down the journey?

Congratulations you are on your way to specifying your segmentation or customer segments. This will allow you to understand what data needs to be tracked to enroll someone in a journey as well as what data needs to be reported to understand conversion. Now you can start to think about the content you have, or must create, and what channels you could use it on, to move someone from one journey stage to another.

- Is there existing content you can breakdown into further usable segments?
  - That is, a 30-min video that can be trimmed to a 2-min teaser
  - Or even a 30-second short form video

By using this high-level structure, you can start to plan out the boundary conditions of your individual campaigns (and subsequent channels used) connecting your individual campaigns into a complete end-to-end journey.

With high level segments and journey goals (conversion criteria), you can now start to move to the next step of detailed planning, once a contact is enrolled, what are you going to do with them to get them to move to the next stage? Sometimes this is an easy feat if using a single channel (as in with stand-alone paid advertisements).

A simple example:

A contact comes to your page and spends 30 seconds looking at a product and leaves. The average time on page for conversion is right at that 20–40-second window.

This observed behavior is a clear sign of interest given your data at hand, so what do you do? The simplest journeys would be:

- Send a direct message (Email, DM, Notification, etc.) asking them to come back.
- Enroll them in a remarketing ad scheme to come back and convert.
- Have a Customer Service Phone agent call them.
- Send a direct sales force representative to reach out (a bit overkill potentially, but possible).

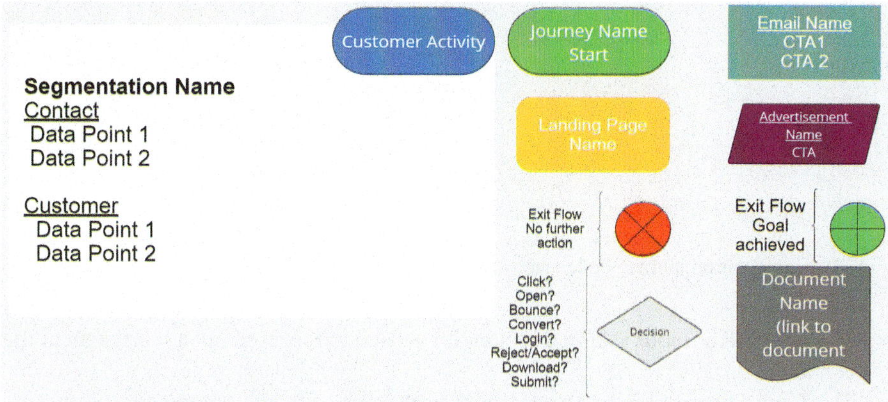

Fig. 3 Basic elements for campaign flow designs

These are easy to manage, but what if we wanted to do a progressive set of channel utilization? This is the next level of integration and planning. Here we advise it's best to leverage any sort of process documentation tool to map out the boundary conditions (i.e., enrollment criteria or segmentation) and the progressive steps and actions you'll take. In some ways it's very similar to a circuit diagram (forgive us our engineering background is showing), but we are sure every industry can relate to this need.

In Fig. 3 you can see a basic selection of icons that can be used to create sophisticated integrated marketing flows. It starts with your segmentation on the left; you'll need to account for all the variables you'll use to enroll someone into the journey. In this example and world, we have two main data objects, the contact and the customer. How you structure your data will help dictate this setup. In the world we are building for this example we have basic data for the contact (such as first and last name, email address, country, and observed behaviors) and basic data for the company, things like what level of customer (basic to VIP, specific purchase history, or even complaints). From there we have various blocks for different activities and steps:

- The green terminator (yes that is the stretched looking circle shape's name) is to indicate the start of one journey.
  - This is useful if you want to be ambitious and indicate new journeys you hand off to or chain into one long flow.
- The blue terminator indicates any activity the customer does outside of flow, specifically if it causes an ending.
- The Yellow Rounded Rectangle is used to represent when a customer encounters a landing page.
- The Teal-ish colored rectangle represents an email that could be sent to the customer.

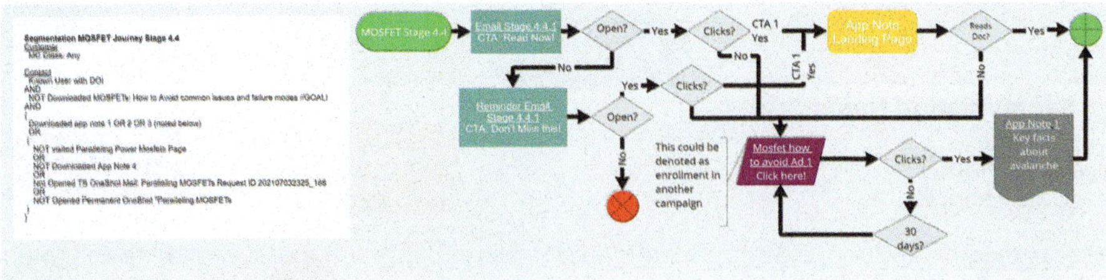

Fig. 4 Segmentation journey code and visualization

- The purple Rhombus (slanted rectangle) is used to represent an advertisement that is shown.
- The Grey Diamond is to check if an event or process has happened.
  - Did they open? Click? Submit the form?
- The normal sized Red and Green Circles indicate the end of unenrollment from the journey with an indication of success (Green) or failure to accomplish the goal (Red).
- Lastly the "wavy rectangle" represents accessing a document, but you can use this for any media or multiple other shapes to represent.

How can these blocks work?

In Fig. 4 this is an example of how a simple integrated journey can work. In this example we are on stage 4.4 of an already existing end-to-end journey (hopefully near conversion!) and the goal is to download App Note 4.4 (as denoted with the rule out clause in the segmentation.). The segmentation should explain or provide the logical rules of who and when someone should be enrolled. Though not observed in this image, we found it's always best to explicitly type out the timeframe for when a triggering action would have occurred. In this example there is really one opportunity to add a time window:

- Downloading App Notes 1 through 3 in the past x days/weeks/year

The remaining segmentation criteria all remain in the future or a contact hasn't had them happen.

If successfully met the customer will be enrolled at the Green Terminator and receives the first email. From there a series of wait stages and checks will occur to ensure the proper routing and receiving of future emails (reminders) or advertisements to get the contact to convert to the goal of downloading the App note. Note: highly sophisticated setups can use per contact data science to send the emails at the right time, account for fatigue of the contact, or even avoid channels with a known low conversion rate for this contact. At this stage of mapping though, it's best to keep it one level at a time. Get your main progressions mapped, and then you can add in such finer details of personalization.

From here you can create a marketing journey "flow diagram" and map out all the possibilities. Something to keep in mind while detailing out what you want to do:

- Don't forget where the customer is coming from and where you are trying to send them (one stage at a time).
- What are the data points you'll need for enrollment and journey branching?
- How will you keep track of success and contact progression? (i.e., your dashboard).

7 Adapting to the Inevitable: Turning to the Unknown

It's also beneficial to keep your change management and communication package in mind. If you are creating a very in-depth and detailed flow, is it something you can easily communicate to someone outside your organization with ease? Is it heavy to digest? Be prepared to identify the core of any flow that will go into making your Minimum Viable Product, the leanest you can make something that is of valuable to your customers. It's ok if you end up going very detailed and map out all possibilities, but it's best to not get too far down if you don't yet know if the first stage is even beneficial.

Once mapped you can then start to give further definition for how intermediary content pieces are needed and can be shaped for personalization. What emails/ads/landing pages are needed that can take into context the persona and their previous actions? You can start to refine the journey and see it more clearly. As you finalize the flow and content needs, you can hopefully create, integrate, and test in your marketing automation platform of choice (a simple statement that can be a very laborious task), but once launched the real work begins. In a Herculean or Sisyphean effort the now arduous task of deciding if you truly care about your customers will come into play: iterating and improving on the campaigns. It would be post launch that you must start analyzing the results of the campaign:

- Are people enrolling?
- Was your data accurate?
- What content is successful in converting contacts from node to node within the flow?
- What flow pieces are successful in achieving the goals?
- Are there common threads in those who are taking certain actions (conversion, ignoring an email, clicking an email?)

By looking at these results, and reviewing them with stakeholders, you can start to refine and improve your campaign. Create new branches, incorporate new data if needed; even find new personas! This is where it takes effort, focus, and discipline, and seemingly a repetition of the same actions but each time looking for new clues into what your customers are looking for, which honestly to me is the exciting stuff. This is the real power of engagement marketing, taking a systematic and repeatable approach to digital marketing that allows you to scientifically understand your customers and provide scalable and profitable experiences that make their lives better.

This is something you can start with from day one (but hopefully you have some idea of where your customers are!), but if you don't, you'll need to start with two main worlds: the unknown (broadcast marketing) and the known (engagement marketing).

8 Being the Change You Want to See in the World

Hopefully by now we have given you enough understanding of what engagement marketing is and is not, and how both broadcast combined with engagement marketing can yield the highest likelihood of success. Great; then job done...

Just kidding, now how do you convince others? Well obviously, give them a copy of this book to start, but the next piece to understand is that digital transformation is not a single party affair. Identifying the need to leverage engagement marketing (or a larger digital transformation) is most likely one of the most underestimated efforts in change management activities. There are numerous sources and documents on how to facilitate change management; our recommendation is one of the numerous forms of Kotter's 8 steps of change, from high level to deeper text:

- His HBR paper covering the essential 8 steps (Kotter, 2007).
- *Our Iceberg is Melting* is a very easy to understand story telling version (Kotter et al., 2006).
- *Leading Change* – his thoroughly detailed book with more technical depth (Kotter, 2012).

The greatest argument on the need for change and digital transformation comes from two potentially conflicting, if misinterpreted, statements:

- You cannot grow your business if your base (revenue) is declining.
- Defending the status quo is not a sustainable business model.

With these two guiding principles, the need to transform a business becomes more apparent, and hopefully the necessary strategies clear. That clarity though can be muddled and occluded when transmitted across various mediums, cultures, and environments. To paraphrase the title, you may see the iceberg is melting, but there will always be those who deny it (the aptly named No-No in the story[5]), as ignoring the evidence of change is easier to accept than the hard work of finding a solution.

In your journey to convince others, you must find the starting evidence that change is needed, as every industry is different in terms of their development and evolution, except for the fact that digitalization of industries *is happening*, and has effectively been accelerated by 10 years compared to the previous rate of change prior to COVID-19[1]. If you have your evidence of the need to change, start with building a trusted coalition to drive that change. You must find your allies to ultimately find and convince a sponsor. With a sponsor in hand, you must plan out your path. Much like your customers/partners, each unique company has their own needs. Given the outlined previous requirements, do you have your fundamentals in place?

- How will your corporate culture respond to this call to action?
- Are you creating customer-centric feedback loops?
- Do you have the infrastructure needed for data collection and full actualization?
- Do you have tailored content/end-to-end journey mentalities?

Given your analysis you must start to decide what really is the best course of action.

- Can you create a safe space to pilot and learn?
- Can you setup "island mode" technological landscapes before investing in the needed infrastructure to connect systems together?
- Who else do you need to work with to launch a pilot?

Your guiding coalition and team must make a best plan of action, but the biggest caution to all of this is to **be flexible**. The best of intentions can yield unanticipated negative results.

Once you know or at least have an idea of how to move forward, then the next set of questions will allow you to decide the next steps more easily. Essentially do you seek out a partner, or try to do it yourself. Our advice is always to seek a partner, be it a friend, or vendor (in this case). It's a good idea to seek outside counsel to ensure a best chance of success and reduce numerous "big" iterations. Again, this is all subject to your company's size and appetite for change. Given the automotive world's environment, an outside counsel is a prudent move.

So now you have your guiding council, and a plan. Next is to put it into action! Start small and focus on crawling before you start running (or sprinting #AgilePun). Find one neglected experience and map it out completely. Find a small test area where you believe you can make an impact with this improved engagement marketing journey. Find the other necessary stakeholders required to make this change. Chances are you'll need the support/buy in of the following players:

- Business/product line management and marketing
- Marketing/corporate communications
- Information technology organizations
- Digital marketing
- Content generation

With enough rounds you'll find out who should take a more prominent view or more prominent role in the working teams. Combined with good data discipline, you'll be able to provide insights from your iterations when relevant to share your learnings and (justify the actions taken) easing any of the inquisition that may pop up during alignment sessions. These first few sessions and iterations will be crucial moments so take your time to lay a foundational level of trust and empowerment that you know what you are doing or are at least getting to the bottom of it. Over time you will set into motion an avalanche of change, but don't take it as granted; keep the discipline focus and rigor of reviews (or agile ceremonies) or else you will be swept up by the wave vs ride it to where you want to be.

<DING>

Uh oh, unfortunately that ding means our time for this session is up. We hope you found the information insightful and actionable. We can tell you that making these sorts of decisions and changes is not easy, but it is also not impossible. The best thing you can do is maintain an open mind and be prepared to learn quickly, be open to ideas from others, but dig down and validate that it's possible or map out the contingencies so you can ensure to bring in others needed into the fold. The journey, or dare we say quest you are embarking on, is challenging, but also full of excitement; you have the power to fundamentally change a company. To become a digital Prometheus, bringing forth the engagement marketing fire to humans, so you can set forth a change in you and your company's destiny. If that isn't enticing, then you might want to question why you are still reading (j/k). Best of luck!

References

Corish, B. (2022). *Digital transformation in the 21st century*. Accenture.

Fitzpatrick, M., & Strovink, K. (2021). *How do you measure success in digital? Five metrics for CEOs*. https://www.mckinsey.com/capabilities/mckinsey-digital/our-insights/how-do-you-measure-success-in-digital-five-metrics-for-ceos

Kotter, J. P. (2007). Leading change: Why transformation efforts fail. In *Museum management and marketing* (pp. 20–29). Routledge.

Kotter, J. P. (2012). *Leading change*. Harvard Business Press.

Kotter, J. P., Kotter, J., & Rathgeber, H. (2006). *Our iceberg is melting: Changing and succeeding under any conditions*. Pan Macmillan.

Robuck, M. (2020). Digital transformation spending will catapult to $6.8 trillion by 2023. https://www.fiercetelecom.com/telecom/report-digital-transformation-spending-will-catapult-to-6-8-trillion-by-2023

Advancing from a Scalable Marketing Approach into a Digital Self-Service Sphere

Alexander Schwertlein, Uli Schneider, and Jürgen Hoika

To stay ahead in the dynamic semiconductor industry with its highly complex products, continuous development is required at all levels. So, it's not enough just to offer the most innovative products, but you also have to stay one step ahead of the competition in the marketing of the products.

One of the challenges the industry is currently facing is the transition from a scalable marketing approach to a digital self-service sphere that enables digital sales. Research suggests that 80% of B2B sales interactions between suppliers and buyers occurs in digital channels by 2025 (Gartner, 2020). Enabling digital sales are especially important for semiconductor manufacturers whose customers are in the automotive industry, as the design-in cycle for semiconductors that are built into cars can take several years. Therefore, it is crucial to accompany automotive customers through the customer journey to the purchase of products and beyond with the help of digital self-services. This can be done by replacing physical touchpoints. It can also be achieved by enriching already existing digital customer touchpoints. Another option is to come up with a new solution that is detached from existing touchpoints across the entire customer journey. Digital self-services enable customers "to find the answers to their questions without having to contact customer support." This can be achieved by providing "a solution or a group of solutions enabling web users or employees to be completely autonomous on a website or intranet" (Verani, 2021).

Infineon Technologies AG generates more than 40% of its consolidated revenues from customers in the automotive industry. To enable further growth in the future, core and mass market customers with high growth potential and higher margins are increasingly coming into focus. The introduction and expansion of digital self-services can support the customer journey of both customer groups and thus

A. Schwertlein (✉) · U. Schneider · J. Hoika
Infineon Technologies AG, Neubiberg, Germany
e-mail: Alexander.Schwertlein@infineon.com; Uli.Schneider@infineon.com; Juergen.Hoika@infineon.com

U. Schneider, J. Hoika (eds.), *Digital Marketing in the Automotive Electronics Industry*, Management for Professionals,
https://doi.org/10.1007/978-3-031-30720-1_11

scale revenue of Infineon's Automotive Division. Additionally, engineers and decision makers of direct customers also benefit from digital offerings and digital self-services, so they are critical for scaling the design-in support of all customers. Thereby, future growth is ensured by winning additional customers and at the same time satisfying existing customers, who expect these digital services in addition to analog support. With a growing number of customers, at one point it is no longer feasible to provide analog, in-person feedback on product-related content. Therefore, it is crucial to advance from a scalable marketing approach into a digital self-service sphere in order to still convince all customers of the product offering. The need to move into the digital self-service sphere is amplified by three factors. General changes in the B2B business, fundamental changes in the automotive industry, and the impact of the COVID-19 pandemic.

The following chapter aims to present companies in the B2B sector which ongoing changes make digital self-services crucial to ensure sustainable growth and customer satisfaction. It will also show practitioners and managers how to set up a project to identify digital self-services relevant to their business context and capture the requirements necessary for implementation. As a proposal for setting up such a project, we describe the approach we followed in a digital customer engagement project of Infineon's Automotive Division and the experiences we made in this process. To enable practitioners and managers from the B2B sector to derive implications for their business context, the following sections first address ongoing changes that accelerate the need to implement digital self-services. On this basis, in a next step we present our approach and disclose insights gained. Finally, we summarize our results and give an outlook for the transition into a sustaining project setup and the technical implementation of the services.

1 Changes in the B2B Context That Drive the Change from a Scalable Marketing Approach into a Digital Self-Service Sphere

The standards that leaders in B2C business have set in using digital technologies for their customer relationships in marketing and sales are also putting B2B companies on the spot. As they try to catch up, enabling future growth, differentiation, and an improved customer experience, B2B companies are looking for new ways to leverage the various digital technologies available.

Digital self-services can provide a rather large level of leverage. They can guide customers through various stages of the customer journey and enable customers to find answers to their specific problems themselves without having to wait for analog resources. Moving touchpoints into a digital sphere enables a smoother and more efficient customer journey (Verani, 2021).

The attempt of B2B companies to catch up with the established standards is described in more detail in Sect. 1.1 General Changes. In addition, we will look at changes in the automotive industry and how they are driving the need for digital self-services. Finally, we will explain why the Covid19 pandemic further reinforces these trends.

1.1 General Changes

The B2C industry has long demonstrated how digital technologies can significantly improve the customer journey. Numerous interactions and transactions between consumers and providers have moved into the digital sphere. Many consumers have become accustomed to everyday services such as access to information at any time, online purchase of products with just a few clicks, or product suggestions based on user behavior. Now similarly sophisticated functions are expected in their professional context in B2B customer relationships as well. This is exacerbated by the upcoming younger generation of engineers and buyers. Over time, the proportion of customers who have grown up with permanent Internet access via smartphones is steadily increasing, forcing vendors to adapt to the changing expectations of these younger generations, who are seeking the same level of B2C customer experience in their daily work in the B2B environment (Forrester, 2021). Already today, the vast majority of the customer journey is completed digitally before a buyer engages with a supplier (Gartner, 2019).

1.2 Changes in the Automotive Industry

The automotive industry is currently undergoing the biggest transformation in decades, driven by government regulations that impact mobility in general and push the electrification of vehicles. This unleashed change has opened up opportunities for new players to enter the market. These new players are joining the established OEMs and Tier 1s and softening the old structures. The new players are not only innovative startups, but also new entrants with a background in the Internet industry or consumer electronics that are also looking to take advantage of the opportunity to enter the automotive market (Chanias & Hess, 2016). To secure future growth as a semiconductor manufacturer in the automotive industry, it is essential to integrate its products into the mobility concepts of the new players in case they turn into the next market leader. This results in the balancing act of offering old customers the service they are used to and at the same time not missing out on new opportunities in the form of customers. Given the large number of new entrants and the change in preferences brought about by the pandemic, it is no longer possible to serve them all with human resources, so a scalable solution is needed to meet customer needs. This results in the need to evolve one's marketing approach towards digital self-service and shift resources intensive customer touchpoints to a digital sphere. To accomplish this balancing act, digital sales are essential to enable a smooth customer journey for customers who are too small for direct service. To make this work, you need content that speaks for itself and is easily accessible so that customers don't get lost on their customer journey.

Because of increasingly complex products, it is becoming increasingly difficult to make purchasing decisions without sufficient guidance or advice. Therefore, the overall convenience and ease of buying products as well as the quality of the content available online play an important role when buyers decide for or against suppliers operating in highly competitive markets (Gartner, 2022).

1.3 COVID-19 Pandemic Accelerated the Digital Transformation and the Need of Digital Self-Services

The pandemic acted as a catalyst as companies had to adapt their sales strategy to the restrictions imposed by several countries in response to the global COVID-19 pandemic. Face-to-face interaction was mostly no longer possible, making it necessary to shift interpersonal interactions to a digital sphere.

Activities and problems that were previously solved in person needed to be tackled virtually (Simon-Kucher, 2022). Thus, the COVID-19 pandemic has accelerated digitalization drivers that were already in place. Although the restrictions are being eased again worldwide, customers have become accustomed to this digital collaboration and, as a result, customers are relying more and more on digital experiences to guide them to informed purchasing decisions (Forrester, 2021). This applies to all areas of the customer pyramid, including OEMs and tier 1s, making digital self-service crucial to serve the additional virtual encounters.

The above changes are the reason why Infineon's digital marketing departments are focusing its digitalization efforts on digitalizing the customer journey and moving the various touchpoints into a digital sphere. In this context, efforts are being made to leverage and establish the various opportunities offered by digital self-services to provide the best possible user experience, to satisfy the needs of engineers, especially those of the next generation, and to successfully guide the entire customer pyramid through their respective customer journeys.

2 Identifying and Prioritizing the Most Important Digital Self-Services for an Automotive Semiconductor Manufacturer

The specifics of the automotive industry have their own influence on the need for digital transformation and its outcomes. Infineon has four divisions with very different customer groups. For example, one division focuses on customers who manufacture consumer goods, which is a different customer group than the automotive industry. Infineon's Automotive Division faces the challenge of digitalizing the go-to-market approach of sales and marketing and identifying the digital self-services that are most important for its customers in the context of digital transformation.

The following section shows how a customer-oriented identification of digital self-services can be approached along the customer journey. This is illustrated using a digital customer engagement project from Infineon's Automotive Division. The goal is to show practitioners and managers how they can set up a similar project to identify digital self-services that are relevant to their business context and capture the requirements needed for implementation. To enable this, we present the specific approach and disclose some of the most important lessons learned. The focus is on the approach itself rather than the specific digital self-services we identified. As will be shown below, the digital self-services relevant for a company result from a mix of different variables. These variables include the company-specific customer journey, customer buyer persona, available resources, existing IT backbone, ongoing digital transformation efforts, and many more. This mix is very individual for each company, and therefore a focus on the digital self-services identified by Infineon's Automotive Division has only limited added value for the reader.

The many different ways of structuring a company may mean that the approach presented here cannot be transferred one-to-one. However, the basic stakeholders and necessary processes should be similar in most companies of comparable size. Therefore, Sect. 2.1 first introduces the stakeholders of the project setup and their function. This approach allows practitioners and managers to apply the project setup to their company. For example, IT is centrally organized at Infineon Technologies AG and is therefore listed under "other relevant stakeholders." If IT topics are organized differently in another company, describing the functions that IT assumes in the context of the digital customer engagement project at Infineon's Automotive Division still makes it clear to the reader which stakeholder to involve, regardless of the organizational structure.

To sum it up, even though the section is written from the perspective of the Digital Marketing Department of Infineon's Automotive Division and the reasons for starting such a project, the company structure, and the relevant digital self-services may vary, the general approach is still relevant and applicable for other companies of similar size.

2.1 Stakeholder

Anyone involved in project initiatives that involve the development of innovations should have a clear understanding of the underlying goals. In this case, the goal of digital self-service is to strengthen customer relationships by delivering a superior digital customer experience, thereby gaining a competitive advantage.

Given the many opportunities that digital self-services present for the entire customer journey, it is important to create a common understanding of how to achieve this. This can be a difficult undertaking, as business units may have very different needs.

The project manager that gets nominated by the project owner who is usually part of the top management team breaks down the agreed project targets into manageable parts and defines an adequate team with which he or she will work to achieve the overall project target. To ensure a smooth transition once completed, the final results are then handed over to a Sustaining Function that maintains and sustains these results and makes them available for the internal or external users and customers. The core project team should consist of representatives from the division, who are close to the day-to-day business. In particular, employees from the areas of marketing and sales should be selected, since they can map the most important parts of the customer journey. In addition, the project setup should include an interface to the IT department so that the digital self-services can be integrated into the existing IT infrastructure if possible. To ensure that digital self-services that go beyond the existing IT infrastructure are integrated into ongoing company-wide transformation projects, it is also important to have an interface to the department that enables digitalization to drive these company-wide projects.

The stakeholders involved in the project to identify and implement digital self-services at Infineon's Automotive Division are presented below. The project setup selected and the advantages and disadvantages resulting from it are then explained.

Top management for sales and marketing:

Infineon's Automotive Division has involved top management in the role of the Project Portfolio Manager. This is to make clear that the initiative is a top priority on their agenda. This approach creates the necessary internal and external visibility and ensures the motivation and commitment of the project participants. In addition, it is their responsibility to ensure that projects are pursued according to the company strategy. Based on the information presented by the project management, the top management decides which projects shall be started and prioritizes between different projects within the project portfolio.

Business units of the Automotive Division:

Infineon's Automotive Division consists of different business units. These business units differ to some extent in the products they sell. The different degree of complexity of the products also results in different requirements for digital self-services. Therefore, it is important that all business units provide resources and have the opportunity to contribute their requirements.

As mentioned above, we choose as project team member (PTM) representatives who are close to the day-to-day business, such as employees involved in marketing and sales, since they can cover the most important parts of the customer journey. Within the project, it will be the task of PTMs to identify and prioritize the most important digital self-services and define sustaining processes for their business units. For each sub-project we nominated a representative from a business unit as the sub-project manager (sub-PJM). The buy in of the top management is necessary to authorize each sub-PJM to drive the implementation of the respective digital self-services in the name of Infineon's Automotive Division for the duration of the project. This approach gives the sub-PJM more weight with other departments and functions as the backing of the entire division is ensured.

Functions and units outside of Infineon's Automotive Division:

Other relevant functions and units you should consider to include into your project team can be identified by the following criteria: a function or unit should be included for those digital self-services that touch upon their field of responsibility. In the context of our project, this applied to the following departments: digital marketing department of the Automotive Division, supply chain management, central department that enables digitalization (CDD), and the IT. Potentially, all digital self-services affect the digital marketing department, as it is responsible for maintaining the website, which is typically the customer's interface for digital interactions. That is why we decided to integrate them into the project in a meaningful way, by assigning the role of Project Management Office (PMO). In this role, their main tasks include consolidating input from the business units, ensuring project governance, and orchestrating management readouts.

Unlike the digital marketing department or the business units that were part of the project team from the beginning, the supply chain management department only became involved when a digital self-service emerged in the idea generation phase of the project that touches their responsibility. When the prioritization of potential digital self-services by the business units revealed that the service with supply change management touchpoint was a top priority project, a top management readout was held to ask whether the department would be willing to make resources available for this project. Without these resources, the project would not have been realized as it makes no sense to define requirements without involving the department that it would ultimately affect in day-to-day operations.

If you want to drive a digitalization project out of the division, for efficiency reasons you need a function in the project setup that ensures that these digitalization efforts fit into a holistic company-wide picture. This harmonized, long-term vision should lay the foundation for every single future activity around digital self-services in order to ensure a certain scalability of the new functions through a company-wide rollout. Digital transformation initiatives, even if they originate in a Division, often have to be combined with a company-wide transformation project, since both the business models and the underlying internal processes can be affected. Therefore, the involvement of the CDD is essential to enable the implementation of digital self-services after identification and prioritization.

Integrating them into the project was critical for the reasons mentioned above, and close coordination with the department was crucial for the project's success. In addition, the CDD also acts as an interface between the divisions and IT and also deals with external implementation partners. While the division project team is a temporary setup, the CDD can be seen as a permanent project team that continuously drives digitalization in the company across departments (see Fig. 1).

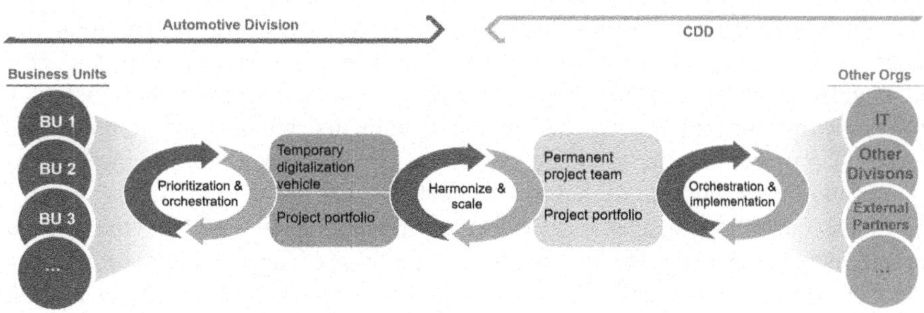

Fig. 1 Interaction of key stakeholder

2.2 Project Context

To successfully launch a digitalization initiative driven from within a division, you need a vehicle to share ideas across business units, create a common understanding of defined goals and priorities, and decide together as one division. This vehicle also serves as a roadmap to prioritize and orchestrate existing and newly launched projects (see Fig. 1).

An orchestration is necessary because, in many large companies, important and effective digitalization projects and experiments run on a small scale (Chanias & Hess, 2016). For example, one business unit digitalizes a process using an available tool, and it turns out to be a real improvement that can benefit other business units. However, it is often not possible to communicate and implement this improvement across departments.

This is where the digitalization vehicle (see Fig. 1) comes into play at Infineon's Automotive Division to draw attention to this project, orchestrate it within the division, and then scale it across the company via the CDD by providing the necessary IT resources and setting up binding processes. This is often something that the people who came up with the original idea cannot do themselves because they don't have the resources and skills in their role. Optimizing existing functions for new use cases, such as digital self-services, leads to the efficient use of resources. At Infineon's Automotive Division, there are many important and effective digitalization projects that were already running before the digitalization initiative started. But with the digitalization vehicle, the important projects can be extended to meet the needs of the entire department and get the support they need, while also ensuring that the projects are also scalable to benefit the entire company. Centralized management within the digital customer engagement project enables prioritization of the projects that are of strategic importance and have the greatest potential to ultimately make a significant contribution to customer satisfaction and customer engagement and therefore business performance.

The implementation of digital self-service interacts with the (technical) infrastructure as well as with new or existing processes. Thus, the timely definition of the needed processes should be a project outcome to ensure a smooth roll out into the daily business. The maturity of the existing IT infrastructure is another crucial factor, as the implementation of digital self-services depends on the existing IT backbone and the corresponding IT infrastructure can only be influenced at certain time intervals and is largely stable the rest of the time. It is therefore important to distinguish between projects that can be integrated directly into the existing IT infrastructure and projects whose implementation first requires the completion of larger IT projects in order to create the necessary IT backbone for the implementation of more sophisticated digital self-services.

In the customer engagement project of Infineon's Automotive Division, the requirements on the IT infrastructure of these more sophisticated digital self-services are handed over to centrally managed digital transformation projects. Even after the requirements have been handed over to long-term IT projects, the project manager should ensure that the formulated requirements are considered in the redesign of the

IT backbone and should be available for further inquiries of the respective project team.

3 Specific Approach

In this section, we present the approach Infineon's Automotive Division used to identify relevant digital self-services and collect the necessary requirements. In particular, we address those topics that have proven to be especially important for us in practice.

These include factors such as having the right people on board, a robust approach, generating top management support early on, and close collaboration with functions such as IT. It has also proved essential to create a basis for discussion within the project team through a shared understanding of digital self-services, buyer persona, customer journey, project goal, and expected deliverables. The buyer persona analysis ensures the scalability of measures by targeting a class of relevant persons and enables discussions across business units even if different specific customers are addressed. When assessing customer issues, the investigation of existing weaknesses should always start with a comprehensive look at the customer journey. The same understanding about a generic Customer Journey helped to show the purpose and the phase the customer is in in the buying process with typical touch points, enabling a cross-departmental discussion about use cases.

For the digital self-services we encouraged Project Team Members to think beyond their core processes and products and focus their ideation efforts on customer-centric solutions that solve a customer problem or satisfy an unmet customer need. This could be problems such as time-to-market, finding best-fit products, finding complementary products, or accessing contextual information easily and efficiently.

The project goal, to create a common divisional picture of the most relevant digital self-services tailored to the needs of automotive customers, was specified by the project manager and then approved by the top management of Infineon's Automotive Division before being communicated to the business units.

The digital customer engagement project will act as an umbrella for the preparation of the most relevant digital self-services, based on feedback, priorities, and support from the business units. The focus will be on the project ideas that have the potential to make a significant contribution to business performance. To achieve this, the project shall define and prepare the digital services technically and in terms of processes and behaviors. The technical implementation will be synchronized with ongoing company-wide digital transformation projects.

The deliverables expected from the sub-projects include digital self-service concepts that include the following:

For IT, a detailed description of the digital self-service informs of user stories, and a set of technical requirements is needed.

For the business units, the definition of processes and resource requirements to operate the digital self-services after implementation is needed.

To avoid misunderstandings and conflicts of responsibility, we have also formulated the following non-objective: The project is not a technical implementation project. The technical implementation is the responsibility of the IT and, as already explained in Sect. 2.1 Stakeholder, the CDD serves as our IT interface. The implementation and schedule for the implementation of the digital self-services depends on the IT implementation roadmap, and the digital customer engagement project only represents the requirements and priorities of the Automotive Division and its customers.

Due to these corporate structures and responsibilities, there are also certain risks for the project. For example, other divisions might have different priorities for digital self-services, which in turn have an impact on the overall priorities of Infineon as a whole.

3.1 Identification of Digital Self-Services

In this section, we now begin to describe our approach so that managers from the business units of companies of comparable size can use this as a basis for their own digitalization efforts within their company context.

We have already talked about the Digital customer engagement project of Infineon's Automotive Division at various points in the previous sections.

However, before you can define the project setup, a number of steps must be taken.

First, a person is needed who recognizes the need for digital self-services and the need to streamline the ongoing digitalization efforts of the business units as described in Sect. 2.2. This impulse came from the digital marketing department of Infineon's Automotive Division. The digital marketing department is considered the interface for all business units in the Automotive Division when it comes to digitalization issues and is thus able to identify the emerging needs of the business units (which are ultimately attributable to customer requests). In addition, it is usually informed about individual digitalization efforts in the different business units. The knowledge about these efforts is not necessarily known across all departments due to the complex company structure.

With this knowledge, we sought management support to launch activities to identify the most relevant digital self-services for automotive customers.

The initiator was chosen as project manager for efficiency reasons, as it was not yet clear how the project would unfold. At this point, involving a colleague who is pursuing a career as a project manager and then boarding the project as a full-time job could have led to a waste of resources, which is why we opted for the less resource-intensive and therefore safer option.

As a first step towards identifying suitable services, we decided to hold an ideation workshop with the two business units that had already excelled in the past with digitalization projects on their own initiative. These own initiatives were started because they sell rather complex products and therefore also require a distinctive tool and software infrastructure that was not yet covered by the IT backbone. Our selection of workshop participants was based on two main considerations. First, to only include two of the business units would require fewer initial resources, and second, it is easier to find a common ground. This can be a difficult undertaking because the business units have very different needs. For example, one business unit sells highly complex microcontrollers with an extensive tool and software infrastructure, and another sells comparatively simpler power supplies. Nevertheless, a common basis must be found within the Automotive Division to ensure that our requirements are given a higher weighting in the project roadmap of the CDD and IT. The basic idea is that the less complex use cases of the business units with less complex products are also covered by the identified digital self-services, which cover the highly demanding requirements of the business units with highly complex products.

We made a proposal of fitting workshop participants of the two business units with complex products and ongoing digitalization initiatives, and aligned it with their management. We primarily selected employees who were either already proactively and intrinsically motivated to work on digitalization topics within their department in addition to their main job, or employees who maintain close contact with customers and thus have a good understanding of the customer pain points.

After the appropriate workshop participants are identified, the next hurdle is to ensure the right integration of digital technologies and digital self-services respectively into the customer journey of different customer groups. Especially with workshop participants from different business units with diverse backgrounds, it is important to create a common ground for discussions first. Therefore, in the first half of the workshop, we shared the following definitions from literature with the workshop participants.

Digital self-service:

Digital self-services represent "a solution or a group of solutions enabling web users or employees to be completely autonomous on a website or intranet" (Verani, 2021). These types of services thus enable customers "to find the answers to their questions without having to contact customer support" and "affect actions that are quite simple, such as asking for a quote or even managing a contract" (Verani, 2021).

Customer journey:

According to Følstad and Kvale (2018) the customer journey addresses processual as well as experiential aspects of service processes as seen from the customer's perspective and describes reoccurring interactions between a solution provider and the customer. In simple terms a customer journey is "walk in the customer's shoes" (Blomkvist & Holmlid, 2010).

Buyer persona:

In theory, these archetypes of customers are called buyer personas (Revella, 2015), and they guide decisions about offering, the solutions' value proposition, omni channel interactions, and the customer's journey towards purchase (Cruz & Karatzas, 2020).

In the second half of the ideation workshop, we formed two breakout groups. We mixed the nominated participants from the two business units. With this approach, we want to promote the exchange of information about current digitalization initiatives and at the same time ensure that the results are services that deliver added value for both business units. In addition, two discussion groups offer the advantage that an initial sanity check is done while the results are presented. If both breakout groups identify similar digital self-services, these are likely to have a certain relevance in the market. This way, we have identified a total of ten digital self-services that help the buyer persona through key points in their customer journey and address existing customer pain points. In order to define the strategic direction of the Automotive Division in terms of digital self-services, we next brought the other business units that did not participate in the idea workshop on board. This follow-up to the workshop can also be seen as a second sanity check of the identified digital self-services through the other business units. With the agreement of all business units to initially pursue the ten services identified, we have defined a set of digital self-services that form the basis for an digital self-service roadmap.

3.2 Prioritization of Digital Self-Services and Resulting Project Setup

Initially, we only had the business units' assessment that the identified digital self-services address important pain points for their customers and thus help to guide them smoothly through their customer journey. However, substantial resources were required to achieve the stated goals of the project. To obtain these resources from the business units, we approached their management directly and used a readout to convince them of the value of our project. The execution of a prioritization assessment conducted by a responsible counterpart in each business unit allowed us to calculate an average prioritization of all the services. In addition, we asked which services the respective business unit would like to contribute resources to. We distinguished between two types of resources. PTMs who should dedicate 10% of a full-time employee's working time to the project and sub-project managers who should contribute up to 20% of a full-time employee's working time. In parallel, we have developed an estimate of the project complexity of each service. The complexity is based on a relative comparison of the digital self-service projects and an assessment of three factors, cross business unit support needed, complexity of processes that need to be defined, and sustaining efforts that will be required after implementation. Thus, we have created three points of reference based on feedback from the business units, which we can use to prioritize the digital self-services: average business line priority, complexity assessment, and resource commitment. The result can be seen in Fig. 2.

In case of the customer engagement project, we had six sub-projects that had a resource commitment from the business units and a high average priority. Despite different requirements of the different business units, no resources were made available for the other four sub-projects. This seems logical at first, because resources are a precious commodity and are limited in the business unit and therefore not made available for the low priority projects. However, since our approach uses an average of the priorities across all business units, it could be that one of the

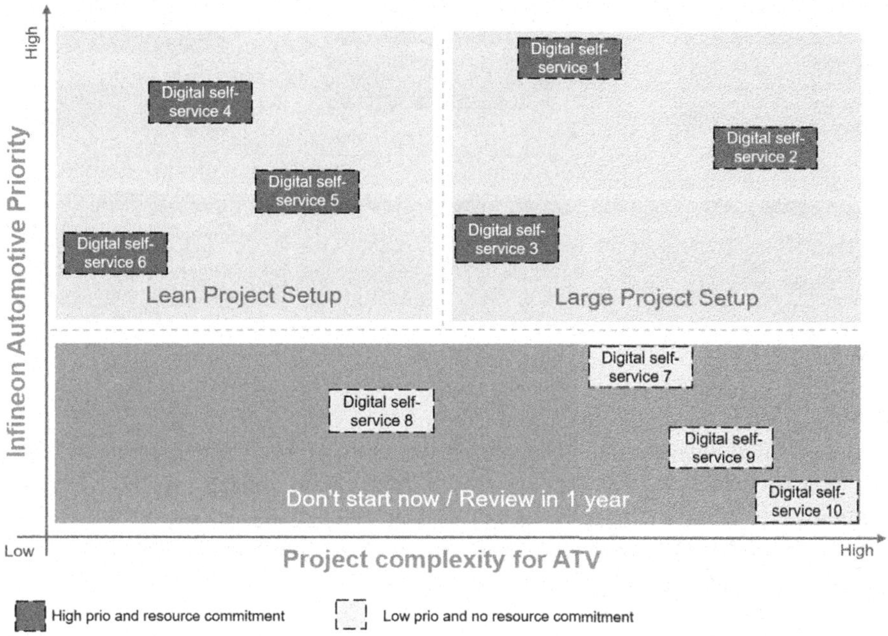

Fig. 2 Prioritization approach

business units also provides resources for a project that has a low priority on average but a high value for this business unit individually. In this case, it must be carefully evaluated whether the project can also be accomplished with few resources. In the case of a high project complexity, we would rather advise against it because in these circumstances the entire division is not behind the project, and therefore it does not get the necessary attention from IT. This way you run the risk of the project going nowhere and still waste the resources.

Therefore, we have grouped the projects without sufficient resource commitment in the category "Do not start now and review in 1 year." In case of a review at a later point in time, the priorities and therefore also the resources provided by the business units may have changed.

For high priority projects with resource commitment, we distinguish between a "Lean project setup" and a "Large project setup." The distinction is based on the complexity of the projects. For comparatively less complex projects, part of the PTM provided by the business units is made available as "on demand" (see Fig. 3). If the assessment of complexity proves to be incorrect, these resources can be activated at short notice, and the project can be driven forward. If the assessment is correct, resources can be saved and the project can work more efficiently in a smaller set-up.

For the six focus services we want to pursue, we need a project release from the management. To convince them to start these projects, we have defined a thorough but pragmatic program structure that is supported by Infineon's Automotive Division as a whole. Each service will be managed in a sub-project that is owned

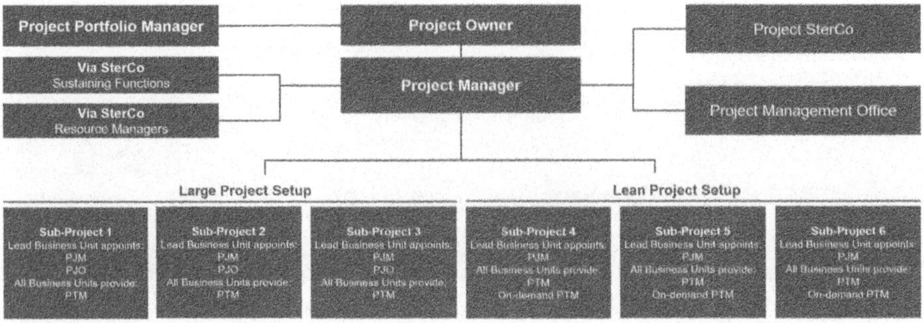

Fig. 3 Project setup

by a dedicated business unit. The sub-project manager will be empowered to drive the topic on behalf of the entire division for the duration of the project. For the more complex topics that are in the Large Project Setup category, we engaged high-level business unit managers as project owner (PJO). In this function, they should serve as supporters to get the necessary weighting, for example, when it comes to setting up cross-departmental processes.

The project steering committee consists of representatives of the stakeholders introduced in Sect. 2.1.

This rather complex, cross-divisional and cross-functional setup requires a structured approach of a project that drives the involved people towards reaching the agreed objectives within the defined timeframe and acceptable expenses. The individual tasks and responsibilities of the people involved must be clearly defined to avoid non-acting, over-acting, or decision-avoiding behavior and lengthy discussions about responsibilities. To achieve that we used a standard and well-established project approach within Infineon Technologies with standardized roles and responsibilities. This includes that once the project is completed, the final results are then handed over to the CDD and to the IT. They will maintain and sustain the project outcome and make them available to the customers. Part of the setup is also the agreement on project governance including collaboration and documentation of results. We chose to do regular readouts on different levels: project team readouts, cross-functional readouts, and leadership team readouts. The other divisions are not part of the project setup that we choose. But we still decided to have regular sanity checks with them to increase the credibility of our project results.

3.3 Project Outcome and Transition into a Sustaining Function

The most important deliverables of the project are the requirements and user stories that the IT department needs to set up and implement the respective digital self-service. The requirements and user stories are developed by the PTMs in the sub-projects and regularly reviewed with the relevant contacts in the IT department to ensure that they can also work with and fully understand them. The evaluation by the IT department showed that three of the projects can be implemented relatively quickly, since no new IT infrastructure needs to be set up for the requirements and user stories described. For the remaining projects, a step-by-step implementation is necessary because the required infrastructure has to be created in extensive IT projects. For this more elaborate and complex implementation process, we have set up an intact feedback loop between project setup and CDD for continuous review of the implementation, including deep dives on the collected requirements and user stories.

Another key outcome of the project is the establishment of processes within the business units that become relevant after implementation and ensure a smooth rollout of digital self-services through clear responsibilities and tasks. In order for customers to reap the expected benefits of digital self-services, you need to maintain, nurture, and operate the digital self-services even after the project has ended. We developed a proposal for the respective service in the sub-projects and then coordinated it with the CDD team to enable a cross-divisional rollout. We expect a company-wide standardization of processes to result in greater efficiency in day-to-day business, a uniform appearance to customers, and the necessary commitment to the execution of tasks by the stakeholders concerned.

Another, albeit less tangible, outcome of the project is the setup that has been created. Even though the individuals involved may return to their main tasks, we will use the established framework and structures as a vehicle to prioritize digitalization topics going forward. As we are convinced that the six digital self-services are just the beginning and that these topics will become increasingly important in the future in order to be able to grow in a scalable manner, to satisfy customer needs and to become more profitable, we have decided to move from a temporary project setup to a permanent one. Due to the lack of transparency regarding workload, commitment, and resources of the business units, the project approach was the right one to get started quickly and to get the business units on board. The disadvantage is that the project participants have always contributed as side business and thus the focus was taken away from their main task.

The reasons why stakeholders from the business units, IT, and CDD were part of the project structure are still intact, and a close coordination with them will remain crucial. Close interaction with the business units is not needed in phases where the main focus is on the realization and implementation of the digital self-service ideas. With this new setup we feel better prepared to face the fast changes in technologies and the resulting needed continuous improvement to stay ahead in the Automotive Semiconductor industry.

4 Summary and Outlook

The aim of this paper was to show companies in the B2B sector that digital self-services are crucial to ensure sustainable growth and customer satisfaction due to ongoing changes in B2B business in general, and the impact of the COVID-19 pandemic. This is especially true for companies operating in the automotive sector due to fundamental changes in the industry.

Digital self-services that enable digital selling and move formerly analog touchpoints into a digital sphere create a smoother customer journey for automotive customers and ensure future growth and higher profitability.

To enable practitioners and managers from the B2B sector to derive implications for their business context, the example of a digital customer engagement project from Infineon's Automotive Division was used to show how to set up a project to identify digital self-services that are relevant to their business context and how to capture the requirements needed for implementation. The two most important insights we gained during the project are briefly summarized below.

Be customer-centric and ensure that project participants and other project stakeholders have a common understanding of the customer and how the project will support their customer journey. To decrease complexity, we recommend to use concepts like the customer journey and buyer persona. To ensure customer centricity, you should also drive the project out of a division as they are closer to the customer needs as any central function.

Do not start the project with the goal of being perfect – start and actively develop it to meet emerging challenges and needs.

It has also proven beneficial to us to start with selected employees who were either already proactively and intrinsically motivated to work on digitalization topics within their department. We recommend to add to these digital pioneers some employees who maintain close contact with customers and thus have a good understanding of the customer pain points.

If one decides against the introduction of a permanent and sustainable vehicle to prioritze digitalization topics, you should use the described approach at regular intervals. Ever new technologies, faster computing power, and data processing through cloud applications will enable increasingly sophisticated digital self-services to guide customers through their digtial customer journey. Digital marketing, which often focuses on the early stages of the customer journey, will be able to cover the entire customer journey and thus enhance customer engagement.

Leveraging the megatrend of digitalization by introducing and continuously improving digital self-services ensures the transition from a scalable marketing approach to a digital self-service sphere. Using the diverse capabilities of digital self-services helps to serve more customers efficiently through digital channels. This leads to increased customer satisfaction, sustainable revenue growth, and profitability.

References

Blomkvist, J., & Holmlid, S. (2010). Service prototyping according to service design practitioners. *Conference proceedings, ServDes. 2010, exchanging knowledge, Linköping, Sweden, 1–-3 December 2010*, *2*, 1–11.

Chanias, S., & Hess, T. (2016). *Understanding digital transformation strategy formation: Insights from Europe's Automotive Industry.*

Cruz, A., & Karatzas, S. (2020). Understanding your buyer persona. In *Digital and social media marketing* (pp. 69–97). Routledge.

Følstad, A., & Kvale, K. (2018). Customer journeys: A systematic literature review. *Journal of Service Theory and Practice, 28*, 196.

Forrester. (2021, March 3). *New research revealed at Forrester's SiriusDecisions summit 2020 shows coronavirus pandemic is accelerating modern B2B buying behavior.* https://www.forrester.com/press-newsroom/new-research-revealed-at-forresters-siriusdecisions-summit-2020-shows-coronavirus-pandemic-is-accelerating-modern-b2b-buying-behavior/

Gartner. (2019). *The buying experience: The most important thing in sales and marketing*. https://www.gartner.com/en/articles/the-buying-experience-the-most-important-thing-in-sales-and-mark

Gartner. (2020). *Gartner says 80% of B2B sales interactions between suppliers and buyers will occur in digital channels by 2025.* https://www.gartner.com/en/newsroom/press-releases/2020-09-15-gartner-says-80%2D%2Dof-b2b-sales-interactions-between-su

Gartner. (2022, July 28). The new B2B buying process | *Gartner*. https://www.gartner.ca/en/sales/insights/b2b-buying-journey

Revella, A. (2015). *Buyer personas: How to gain insight into your customer's expectations, align your marketing strategies, and win more business*. Wiley.

Simon-Kucher. (2022, July 28). *B2B sales 2.0: Remote selling in the midst of COVID-19*. https://www.simon-kucher.com/de/blog/remote-selling-midst-covid-19

Verani, E. (2021, June 8). Digital self-service: How to optimize customer relations. *Inbenta*. https://www.inbenta.com/en/blog/digital-self-service-definition/

Separating the Useful from the Harmful: How the Core Competence of Filtration Drives Digital Marketing Transformation

Julia Remmele, Gudmund Semb, and Marian Wenking

"Separating the useful from the harmful" is not only the title of this chapter but also the mission of the MANN+HUMMEL Group, a leading global filtration company. This statement perfectly describes the company's purpose: to provide cleaner mobility, cleaner air, and cleaner water without harmful elements. At the same time, it is also well suited as the central theme for this chapter: identifying the "useful" (contributing to the company's goals) and stopping the "harmful" (counteracting the achievement of those goals) is a key capability for mastering the digital marketing transformation. This competence is particularly relevant in marketing, as the seemingly endless possibilities that have arisen through digitization do not only have positive effects. In marketing, close observation of user behavior and media consumption habits is core for success; however, it is sometimes difficult to measure this success and demonstrate its direct financial impact on a company's performance. Therefore, new channels and tools providing new technological possibilities and analytical capabilities are gamechangers toward significantly better market insights and results; however, they can also be a threat with regard to wasting resources due to a lack of focus or due to an incorrect assessment of truly value-adding solutions.

This chapter describes how the useful was separated from the harmful in MANN+HUMMEL's digital marketing transformation journey and provides insights into what belonged to which category. It is written from an internal perspective outlining the authors' practical experiences and opinions.[1]

[1] In addition to the authors, Thomas Fischer contributed substantially to this work. As Chairman of the Supervisory Board of MANN+HUMMEL since 2002 and grandson of founder Adolf Mann, filtration has accompanied him throughout his life. He brought his accumulated knowledge and

J. Remmele (✉) · G. Semb · M. Wenking
MANN+HUMMEL Group, Ludwigsburg, Germany
e-mail: Julia.Remmele@mann-hummel.com; Gudmund.Semb@mann-hummel.com; Marian.Wenking@mann-hummel.com

U. Schneider, J. Hoika (eds.), *Digital Marketing in the Automotive Electronics Industry*, Management for Professionals,
https://doi.org/10.1007/978-3-031-30720-1_12

1 A Digression into the Filtration Industry

To provide some context before elaborating on the "why" and the "how" as well as the transformation journey and the key learnings, this chapter provides a brief overview about the company MANN+HUMMEL, the filtration industry, and the external and internal developments that facilitated or complicated MANN +HUMMEL's digital marketing transformation.

1.1 The MANN+HUMMEL Group: A Leading Global Player

MANN+HUMMEL is a family-owned company providing filtration and separation solutions for cleaner mobility, cleaner air, and cleaner water to various industries and markets through its two business units: Transportation and Life Sciences & Environment (LS&E). The group has its roots and global headquarters in Germany and has grown into an international company with over 23,000 employees and more than 80 locations worldwide.

Founded in 1941, the company transitioned into industrial mass production by implementing assembly line production in the 1950s. In the following decades, MANN+HUMMEL evolved into a development partner for the original equipment manufacturers (OEMs) within the automotive industry thanks to its product and production innovations. These partnerships impacted the company's global expansion strategy. With a focus on the improvements to the consumption and performance of engines and the reduction of pollutant emissions, MANN+HUMMEL grew steadily from a small manufacturer to a global automotive supplier and, with its expansion into new business fields, to a global filtration specialist. In 2009, MANN+HUMMEL's vision of "leadership in filtration" was established as its long-term group strategy, with customer centricity being a core element. In 2021, the group generated a turnover of 4.2 billion euros, which resulted in earnings before interest and taxes (EBIT) of 191 million euros representing an EBIT margin of 4.6%.

Ever since its foundation, the original business of MANN+HUMMEL has been to supply the automotive industry with filtration solutions. Today, the company's automotive business is part of the business unit Transportation along with the development of solutions for industrial applications. This business unit has, to a large extent, grown organically but also through strategic acquisitions, the largest one being Affinia Group's filtration segment. This acquisition added two established product brands to the existing MANN+HUMMEL brand portfolio in 2016. The group diversified its business to and within LS&E providing technologies to the air filtration and water and membrane solutions business segments. This business unit has been built mainly through acquisitions, starting in 2010, and continually expands

experience to this work, particularly on the developments of the company, the filtration industry, and the associated changes in the role of digital marketing.

with the latest acquisitions of Tri-Dim (2019), Seccua (2019), HELSATECH (2020), and Pamlico Air (2021).

With more than 80 years of existence, via its global footprint and the broad product portfolio, MANN+HUMMEL has significantly contributed to the development of the filtration industry and to defining today's technological standards. As a leading player in filtration, the group also takes responsibility for strengthening public awareness for the relevance of filtration, particularly in the context of achieving global sustainability goals. This responsibility also influences the role of marketing within the company, which the following subsections discuss. Before, the authors describe the filtration industry in more detail to provide indications as to whether the selected approach and the identified learnings for digital marketing transformation are applicable to other industries and companies.

1.2 Customer Structures and Sales Chains

MANN+HUMMEL's business is, except for some small initiatives, based on business-to-business transactions. Across the Transportation and LS&E business units, MANN+HUMMEL's business consists of original equipment (OE) and (independent) aftermarket (IAM), which both have great importance for the company. Main Transportation OE customers are manufacturers of passenger cars, trucks, and other on-road vehicles, and manufacturers of construction and agricultural machinery as well as other off-road applications. Additionally, some of these OEMs are selling MANN+HUMMEL filters as OE spare parts labeled with their own brand in the aftermarket. In the IAM, on the other hand, MANN+HUMMEL operates using a multi-brand approach with five product brands, each one with different value propositions. The Transportation IAM customers are, in general, large distributors servicing and supplying a multi-stage sales channel and similar players. MANN+HUMMEL is mostly approaching a decision-making process facing buying centers while, at the same time, being confronted with the challenge to build end-user value propositions for its products and filtration in general. Considering that the pure filtration product itself is an ingredient to a full solution or service such as an oil change and an element with a technological focus, there is little to no attraction and awareness at the end-customers level. On the other side, indirect customers, such as workshop employees, are often frequently exposed to MANN+HUMMEL product brands without a direct buying relationship, as standard services are often performed multiple times a day.

In contrast to the relatively clear and established structures within the transportation industry, the LS&E business (as well as its OE and aftermarket customers) is heterogenic and spreads across fundamentally different segments. The range of OE customers covers manufacturers of air conditioning systems and household applications, wastewater treatment plants, as well as general contractors of governmental projects and similar companies who install filtration solutions directly in their applications. Larger aftermarket customers within LS&E are retailers and maintenance companies such as facility managers. Across both OE and aftermarket, highly specialized niche players such as pharmaceutical companies or food and beverage manufacturers represent an important part of MANN+HUMMEL's business.

All these industries and customer structures are determining the setup, the focus areas, and, ultimately, the investments into marketing within MANN+HUMMEL. To provide some context on the starting point of the digital marketing transformation, the following subchapter describes this setup.

1.3 Relevance and Structures of Marketing

As mentioned in the context of MANN+HUMMEL's long-term vision, customer centricity is a core element of reaching the company's strategic targets; this applies to regional proximity and products, as in technological specs and product portfolio, as well as marketing approaches and customer-oriented service offerings. As the number of potential customers is limited in the traditional transportation business unit, marketing within MANN+HUMMEL was typically perceived as a supporting unit that strongly focused its activities on supporting the relationship-oriented sales model with the strategy to be recognized as a business-enabling partner and build the ingredient value proposition "MANN+HUMMEL inside."

For companies operating in the (independent) aftermarket segment, another core competence is to support direct customers in reselling the products to their customers as easily as possible. Building brand awareness for MANN+HUMMEL product brands and supporting customers' sales activities through high-quality product and marketing content as well as sales push activities are, therefore, additional focus areas of MANN+HUMMEL's marketing efforts. Consequently, capabilities within the areas of cataloging, product data creation for both the company's and customers' digital platforms, trade fairs and events, sales promotion, traditional marketing materials including point-of-sales materials, brand items and giveaways, brand awareness (e.g., through sponsoring), and customer relationship management (CRM) are strongly developed within MANN+HUMMEL's marketing teams.

With increased connectivity, data access, and analytical skills, digital revolution also came to MANN+HUMMEL's marketing teams in the early 2010s. However, digitalization did not mean that the traditional relationship-oriented marketing activities were substituted – quite the opposite has happened: new technological possibilities were selectively added to the MANN+HUMMEL marketing portfolio based on how they supported the business' existing activities, which were digitized, improved, and complimented with new digital measures. As an example, the aftermarket marketing teams strongly focused on developing their digital cataloging and CRM competencies as well as supporting the general brand awareness through online and social media presence; however, skills such as online marketing campaigning and active lead management did not belong to the marketing teams' core focus areas.

The value of digitalization for MANN+HUMMEL's marketing as well as the general importance of marketing and communication within the group were directly fueled by the influence of globalization, the increasing relevance of the LS&E

business, and the general growth of the company. The numerous acquisitions within a short period of time not only led to more complexity due to new brands and new product portfolios but also made it necessary to understand and serve completely different markets and customer segments with their structures, behavioral patterns, and channels simultaneously. Approaching these new markets as a mostly unknown player, attempting to build brand awareness from zero, and connecting with a much larger size of unknown potential customers required a drastic change in the company's marketing and sales approach. Additionally, diversifying the business by entering water and air filtration immediately changed the purpose of MANN +HUMMEL's business from a purely technological orientation to a personal, individual relevance, which had major implications on the corporate brand strategy and led to the formation of new marketing teams with different skillsets and execution capabilities.

From an organizational perspective, the marketing teams are mainly spread across local markets and report to the business units, with a lean central team and some expert roles organizationally located in other functional areas such as human resources. Within the local business unit teams, capacity for marketing can be limited, as some of the responsible employees are covering different roles (such as sales and marketing or product management and marketing) at the same time, and some of those responsible for marketing do not have a dedicated marketing background. Therefore, the enablement of the business unit teams through technologies, tools, and trainings as well as the assurance of quality is a core task of MANN +HUMMEL's central functions.

2 Digital Marketing Transformation: The Why

In parallel to MANN+HUMMEL's growth, the industries and markets the company was entering or already operating in simultaneously evolved in different directions, which was impacted by various parameters such as regional and cultural characteristics, technological developments, and social or economic factors. This resulted in strong variations of market structures and end-consumer behaviors. While MANN+HUMMEL is not in direct contact with the end consumers in most cases, their behavior significantly impacts MANN+HUMMEL's direct customers' customers and, consequently, the direct customers' needs and expectations. For various reasons, no central solutions existed that effectively supported the company's local organizations in fulfilling these diversified expectations from markets and customers. Therefore, the local organizations had to develop individual solutions for sales and marketing. The portfolio of channels, platforms, systems, tools, and technologies grew accordingly, and MANN+HUMMEL's various acquisitions brought further complexity into this landscape.

2.1 External Factors Impacting the Digital Marketing Transformation

While the local approaches were necessary to meet the short-term customer needs, they were not sufficient in the long term due to various external developments encountered by MANN+HUMMEL:

Rising Expectations
With evolving technologies offering more possibilities for automation and connectivity, new behavioral patterns are constantly emerging in the (end-)consumer landscape. Simple product sales, for example, have evolved into fully connected service offerings that switch (sometimes multiple times) between online and offline touchpoints. Offering such services creates new demands for companies at the consumer interface, often leading to additional requirements for their supply chain – such as providing product data in special formats or through unique technological interfaces. For suppliers like MANN+HUMMEL, this results in highly specialized requirements for certain industries or countries that are driving new trends, such as China.

Rising Individualization
Equally supported by the evolution of new technological possibilities, MANN +HUMMEL's direct customers are trying to gain competitive advantages through innovations. These new solutions often affect their go-to-market channels or digital service offerings and can result in additional demands from their suppliers. To differentiate themselves from their competitors by offering unique added values to their respective clients, the innovations increasingly deviate from existing market standards and cause highly individualized demands with limited scalability for MANN+HUMMEL.

Rising Market Power
Due to a strong consolidation of players within the aftermarket industry, some market participants are gaining more power within the aftermarket. With this market power, these players are able to enforce compliance with their individual requirements.

Rising Complexity
More possibilities, higher expectations, and higher degrees of individualization result in an increased level of complexity with businesses fulfilling their customers' needs. Solutions do not only consist of a frontend but often require deep integrations into databases or multi-staged processual integrations into internal and/or external systems. Additionally, an increasing number of different systems and technologies are used. With this increasing complexity, the need for more expertized skills and diversified skill sets is growing.

Rising Security Challenges
With the increasing trend of digitalization, protection against cybercrime is becoming an important task for companies like MANN+HUMMEL. Due to the constantly growing number of malware, maintaining high security standards is as relevant as it is challenging and requires regular security updates and continuous monitoring on all digital platforms.

These external developments, separately and especially in combination, meant that the previous strategy of individually developing complete marketing solutions in MANN+HUMMEL's local markets, which was often based on short-term planning depending on immediate customer needs, no longer worked well. It was crucial for MANN+HUMMEL to move away from its reactive role and into a position of proactive steering, including active decision-making and prioritization. To do this, a certain centralization of technological solutions and know-how as well as strategic direction was required.

2.2 Internal Factors Impacting Digital Marketing Transformation

As stated in the beginning of this chapter, various **internal factors** hindered the centralization within MANN+HUMMEL's digital marketing despite the outlined external challenges. These factors focused mainly on four areas: (1) disconnected marketing teams, (2) lack of communication between marketing and IT departments, (3) limited resources in central teams, and (4) technological limitations. In the following paragraphs, these factors and their development from barriers into transformation drivers are explained in more detail.

1. Disconnected marketing teams
   The top priority in customer-centric organizations, especially in a relationship-based sales approach, is to meet customer expectations quickly and without compromise. Within MANN+HUMMEL, central solutions often failed to support its local teams effectively, especially in markets outside of Europe where structures strongly varied from the well-known German market. This led to a strong decentralization of digital marketing and a fragmented landscape of local, market-specific approaches and highly customized, non-scalable solutions. For a significant amount of time, the markets were satisfied with their freedom, and the demand for central solutions in digital marketing was, therefore, low. Consequently, the alignments between central marketing and local business teams were irregular and resulted in little understanding for the actual customer needs on the central side. In addition, any exchange between the locations, in terms of know-how and the marketing solutions implemented, typically occurred on a voluntary basis. With the increasing demands and requirements outlined in the external developments, however, the situation changed. The local teams were no longer able to meet customer expectations on their own. Support from the central functions was needed to fulfill complex technological requirements, learn from

the experiences of other markets, and orchestrate the development of global marketing tools and capabilities.

2. Lack of communication between marketing and IT departments

While the IT department was moving into a centralized structure, the marketing teams remained fragmented across locations, brands, and business units. There was no dedicated unit within marketing that focused on digitalizing the company's existing processes and activities; therefore, alignments between business and IT happened in a decentralized manner, with different contact persons for different locations, tools, and platforms, varying from regular and close alignments to no alignment at all ("shadow IT"). As a result, the technological know-how was spread across the entire organization and no overview about the current state of the IT landscape supporting the company's digital marketing existed. Due to the lack of a unit responsible, there was also no overarching target vision for digital marketing to provide a direction for IT to identify the needed structure and solutions supporting these goals; hence, MANN+HUMMEL's IT processes were often slow compared to the business' pace, and, due to the disconnect of marketing and IT in some areas, any developed technological solutions did not typically meet its business needs. Local solutions were able to compensate this toward the customers for a substantial amount of time, but with the increasing complexity, the locations were becoming more dependent on IT support. To provide an example, many solutions requested by customers required data such as pricing information to be updated frequently or in real-time. Consequently, the local organizations requested the integration of their solutions with central systems such as MANN+HUMMEL's Enterprise Resource Planning System; however, MANN+HUMMEL's IT often blocked these requested integrations due to security concerns, as many local third-party solutions did not run through the standard IT processes. To fulfill the customer requests as their primary target, the locations had to invest in further local developments or manual administrative work steps; this resulted in a vicious circle: more local solutions leading to further security concerns and, therefore, less of a possibility to integrate with existing central platforms. In addition, maintaining the multitude of existing platforms, interfaces, and tools was highly challenging for MANN+HUMMEL's IT department. In early 2020, more than 120 different system environments, technologies, and tools were actively used to support MANN+HUMMEL's global digital marketing solutions. As IT was often hardly or not at all involved in the development of these solutions, risk prevention was challenging. Reactive maintenance work on selective local channels consumed valuable IT resources and further slowed down the development of new solutions needed for business purposes. A change in this setup was imperative to be able to maintain the required IT security standards and support the local businesses effectively (Figs. 1 and 2).

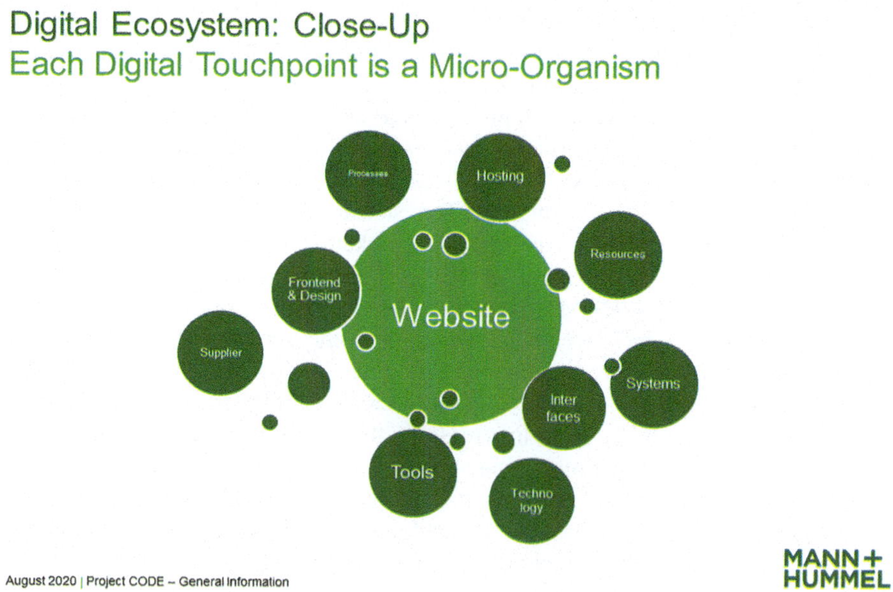

Fig. 1 More than a frontend (This figure was taken from internal MANN+HUMMEL project documents. The slide was originally created in October 2019 and was used to illustrate the major efforts *behind* the frontends of the company's digital marketing touchpoints)

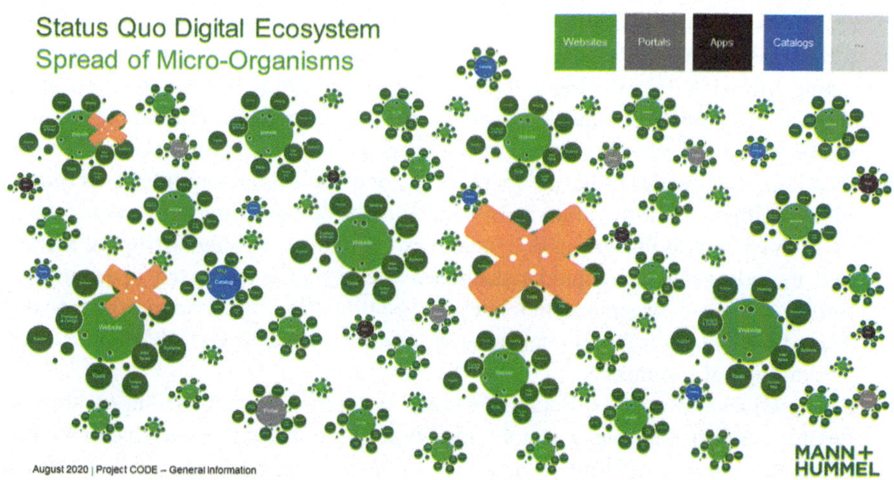

Fig. 2 The spread of digital "microorganisms" (This figure was taken from internal MANN +HUMMEL project documents. The slide was originally created in October 2019 and was used to illustrate the effects of the strong localization in the development of digital marketing solutions: efforts spent on these individual channels were mostly not sustainable and not scalable)

3. Limited resources in central teams
   As a result of the strong decentralization in MANN+HUMMEL's digital marketing, its investments in central functions were made reluctantly. Accordingly, the company's central marketing teams tended to be lean and were primarily considered as supporting sales functions instead of active business drivers. Moreover, overarching initiatives were mostly limited to the exchange of experiences and the development of brand standards. This starting point seemed to be not favorable at all for a centrally driven digital marketing transformation. Due to the described external developments, however, the decentralized approach to digital marketing at MANN+HUMMEL had reached its tipping point from an economical perspective, which went unnoticed for some time, as the real decentral expenditures for building, maintaining, and developing the company's existing landscape of digital marketing solutions were much higher than reflected in its cost reports. This was due to five reasons: first, the costs were "hidden" in the global complexity of the marketing structures, as there was no standardized cost reporting for marketing expenses implemented across all business locations. Second, as technological complexity and customer demands were continuously growing, the company's local projects consumed more resources for their realization and maintenance, which made them less cost efficient. However, the reported costs for digital marketing were small compared to other positions due to the unaligned expense reporting structures; therefore, not much attention was spent to the monitoring of the cost development in digital marketing. Third, the tasks to build and maintain local digital marketing solutions were highly administrative due to the lack of IT integration and automation. Using local business resources for administration instead of value adding, customer-oriented work further decreased the efficiency of MANN+HUMMELs' decentral digital marketing approach. Fourth, due to the high level of individualization, most solutions were not scalable in many locations, so the development and (manual) maintenance efforts were performed multiple times simultaneously across several locations worldwide. Fifth, the increasing trend toward outsourcing tasks outside of the company's core value chain instead of building up internal resources and know-how resulted in strong dependencies from local suppliers in digital marketing, including the associated risks when these suppliers ceased operating. To further ensure economic efficiency and stability in digital marketing, a shift toward a more central approach was required for MANN+HUMMEL.
4. Technological limitations
   As digital technologies were (and are still) evolving, fulfilling local needs through flexible, central solutions was not typically feasible. First, this was due to the lack of technological possibilities available. When the required flexibility became technologically possible, the solutions were mostly unaffordable upon their development. Additionally, the internal knowledge about innovative and state-of-the-art solutions in marketing did not exist, as the lean central teams within MANN+HUMMEL primarily focused on supporting the existing business landscape. Another factor to consider is the ever-increasing complexity and, thus, increasing duration of implementation projects for new solutions within the company in contrast to the increasing speed of the general technological

developments. Particularly in the case of central, large-scale waterfall projects, it could happen that once a technology was finally introduced at MANN +HUMMEL, it was already considered to be outdated in the market. Given these circumstances, it often made more sense for the local organizations to perform small-scoped local projects to enter the market quickly with state-of-the-art marketing solutions. While this approach provided short-term relief for local requirements, it resulted in the exact challenges described earlier with regard to maintenance and security. With the trend toward Agile project management enabling faster time-to-market and the technological development of flexible systems and affordable middleware solutions for marketing applications, the limiting factors for a centralized digital marketing approach were finally eliminated.

Evidently, the internal factors that originally stood in the way of a centralized digital marketing approach ultimately evolved into its main drivers. Together with the external factors described above, the situation became more challenging for MANN+HUMMEL, and in addition to the external and internal pressure, there were also promising business reasons connected to a digital marketing transformation:

1. Robust growth and integration demands
   Mergers and acquisitions are an important part of MANN+HUMMEL's growth strategy. In general, the acquired companies are smaller and have fewer resources and less experience within digital marketing. Vital to the return on invest of an acquisition is the speed within the post-merger integration process. The faster business processes and new customer interfaces can be synchronized, and the faster the new business can be enabled to adopt data-driven, lead generating marketing activities, the higher the potential of the organization's success. The integration of these acquired companies, however, created high additional workloads for the central functions, especially for the IT departments. As a result of the resource bottlenecks, technological integrations sometimes took a significant amount of time to accomplish. Due to the inflexible solutions within digital marketing, the delay in technological integration made an integration from a business perspective complex and expensive. Furthermore, the same applied to the launch of new business models from within the company that were crucial to enable innovative ideas and the expansion into new markets, as creating marketing and customer-facing channels for these businesses involved high administrative work and economically disproportionate efforts. This caused the need of a change in the group's strategic digital marketing approach.
2. Lead generation
   The approach of new business fields within MANN+HUMMEL marked a change in its traditional relationship-based sales model. The shift toward a data-driven, conversion-oriented marketing methodology and approach (especially for LS&E) required a redefinition of the strategy, skills, and importance of marketing within the company, and new competencies such as brand and product awareness

building, attention activation, customer needs definition, interaction fostering, and customer journey management had to be developed. The technology needed for this – from flexible platforms connected with a CRM system to an integrated tool suite for marketing, personalization, and analytics – did not exist in the company, and the need for interconnectivity across the whole IT landscape made it impossible for the local markets to introduce these tools without the central organization; therefore, digital marketing transformation was required to enable profitable business growth.

3. Digital business enablement
   Digitalization does not stop at the gates of the filtration industry. New, fully digitalized players have entered the industry and created changes in established market structures. Existing customers have (partly) digitalized their business models and demanded advanced digital interfaces from MANN+HUMMEL. In some smaller segments, such as the sales of air purifiers during the pandemic, even owned eCommerce activities became relevant for MANN+HUMMEL. Based on the existing landscape, it was not possible to efficiently leverage digital business and eCommerce capabilities due to the technological limitations present. This primarily affected the backend and middleware systems that enable data-based transactions with customers, especially in the IAM, and feed MANN+HUMMEL's own web frontends. For example, a structured digital asset management (DAM) system integrated with an equally structured product information management (PIM) system was needed to connect marketing assets with the right product information, remove redundant data storage, and build automated interfaces to owned and third-party platforms. None of these systems existed, nor did they align data structures, quality, or formats globally, so to keep existing business running and build up new business fields, the digital marketing transformation was a fundamental factor for MANN+HUMMEL.

   With the target to overcome the challenges and enable the business potentials, a project was initiated to design and build centralized, standardized, and scalable solutions for digital marketing, ensuring flexibility and individualization toward markets and customers based on an integrated, harmonized, secure, high-quality, and connective technological and data backbone. This project was called **CODE** (**C**ustomer **O**riented **D**igital **E**cosystem).

3 Digital Marketing Transformation: The How

MANN+HUMMEL's CODE project was concepted as a holistic approach toward increasing its customer focus and standardization within digital marketing as well as other business areas creating customer-facing platforms. In this case, the holistic aspect is a crucial factor, as fragmentation at various levels has been one of the core challenges of MANN+HUMMEL's previous decentral approach to digital marketing. In this context, holistic refers to three different aspects: (1) the global and cross-business-unit scope, (2) the end-to-end consideration of platforms from frontend to enabling IT systems and databases, and (3) the dimensional approach including the technological, architectural, processual, and organizational perspective across all relevant phases of technology-driven projects (plan, build, run). CODE launched in August of 2020 and focused on five core topics derived from the external and internal challenges and drivers:

1. Connect business and IT and adapt working mode to intensify collaboration.
2. Create standards for hygiene factors to decrease efforts and time to market.
3. Build translators to make standards usable for individual needs and enable future business.
4. Learn about customer needs and user behavior to initiate proactive, data-based actions.
5. Establish a target operating model to secure long-term and stable operations.

With this focus, the CODE project was not only the initiator but also the catalyst for the transformation of digital marketing at MANN+HUMMEL. In the following subchapters, the authors explain the five focus topics and how MANN+HUMMEL approached them after discussing CODE's project approach.

3.1 The Approach

The CODE project was executed with Agile project management methods by building upon the Scrum methodology. The general framework of the project was a three-phase approach consisting of the **conception phase** (including both the as-is process analysis and the definition of the to-be scenario), the **implementation phase** (including the realization of a new technological setup and resulting in the delivery of a minimal viable product (MVP) or lighthouse project), and the **rollout phase** (including the migration of existing channels and the expansion of the new solution to other markets and/or brands and business units) that marks the gradual transition of the new solution into running operations.

The **conception phase** consists of two phases. For the original conception of new CODE solutions, its essence is to identify the core stakeholders across the organization who need to be involved to represent the different business units, brands, and regions and to form a team with these stakeholders. In different setups such as one-to-ones, group discussions, or workshops, the existing digital marketing solutions, local needs and expectations, as well as the current best practices, customer value-adds, and pain points are collected, clustered, discussed, and prioritized. The target of this extensive, but time-boxed, original conception is to create the concept for a white-labeled standard, ensuring the fast, cost-efficient scalability of the new CODE solution after the first implementation. Thanks to this approach, MANN+HUMMEL has managed to launch six major brand websites within 14 months, which is a significant decrease of time-to-market, and was able to reduce implementation costs for new brand websites by up to 75%. New websites for existing brands can now be built in less than one day without any external costs. Another important part of the original conception phase is the identification of the lighthouse project for the new solution. The lighthouse is an actual business use case that is used as a vehicle to build the standards that will be scaled to other brands or use cases. In the second part of the conception, the lighthouse solution is planned, and the requirements are captured in a product backlog.

The **implementation phase** of the first lighthouse is following the Scrum methodology and focusing on delivering fast results. Measures to support this are the work in sprint cycles, the frequent testing in parallel to developments, and the early launch of the new solutions after reaching an MVP stage. Within the implementation phase, the respective business unit responsible acts as the product owner, whereas a central CODE project manager ensures the global scalability of the product owner's requirements based on the findings of the conception phase. During this phase, the testing releases of previous sprints can also be shared with other project members who use the same solution after the implementation of the lighthouse, which ensures continuous involvement of all stakeholders as opposed to handing them a ready-made, one-size-fits-all solution.

After the go-live and hyper-care phases, the project is moved into the running operations stream. In this stream, the solution is maintained and developed further. The former product owner is now responsible to migrate all existing pages on old systems to the new solution environment and shut down the old systems. Additionally, the product owner can expand the solution to new markets fast through live copies of existing market versions, for example. Finally, the CODE project manager is responsible for the **rollout phase** of the new CODE solution to other MANN +HUMMEL brands and business units. Every rollout project requiring customizations of the standard runs through a small three-phase cycle, but thanks to the high focus on scalability and the early involvement of brand stakeholders, the customization rate is mostly below 10%.

CODE was set up using different streams focusing on the digital marketing solutions as Fig. 3 presents. These solutions included frontends like websites and architectural parts such as DAM and PIM. The three-phase approach was applied for each stream but adapted to the status quo of the respective topic.

3.2 The Focus Topics

In this subchapter, the authors briefly explain how the CODE focus topics were addressed in preparation for and during the project. In general, all overarching focus topics aim to drive digital transformation towards the market and internal transformation aligned to customer needs.

1. Connect business and IT and adapt working mode to intensify collaboration
   The first focus topic, connecting business and IT to strengthen customer focus within IT and technological understanding within the business, was initiated through different actions taken at the beginning of the project. First, a central

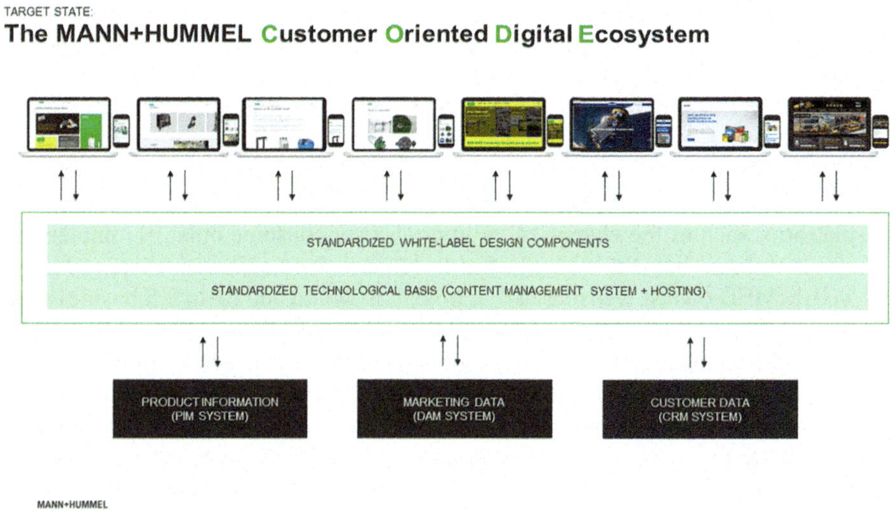

Fig. 3 Target state of the CODE project (This figure was taken from internal MANN+HUMMEL documents. The slide was originally created in 2020 and illustrates the simplified target state of the CODE project with eight overarching brand platforms (one for each product brand), a standardized backend consisting of white-labeled design components, a central content management system and the related hosting infrastructure as well as the enabling data-holding systems)

project team became the responsible unit for all business requirements, and a central IT unit responsible consolidated the knowledge from the IT side. Many alignments happened between the central project team, the local marketing teams, and the IT team to capture the status quo, identify best practices and pain points, and create an understanding for targets and ideas. This process was done internally in the first stage and with external support in the second phase, which involved deep dive workshops. The internal project team participated in every meeting moderated by externals to ensure all knowledge was maintained internally. As the project team was small in the beginning – one full-time person and three to four part-time core team members – all information was consolidated to a high level, which was crucial to enable the identification of similarities and differences. A key factor in this transformative project was the early inclusion of all relevant business stakeholders who were supposed to start using the central solutions instead of their own. This buy-in process offered all the decision takers the possibility to express their expectations and requirements at an early stage. Especially during one-to-one conversations, many doubts and unclarities could be resolved, and a genuine understanding and team spirit between the local business teams and the CODE team manifested. Thanks to the Agile methodology, it was possible to maintain this proximity through a high frequency of alignment meetings throughout the project's duration and beyond. The fast results achieved this way created a positive atmosphere and an elevated level of motivation.

2. Create standards for hygiene factors to decrease efforts and time-to-market
   The strong level of knowledge consolidation supported the identification of standardizable hygiene factors within digital marketing and other customer-facing solutions by discovering recurring challenges from different stakeholders and assessing their added business value and the efforts spent for these tasks. With this information, the project team was able to demonstrate the urgency to project sponsors and management. For example, a small content change in a web platform, such as the change of an imprint, may consume only 10 minutes on a single website, but if this change has to be performed across all existing MANN+HUMMEL-owned websites at that time, this would add up to 2.5 business days of non-value adding work. The understanding and support from the MANN+HUMMEL management, including the Management Board Committee, was a critical factor to start this project, as it brought a high transformational aspect to the existing structures, processes, and hierarchies and required a certain investment. Conversely, the project provided an outlook for efficiency increases and the realization of new business values. Some of the identified hygiene factors for digital marketing solutions that were considered in the course of the project were technology-related tasks (such as the selection of system and hosting providers), administrative tasks (such as vendor selections and internal project approval workflows), design-related tasks (such as maintaining design guidelines), and recurring tasks (such as manual data uploads to internal and external platforms). As part of the project, central approaches were developed for these hygiene factors so that the resources of local markets no longer had to be used for these purposes in the future. The standardization of these aspects also meant that implementations could be realized much faster because numerous work steps were no longer required for scaling.
3. Build translators to make standards usable for individual needs and enable future business
   Historically, the needs of some brands and regions were prioritized during standardizations. Deriving common decisions regarding the priorities of the project was, therefore, crucial for the global acceptance of the transformation. To do so, all input regarding the business targets was consolidated, discussed, and prioritized with business stakeholders from various regions and brands, and the high-level IT target picture was created as a collaboration of IT and project team including some local marketing managers. In contrast to other projects in the past, the considerations on how the standard solutions would be applicable to match individual market needs through processes or tools were incorporated from the beginning. During this phase, two project deliverables formed: the provision of standardized no-code toolboxes ready to use and adaptable by local markets with low efforts and skills and a central data backbone that communicates with third-party platforms through automated real-time interfaces. However, the closer the exchange with the markets became after the start of the project, the more it became clear that the restriction to the defined scope did not sufficiently meet the needs of the markets; this was because the elements of the digital landscape were tightly linked. So, while the original scope was still being implemented, the

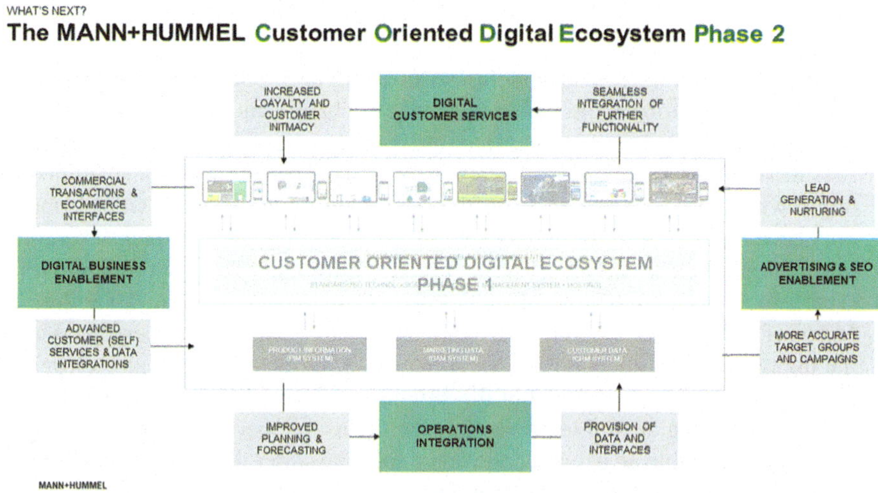

Fig. 4 Digital marketing and beyond – CODE Phase 2 (This figure was taken from internal MANN +HUMMEL documents. It was originally created in 2021 and illustrates the simplified targets of CODE Phase 2: the connection to lead generation via third-party platforms, the integration of digital business elements and customer services as well as the link to the company's operations)

scope of CODE Phase 2 was developed: the close integration of digital marketing with all other business areas, as shown in Fig. 4.

4. Learn about customer needs and user behavior to initiate proactive and data-based actions

   Before CODE was started, there was little to no knowledge about the needs of MANN+HUMMEL's customers and markets in its central business functions, and the existing data in the markets was fragmented. Through the development of centralized standards, the usage of integrated digital marketing analytics tools could be fostered by adding the implementation of these tools to the basic scope of each CODE project delivery. In a dedicated project stream, the harmonization and analysis of existing analytics knowledge and the strategic development of new analytical solutions and understandable dashboards was addressed globally for the first time in digital marketing. The full integration into a standardized CRM system enables marketing automation, strategic lead generation, and lead nurturing along the customer's whole journey. To prevent double work and ensure that the digital marketing data could be connected with data sets from other areas in the company, these activities were combined with the global data analytics program running within MANN+HUMMEL as a shared use case. Additionally, internal knowledge about customer journeys and markets was consolidated in central tools, and qualitative and quantitative customer interviews were performed, initiated by or in close alignment with the central CODE team. Frequent sharing of learnings and best practices and one-to-one exchanges with representatives from brands, regions, and local markets further strengthened the project's knowledge exchange and central understanding for customer needs and business growth plans.

5. Establish a target operating model to secure long-term operations
For a real transformation and a sustainable change in the digital marketing approach without falling back into old patterns, it was crucial for MANN+HUMMEL not to stop at just the implementation of new solutions. While this target was already identified from the beginning of the project, what it meant only became clear after starting, observing, and adapting the approach. Therefore, this paragraph also involves some project learnings. The first intention for establishing a target operating model was to leverage the shared services of MANN+HUMMEL and onboard team members who were experienced with the digital marketing technologies implemented. Over time, it became clear that changes were also needed within the structures of the core organization. On the one side, a lasting central team was needed to ensure operations were running as intended and enable an actual handover of solutions after the go-live phase to free the resources on the project management side to maintain the high speed and start working on the next project streams. For this, the original project team was spilt in two to ensure dedicated focus not only for the development of new solutions but also for maintaining and further optimizing the existing platforms. Moreover, the need for more central digital marketing solutions beyond the original scope of the CODE project grew continually after it delivered the first results. CODE, originally planned to run until end of 2022, transformed into a program to better manage the complexity after running less than a year and established as a lasting area of the central enabling functions soon thereafter; this was the response to the high demand from the markets for support in the development of new digital platforms with the intent to build all of these newly developed platforms in accordance with the CODE approach – standardized, secure, and scalable – from the beginning. In addition to the change in business structures, developing the end-to-end processes of digital marketing solutions into the group's IT structures was crucial to create genuine understanding for IT's impact on customer frontends and highlight the value contribution of all involved departments and stakeholders along the process.

In addition to these five focus topics, numerous other experiences have been gained since August 2020 with MANN+HUMMEL's digital marketing transformation through the CODE initiative. The following subchapter summarizes these experiences.

4 The Useful and the Harmful on the Digital Marketing Transformation Journey

Two and a half years into MANN+HUMMEL's digital marketing transformation journey, some factors can be identified as supportive and, thus, *useful* to achieving these transformation goals, while other factors can be classified as hindering and/or inefficient and, thus, *harmful* to the transformation goals. The following subchapter discusses five aspects that illustrate how the useful was separated from the harmful in MANN+HUMMEL's digital marketing transformation.

1. Prioritization and scope
   Within digital marketing, seemingly endless opportunities, tools, and channels exist, and the areas for action within digital marketing transformation are extensive. To avoid overloads and bottlenecks in the project team and unrealistic expectations among the internal customers of the project, MANN+HUMMEL committed to a certain prioritization logic and a clearly defined project scope. The priorities were transformed into a project plan that was transparently communicated in and outside of the project team and, therefore, became a useful element of the project. Indeed, priorities are subject to changes due to external developments in the markets, customer needs, or internal decisions. During the project CODE, priorities were, in some cases, adapted multiple times during the development of a new solution (even while the MVP use case was already in implementation), and scopes of agreed project streams were expanded or changed due to customer feedback in testing phases. These changes resulted in delays for multiple months for some project streams. Therefore, going forward, the project plan was separated from the selected MVP use case as much as possible to avoid any harmful impact on the achievement of the project goals. Instead of targeting the go-live phase of a certain website, for example, the focus was to identify overarching targets that are applicable to multiple brands and markets, such as "creating technological standards and white-label components for websites," and use the brands' or markets' most prioritized needs as (exchangeable) vehicles to reach this target.
2. Methodology
   At MANN+HUMMEL, the Agile project management approach has proven to be useful for projects with many unknown variables. In digital marketing, for example, the framework has solved many of the drawbacks of waterfall projects, such as a lack of speed, lack of flexibility in adapting to change, and late integration of key stakeholders. To some extent, however, this agility comes at the expense of plannability. This was challenging because, in MANN+HUMMEL's holistic approach, many project streams were interdependent. The websites, for example, are based on a functioning DAM system, just as the product finder solutions are built upon a functioning PIM system. For the orchestration of these interdependent project streams, Agile project management partly turned into a harmful element mainly because the development of architectural components such as PIM and DAM was not planned far enough in advance due to the short-term sprint cycles, and it resulted in a loss of productivity, speed, and ability to communicate transparently and manage expectations of the project's stakeholders. To realign its direction, the project was transformed into a program. The program management was set up according to a Scrum of Scrums logic and included an overarching backlog and a simplified model to estimate work packages. If the estimates were more time-consuming due to a certain

complexity or because more investigation work was required, for example, they were included in the backlog as separate work packages. In addition, a high frequency of coordination meetings was maintained to keep all stakeholders of the related subprojects informed, and before starting a new subproject, it was imperative that the project team jointly agreed on a target delivery date.

Another harmful aspect of the Agile methodology became evident when people could not work on the project full time. This affected the business unit product owners. In this case, the high frequency of coordination meetings consumed sizable amounts of time and led to their inability to fulfill their other project-related tasks, such as the refinement of stories, in a timely manner. This also delayed activities dependent on these tasks. In such cases, the CODE project managers were appointed as "proxy product owners." Once the foundations had been built and the business unit responsible was able to gain experience with the Agile methodology, the CODE project manager started to gradually hand over their responsibility, which ensured that Agile methods could be properly executed from the beginning, while the global teams could be enabled to use new methodologies step-by-step in real-life scenarios simultaneously.

3. External support

External partners are an important source for innovation, experience sharing, application of proven methodologies, and working packages that cannot be completed internally due to a lack of organizational resources and/or capabilities. For all of these reasons, external support was a crucial and, therefore, useful element for ensuring the success of MANN+HUMMEL's digital marketing transformation. At the same time, the right amount of external support was core to keep the feeling of an autonomous, intrinsic transformation movement to secure not only the success but also the sustainability of the project. Having internals driving the transformation was especially important as the project happened within digital marketing, which required deep insights into MANN+HUMMEL's customer landscape and sales approaches and had a direct impact on its customers. Additionally, the project's transformational character made it necessary to have an extensive knowledge about internal structures and awareness about sensitivities. Based on previous experiences, it was obvious that significant external steering could be harmful to the project, as it may become detached from MANN+HUMMEL's internal reality and the much needed central knowledge and skills would be built up externally instead of strengthening its central teams. In MANN+HUMMEL's project, the size of the fully dedicated core project team was, therefore, determined with the requirement to have at least one team member attending every meeting led together with or fully by externals to represent the internal stakeholders. In addition, every step suggested by the external partners was pre-aligned with the core project team and prepared collaboratively to ensure that the external partner had all the needed information in advance and that every meeting or task consuming business resources would be paying into the project targets. Through this approach, the gained knowledge could be consolidated at the right instances, and sustainable internal business intelligence and project skills could be built.

4. Hierarchy and structures
   Learning from existing knowledge or experienced stakeholders can be useful within any project to avoid pitfalls or repeating mistakes. The character of transformation, however, makes it crucial to go beyond the known, as change does not occur within existing processes or thinking patterns. For success with the digital marketing transformation at MANN+HUMMEL, it was necessary to deliberately disregard certain processes and continually challenge certain decisions to trigger the needed changes. As this approach could result in deep disputes that would be harmful to the transformation's success, some supporting elements were needed to avoid these kinds of negative impacts. For CODE, the foundational factors were the identification of project sponsors and individuals responsive to new approaches in all relevant business levels up to the (top) management and the frequent and open one-to-one communication with these stakeholders, which included an active ask for support if needed. In addition, the identification of the strongest partnerships within its organization was a core element of MANN+HUMMEL's approach. With chief marketing officer (CMO) and chief information officer (CIO) closely collaborating and being the top management sponsors and steering committee members of CODE from the beginning, MANN+HUMMEL set a key factor for the success of its digital marketing transformation. Due to its strong centralization and standardization approach, the transformation also strengthened the connection of CMO and chief financial officer (CFO).
5. Change, communication, and stakeholder management
   Even a well-executed change management within a transformation affecting established structures and aiming to dismantle historical silos will most likely create a certain form of the Gaussian distribution with regard to a transformation's early adopters, followers, and opponents. Within the CODE project, a high focus on stakeholder management through individual conversations and the communication outside of known project charters, Excel lists, and status reporting templates has been useful to shift the distribution toward the early adopters and followers. To create a real understanding for the why and the how of this transformation among stakeholders with different professional backgrounds, various marketing experiences, and hierarchical levels, methods such as emotional storytelling and entertaining content formats were used.

   Despite these efforts, the initiative was not immediately supported by all stakeholders for a variety of reasons. For example, standardization fueled fears in the markets about the extent to which local freedom would be restricted and whether customer requirements could still be met satisfactorily in the future. Negative experiences in the past reinforced these reservations about the digital transformation. Another typical example was the more personal concern of the local marketing managers about which additional tasks would come their way as part of the project. As mentioned, many of these local marketing managers at MANN+HUMMEL already fulfill several roles and were, therefore, unable to cover any further tasks – especially if they were not convinced of the project's chances of success. In this situation, the attempt to convince each individual of

Fig. 5 CODE's integrative approach (This figure was taken from internal MANN +HUMMEL documents. It was originally created in 2021 and illustrates how CODE builds bridges between formerly isolated functional departments, also beyond marketing)

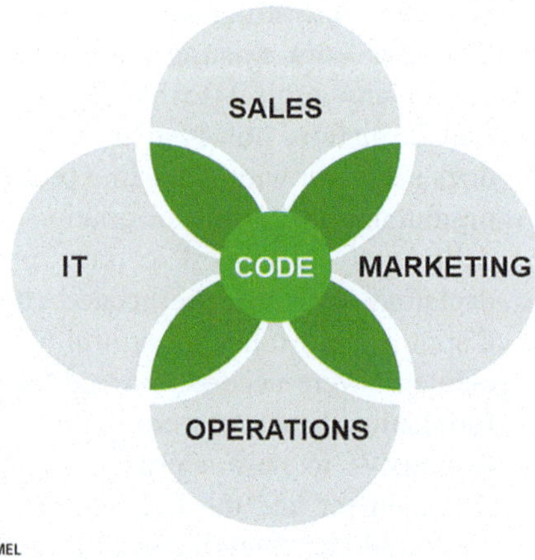

> the transformation through more conversations proved to be harmful in two ways: for the unconvinced individuals, more reasons were found against the project, and for the project team, the repeated negative conversations challenged their intrinsic motivation. What proved to be the one of the best solutions for MANN+HUMMEL was to engage with its numerous supporters, especially the intrinsically motivated stakeholders, to build a strong team that was enjoyable to work with and supported each other. As a result, due to this positive atmosphere, the doubtful individuals gradually became excited about the project, and the last unconvinced ones were persuaded by the quick and successful project results.

As a driver of change at MANN+HUMMEL, CODE connected functional departments that previously acted in isolation from one another. This integration is illustrated in Fig. 5 and was accomplished through cross-functional projects such as digital business and the development of a PIM data model harmonized across all business units, brands, and regions.

To end this chapter, there is one remaining matter to discuss that is also core to distinguish the useful from the harmful. The element that ultimately enabled MANN+HUMMEL's digital marketing transformation is the understanding that mindset determines both short- and long-term business success. This applies to the motivation and empowerment of its global teams to rethink the status quo based on their daily experiences and observations, speak up, take ownership, and drive transformation from within their respective departments. Essential for this culture is a general mindset exemplified from the top down that supports attempts to drive fundamental change from within the organization, which promotes investments into digitalization and transformation and puts belief in compelling arguments on the same level as financial value cases. In MANN+HUMMEL's case, the digital marketing transformation journey has been initiated from within the marketing department early in the COVID-19 pandemic, and it was approved facing an economically uncertain situation with a requested budget much higher than what was ever invested in marketing from a central direction in the company's history. This vote of confidence from the top management has been perceived positively from employees and customers, and this fundamental attitude has proven to be the basis for the success of MANN+HUMMEL's digital marketing transformation.

All the success factors and learnings discussed in this chapter have one idea in common: finding the right mix. Anything that proves useful can turn into something harmful if it is used too excessively or too strictly. To transform an organization successfully and sustainably, the management and execution of the transformation, as well as the individuals acting within, will and must also transform during the process. It is a holistic and continuous learning cycle, constantly striving to separate the useful from the harmful.

Enhancing the Customer Journey with Digital Self-Services

Christoph Tienken, Jonathan Rösler, and Thomas Friedli

1 Digital Transformation in Marketing and Sales: Why Now?

The digital transformation is increasingly gaining momentum in the B2B industry and thereby governs important agenda items of several board members. In this regard, marketing and sales organizations are one of the business areas that seek to seize the different opportunities from using digital technologies. In response to continuously evolving customer and market characteristics, marketing and sales managers employ these digital technologies not only to transform internal business operations, but also to create new digital-enabled business models that provide added value for end customers (Bloomberg, 2018). To master the digital transformation in marketing and sales, companies recognized the need to embrace underlying initiatives as a "customer-driven strategic business transformation" (Muro et al., 2017). By strictly following this approach, marketing and sales leaders draw particular attention to the customer journey and the different touchpoints that characterize the relationship between customers and suppliers.

In this context, the B2C industry has demonstrated how digital technologies can be used to significantly enhance the customer journey. Over the last decade, numerous interactions and transactions between consumers and suppliers were shifted into the digital sphere for the benefit of both parties. Although consumers today are used to informing themselves on websites and ordering articles online, establishing digital customer relationships in the B2B industry is far more difficult and – in many branches – still in its infancy. Looking at reality, major parts of the interactions in long-established customer-supplier relationships are yet predominantly analog. However, with more and more best practices in the B2C industry, even skeptical companies tend to give up their reluctance to engage in the digital transformation.

C. Tienken (✉) · J. Rösler · T. Friedli
University of St. Gallen, St. Gallen, Switzerland
e-mail: christoph.tienken@unisg.ch; jonathan.roesler@unisg.ch; thomas.friedli@unisg.ch

U. Schneider, J. Hoika (eds.), *Digital Marketing in the Automotive Electronics Industry*, Management for Professionals,
https://doi.org/10.1007/978-3-031-30720-1_13

The motivation to embark on underlying initiatives right now is rooted in various external and internal drivers currently pervading almost all sectors in the B2B industry. The external environment is characterized by four major drivers that accelerate the digital transformation in marketing and sales:

- **Implications of the COVID-19 pandemic**: The early months of 2020 marked the beginning of a tremendous turning point for well-established customer-supplier relationships in the B2B industry. All of a sudden, companies had to adapt their sales strategy to the underlying restrictions issued by several countries in response to the global COVID-19 pandemic. Not surprisingly, many companies were caught off guard by new and continuously changing circumstances, making on-site customer visits almost impossible. This shift consequently had huge implications for every organization that was yet relying on numerous customer-facing frontline employees (Simon-Kucher, 2022). For example, salespeople working for pharmaceutical, healthcare, or medical technology companies could no longer meet their contact persons, such as doctors or surgeons, in hospitals to present products or negotiate deals (Bulik, 2020). From one day to the next, they had to find new ways to reach out to customers remotely by setting up online meetings or doing phone calls. In many cases, the shift of common touchpoints into the digital sphere put sales targets at risk since both customers and salespeople often needed several months to familiarize themselves with virtual interactions and the new digital sales tools provided to perform the selling task (Andersen et al., 2021; BCG Global, 2022). On the contrary, companies that were already leaning on digital platforms and self-services with seamless online transactions could get through the first months of the pandemic much more smoothly by simply leveraging existing digital sales capabilities and converting customers to this channel.
- **Shifting customer buying preferences**: Many companies recognize a shift in customers' buying preferences. This shift is caused by younger generations who are increasingly taking over influential positions in purchasing departments. These "millennials" grew up with permanent Internet access enabled by smartphones and are thus used to purchasing goods, services, or digital subscription offerings via web shops and app stores. Consequently, the growing proportion of millennials working in purchasing departments is not only encouraging more "B2C spirit" in procurement but also forces suppliers to adapt to the changing expectations of these younger generations who look for the same level of B2C customer experience in their daily work in the B2B environment (Forrester, 2021). Consequently, supplier companies that have a weak presence in the digital world run the risk of getting marginalized or even ignored throughout the purchasing process. This should be especially alarming because today almost 70% of the buyer's journey is completed digitally before a buyer is engaging with a salesperson (Gartner, 2019).
- **Surplus supply**: Customers today are faced with an overwhelmingly great supply of different options to choose from. Many low-cost suppliers from Asia make use of digital sales channels and promote their products only on platforms that can be

accessed from everywhere, thereby increasing the choice for customers. Making decisions between the different options without sufficient guidance or advice is becoming more difficult and increases the likelihood of the cheapest product winning the race. Therefore, the overall comfort and simplicity of buying items as well as the quality of after-sales services play an important role when buyers decide for or against suppliers that operate in highly competitive markets (Gartner, 2022).
- **Customers seeking efficiency**: Many customers are continuously looking for new ways to leverage efficiency gains in their operations. This applies to both procurement processes that rely on recurring orders and potential improvements in their supply chain, production, as well as maintenance activities. When customers embrace digitalization in their corporate strategy, they tend to proactively demand new digital innovations that promise efficiency gains (Forrester, 2021). Supplier companies that only offer standardized products via standardized channels can soon be viewed as laggards and get excluded from the overall decision-making process of potential buyers.
- **Technological advancements**: To realize digital transformation initiatives, companies can build on continuously evolving digital technologies, such as big data, machine learning, artificial intelligence, or the Internet of Things (Hecker et al., 2017; Ng & Wakenshaw, 2017). The growing availability and quality of advanced technologies used for storing, analyzing, and interpreting data allow for uncomplicated pilot projects that only have limited financial risk and can be scaled individually.

In addition, four company internal drivers accelerate the digital transformation in marketing and sales:

- **Market differentiation**: Numerous industries are characterized by fierce competition from low-cost competitors that relentlessly seek to grow their market share in highly industrialized regions. In this regard, established manufacturing companies are searching for inimitability and differentiation to evade the commoditization trap and resulting price wars (Huikkola et al., 2022). Given the recent competitive landscape, creating customer value and achieving high levels of customer satisfaction solely based on hardware products has become increasingly challenging, and thus urges the need to provide added value with services across the customer journey.
- **New business growth**: To capitalize on investments being made in digital transformation initiatives, companies do not only seek to grow their existing business by leveraging efficiency in marketing or sales activities (Binckebanck, 2015). Digital technologies are further used to transform existing and develop entirely new business models. Consequently, digital offerings, such as standalone software products or digital services, offer ample opportunities for future monetization based on recurring revenue streams (Gebauer et al., 2020).
- **Reducing cost**: Not least because of the COVID-19 pandemic, marketing and sales organizations are recently facing high levels of cost pressure. Additionally,

the breakdown of important supply chains and geopolitical conflicts triggered a disproportionate rise in purchase prices (Ibáñez et al., 2022). Given the new opportunities of remote selling or web-based transactions, many companies began to question the configuration of their sales coverage model and pyramidal customer segmentation respectively. In a lot of cases, this evaluation and re-segmentation motivated the introduction of self-services for small- and middle-sized customers since it was no longer profitable for supplier companies to still serve these customers physically with frontline salespersons (Goonan, 2021).

- **Increasing customer centricity**: Many processes in marketing and sales historically emerged from a company's core value chain – engineering, manufacturing, and delivery of hardware products. Companies realized that this strong internal focus led to unsuccessful product introductions and unsatisfied customers (MIT Technology Review Insights, 2021). To change this way of working, processes are now more geared toward the customer and corresponding problems and needs.

2 Outlining the Vast Opportunities of Digital Self-Services

The previous chapter has proven that there is hardly any way for companies to avoid digital technologies in marketing and sales. One emerging technology specifically catering to the aforementioned drivers is the digital self-service. Digital self-services represent "a solution or a group of solutions enabling web users or employees to be completely autonomous on a website or intranet" (Verani, 2021). These types of services thus enable customers "to find the answers to their questions without having to contact customer support" and "affect actions that are quite simple, such as asking for a quote or even managing a contract" (Verani, 2021). Companies can employ digital self-services across the entire customer journey to enhance single or multiple customer touchpoints. Given the stage in the customer journey, the nature of digital self-services can differ. They can either replace traditional physical touchpoints, enrich digital customer touchpoints, or represent a new solution that is detached from existing touchpoints.

To shed more light on the different opportunities arising from digital self-services, we adopt the notion of Guenzi and Habel (2020) and divide the customer journey into three major phases. This includes the preselling phase (e.g., prospecting and qualifying leads), the selling phase (e.g., presenting a product and negotiating terms and conditions), and the after-sales phase (e.g., servicing customers and making follow-up calls). Each of the three phases is concerned with idiosyncratic customer problems which further lay the foundation for implementing digital self-services. The preselling phase oftentimes represents the most important section as customers become aware of a company's product portfolio for the first time. Digital self-services can help to raise this awareness by providing sufficient product information and guiding the customer through the selection or decision-making process. The selling phase seeks to facilitate a smooth shopping experience for customers.

This includes the provision of pricing information, delivery dates, secure online payments, and the execution of smooth invoicing processes. Lastly, the entire after-sales phase ensures customer satisfaction beyond the point of sale. In doing so, this phase offers many opportunities to improve existing customer support and service structures by leveraging digital self-services. Figure 1 elaborates on the three phases and depicts a general overview of different digital self-services frequently used by companies to enhance the customer journey.

The remainder of this sub-chapter presents six different case studies that outline how leading companies implemented digital self-services to cope with identified customer problems at a certain stage of their customer journey.

2.1 Case Study 1: Preselling Phase – Manufacturer of Building Materials

Situation faced: The German-based case company is producing and distributing building and insulation materials. It is one of the world's largest manufacturers of aerated concrete and calcium silicate blocks. For many years the overall business model of the company has focused on the production of materials and their timely delivery to distributors and wholesale dealers. Consequently, they had no contact to end customer groups ranging from single craftsmen to big construction companies. The entire marketing and sales efforts of the company concentrated on building up and successfully maintaining relationships with sales partners all around the world. The buyer-supplier relationship was characterized by high sales volumes and tiered quantity discounts based on the purchased quantity. This type of business was successful until the financial crisis in 2008 disrupted the construction industry and opened the floodgates for cheaper competitors to enter the market. The company soon realized that the new situation emanating from the crisis significantly jeopardized the leading position in the industry and thus started examining different opportunities to secure the business.

Solution implemented: After carefully examining the customer journey, the company identified a missing connection to its end customers in their overall business model. Since marketing and sales efforts were solely aimed at influencing and persuading sales partners to promote their materials, they paid no attention to craftsmen or building construction companies and their decision-making processes as to the question of why they would choose their materials. This perspective opened up new opportunities to raise the awareness of their materials in the mind of end customers way before they entered a wholesale or dealer store. To enhance the customer experience for end customers, the company found that the planning process of craftsmen is error-prone, inefficient, and time-consuming. In response to the different problems identified, they decided to digitize the planning process with a digital self-service embracing the new Building Information Modeling (BIM) technology. This service is using various 3D planning data to identify areas of improvement – for example, how thick the walls need to be or how many supporting pillars are required in certain buildings. In addition, the company also started to offer

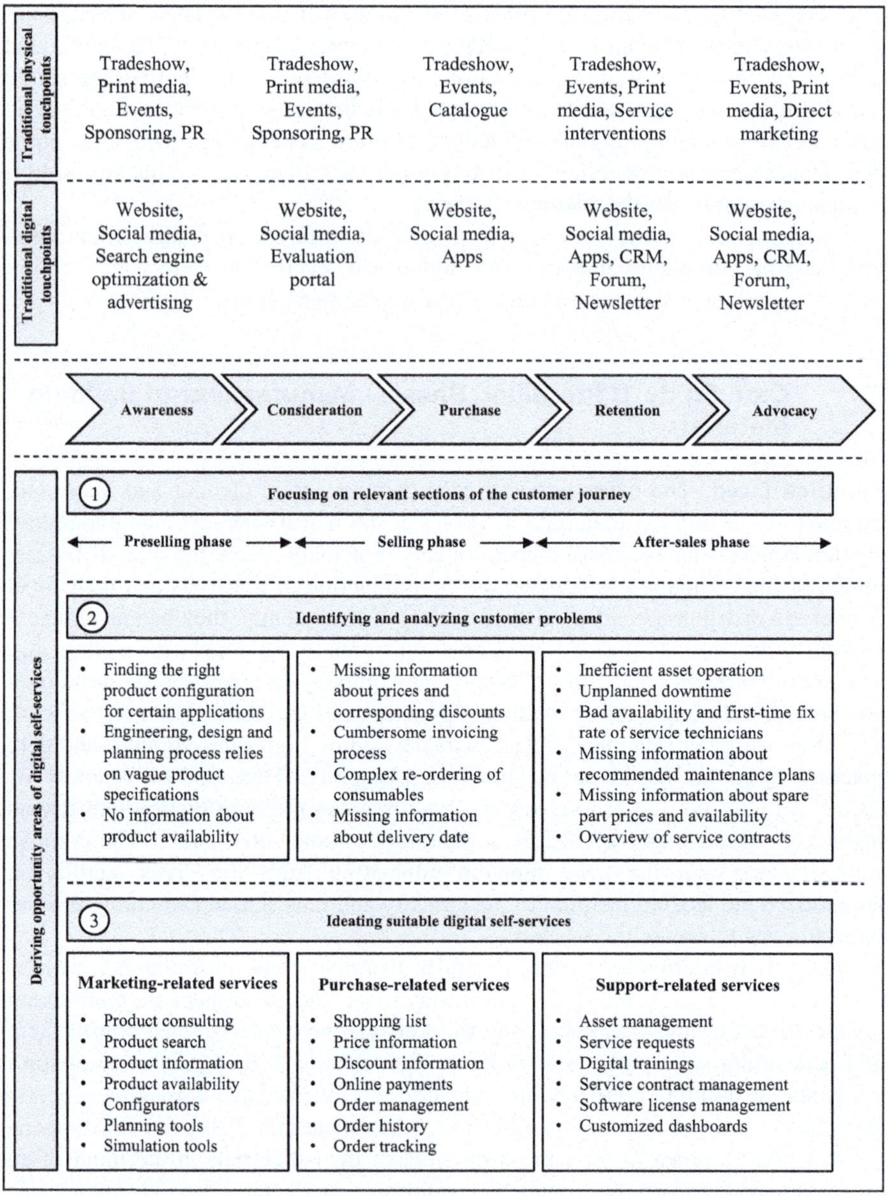

Fig. 1 Opportunity areas of digital self-services across the customer journey (adapted from Hiemeyer & Stumpp, 2020)

planning support from its in-house experts to optimize the sequence planning on the construction site. When finishing the planning process, end customers are smoothly directed to a web shop which automatically creates a shopping list for the materials used in the planning process. Since the digital self-service is both utilizing the case company's materials and offered for free, it creates a strong lock-in effect for customers and thereby shows a positive impact on the overall sales volume of the case company's core products. What initially started as a marketing initiative to enhance the customer journey turned into an independent digital offering supporting customers on their way toward the construction planning of the future. To this day, the company has steadily extended its digital self-service portfolio by transforming its original business model from a raw material supplier to a system provider that strongly addresses the rising expectations of its end customers.

2.2 Case Study 2: Preselling Phase – Manufacturer of Material Handling Equipment

Situation faced: The German-based company is one of the leading manufacturers of material handling equipment, warehousing, as well as material flow systems. The customer groups served are fairly heterogeneous in terms of industry and size. The company's go-to-market strategy includes both a direct sales channel embracing bigger key account customers, such as the world's largest automotive OEMs or food store chains and an indirect sales channel taking care of smaller customers, such as local manufacturing or logistics companies. While the product portfolio of the case company was becoming larger and even more complex over the years due to automation and digitalization, salespeople were facing challenging and time-consuming conversations with customers to configure and select the right equipment for specific use cases. Due to their inability to devote the necessary effort to the sales process, dealerships, in particular, started to struggle with consultative selling approaches. The growing market originating from higher demands in warehousing equipment – which were a consequence of rising E-Commerce shipments – posed a major challenge for dealers to care about customers entering a dealership with no idea about their purchasing intention. To maintain a good relationship with their dealers, the case company needed to act and therefore started to investigate the customer journey.

Solution implemented: The analysis of the customer journey revealed that customers had no chance to obtain any helpful information about product configurations before contacting a salesperson or entering a dealership. This consequently caused a much more time-consuming sales process and degraded the overall customer experience. While diving deeper into this issue, the case company found out that its website solely provided general information about the product portfolio without any link to specific use cases. The marketing department soon came up with the idea of building a product finder guiding customers through the decision-making process more smoothly. The first workshop sessions with dealers served to understand the current sales process and the different questions they were discussing with customers. After finalizing this analysis, the case company started to develop a questionnaire addressing the most important aspects of a guided selling approach. This included, for example, the performed activities with a forklift, the location of

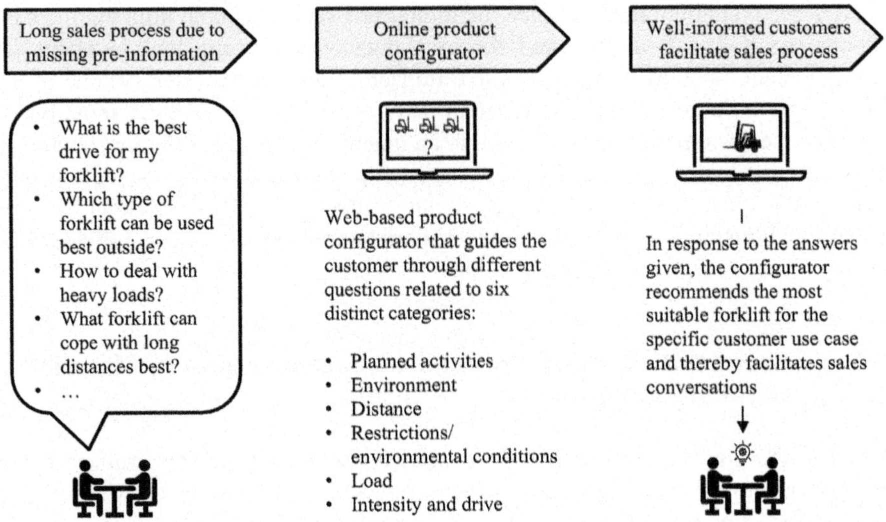

Fig. 2 Description of the product configurator

the site, the maximum weight of loads, the type of drive, or the planned hours of driving per day. Given the specific parameter values chosen for each of these questions or categories, respectively, the tool is recommending a suitable equipment type to the customer without any support from salespersons or dealers. After doing the first pilots, the case company not only provided this tool to their salespersons and dealers but also integrated it – as a digital self-service – on their corporate website. Importantly, they branded the tool and placed it prominently on the landing page of their website. Every customer that is now visiting the website to find information about certain products is consequently stumbling upon the product finder and can start the simplified product configuration process. The recommendation received at the end allows the customer to proactively approach the responsible salesperson or dealer with a much clearer vision about the product needed and enables the case company to nurture leads more efficiently with dedicated marketing activities. Figure 2 summarizes the idea of the product configurator used by the case company.

2.3 Case Study 3: Selling Phase – Manufacturer of Rolling-Element Bearings

Situation faced: The German-based company is a leading manufacturer of bearings, linear technology, as well as mechanical and mechatronic systems. The global sales operations are structured according to four major regions and rely on both direct sales channels serving larger OEMs and indirect sales channels directly serving smaller end customers. The company's products are used in almost all major industry segments, such as energy and infrastructure, transportation, mobile machines and equipment, and industrial automation. Given the long history of the company and the high technical knowledge built up to develop suitable components for different industrial applications, the product business increasingly reached a point of saturation where innovation and differentiation based on technological superiority were hard to achieve. Especially in one of their most important business areas, the standard bearing components, they were faced with fierce competition and commoditization. While having a closer look at the customer journey, the company realized that both their salespeople and their distributors were spending a growing amount of time on consulting customers. The shift toward a rather consultative selling approach became necessary due to the increasing complexity of customer applications and the missing availability of information that allows end customers to obtain relevant product specifications before contacting sales partners. In addition, major parts of the sales process were done manually and caused long response times while answering RFQs or processing orders.

Solution implemented: To cope with the identified inefficiencies in the sales process, the case company started to develop an integrated marketing and sales platform. From the beginning of the development, it was clear that the new digital platform needed to fit into existing sales structures which included both own salespeople and established sales partners. Consequently, the company introduced a link from the sales partner website to their platform to digitally nurture the buying intention. Starting from the landing page which represents a public area, the customers are now able to navigate through the entire product portfolio spanning over 40,000 products with powerful search functions. After finding the right product, customers can register on the digital platform for free to get access to more exclusive functions, such as consulting tools (e.g., calculation and selection assistants or linear configurators) and further product details (e.g., technical information or CAD data). This area of the platform thus aims at guiding end customers toward the right products and encouraging their purchasing intent. While establishing this area of the digital platform, the case company also shifted its buyer persona focus away from purchasing functions toward engineers and product designers. The different digital self-services significantly facilitated the entire decision-making process on the end customer side and prompted engineers and product designers to already approach their corresponding purchasing contact with the specific products recommended by the self-service tools. In the last step of the customer journey, end customers receive requested quotes via mail and are subsequently redirected back to the website of the sales partner side for the payment process. Large OEMs have the opportunity to register for another area of the platform to also purchase products online with an end-to-end, automated ERP integration based on punch-out functions and API interfaces. Figure 3 illustrates the overall concept of an integrated marketing and sales platform.

To also enable its salespeople that were working in the direct sales channel, the company pushed this digital platform as a major sales tool to be used in conversations with customers. This shift further helped to eliminate individual preparation of content-driven presentations. In summary, the new marketing and

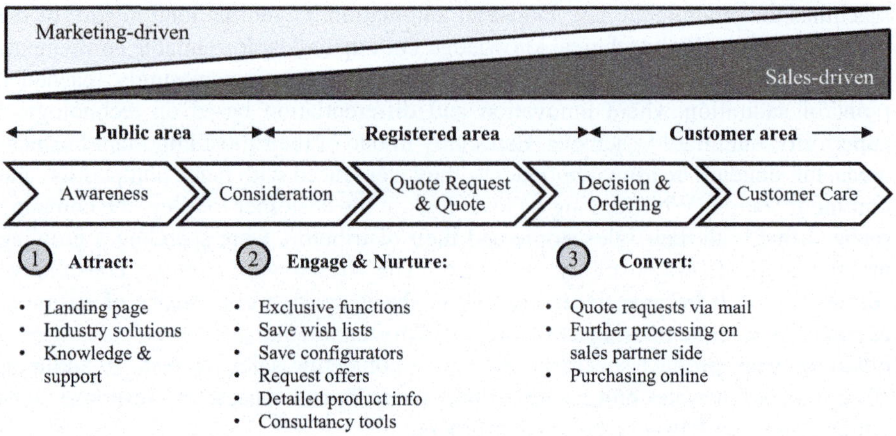

Fig. 3 Overview of the case company's integrated marketing and sales platform

sales platform allowed the case company not only to enhance customer experience with powerful digital self-services but also to lower selling expenses.

2.4 Case Study 4: Selling Phase – Manufacturer of Textile Machines

Situation faced: The German-based company is a market- and technology-leading provider of machines, services, and software for customers in the textile manufacturing sector. Due to the international nature of its business, the long-established company is globally present in its major markets, especially in South-East Asia, China, and the United States. In the past decades, the company expanded through acquisitions and focused on building up a strong service business. Due to the high-cost pressure on the customer side, the company – for quite some time – considered using digitalization to save costs internally and to develop new solutions to increase customer productivity and generate new sources of revenue. In a visionary management decision, it was decided to establish a dedicated "digital unit" to centrally bundle all digitalization activities of the company. As one of the first activities, after an interdisciplinary team was formed, customers and customer-facing stakeholders were surveyed to identify and prioritize possible use cases. The development of a web shop for spare parts turned out to be one of the most promising ideas for internal stakeholders and customers alike. The spare parts business is traditionally the company's biggest margin driver, although many customers, especially in Asia, like to switch to cheaper local, "copycatting" suppliers whenever possible.

Solution implemented: The activities for setting up the web shop started with an in-depth analysis of the product categories and the ordering behavior of individual customer segments. The results revealed three types of order categories: commodity parts, make-to-order parts, and engineered-to-order parts. For commodity parts and most make-to-order parts, the company recognized a great potential to prevent customers from buying such parts externally while providing substantial value add to customers through a seemingly convenient, fast, and 24-hour available order process. For engineered-to-order parts, in contrast, it was clear from the start that personal interaction and ordering via the spare parts hotline would remain a priority. After benchmarking existing web shop solutions and technology suppliers, an external service provider was contracted to set up the web shop by connecting it with the existing e-catalog and integrating it into the ERP system. The core requirements included the ability for customers to program automatic parts ordering, smartphone usability, and a customer-specific login that allows the company to place individual price tags. A challenging and initially underestimated task on the case company's side was to define the correct ordering logic and to record, catalog, and implement all spare parts since some of which were designed 20 years ago. Before going online, the case company defined a pilot market (Europe), scheduled internal training sessions, and launched affirming marketing campaigns for the new web shop solution. Roughly 12 months after the noiseless launch in the pilot market, the web shop was rolled out globally with the target of transferring 50% of spare parts sales within 3 years to the web shop. This target was ultimately missed after additional 36 months by 20%. Although the hoped-for efficiency and convenience gains were visible and resulted in an observable freeing of internal resources which were previously allocated to processing orders, many customers still preferred the old process for the sake of convenience. The company is expecting that it will take further time to convince all customers of the different benefits inherent to ordering spare parts from the web shop. Nevertheless, the project was considered a great success, demonstrating impressively the potential of the digital transformation to the company, and creating a win-win situation with customers.

2.5 Case Study 5: After-Sales Phase – Manufacturer of Plant Equipment

Situation faced: The Swiss-based company is engineering, manufacturing, and distributing machines to process foods and produce advanced materials. Given the cost of the machines and the complexity of the customer's production processes, the sales strategy emphasizes direct sales channels. The different sales organizations all around the world are covering the most important markets and differentiate between salespeople responsible for acquiring new customers and selling costly equipment as well as service salespeople responsible for maintaining customer relationships and selling service contracts or spare parts. The different customer segments are very heterogeneous in terms of industry and size and range from small bakeries or candy factories to medium-sized animal food manufacturers and the world's largest food makers. Over time, the case company developed a strong service business offering a broad portfolio of service contracts and providing both consumables and spare parts. When expanding their business to the emerging Asian market, the company soon realized that customers in this region heavily utilize their assets without purchasing any services or spare parts. This was surprising and concerning at the same time as the overall business model was designed in a way to keep the margins as low as possible on the hardware product while charging higher margins on services and spare parts. Facing missing revenue streams in the service business, the company started to investigate potential root causes for this dilemma.

Solution implemented: The analysis of the customer journey revealed several opportunity areas for the case company to improve the customer experience while securing the service business. On the one hand, customers in the Asian market were seen as very price sensitive and thus refrained from buying services or expensive spare parts. Additionally, the process of ordering a spare part was time-consuming. Due to the limited availability of service technicians being dispersed across the large continent, it took several days – sometimes even more than a week – until the case company could send an expert to identify and order the right spare part. The same procedure was awaiting customers when the spare part was finally replaced on site. Rather than going through this cumbersome process and struggling with unplanned downtime, the customers instead contacted independent, regional service providers which were able to copy a great variety of broken parts and could deliver their services much faster. On the other hand, customers increasingly complained about machine failures and downtimes. The case company found out that maintenance schedules were not met or incorrectly executed by the customers' operations personnel. To cope with these issues, the company introduced a customer portal addressing the identified problems. One of the most important functions is a web shop that allows for a smooth search process of spare parts where customers can easily upload a picture of the broken part and immediately get information about the availability and the price of the missing part. This digital self-service represented a huge improvement for customers and thereby also strengthened the relationship of customers in the Asian region. Moreover, the customer portal offers the opportunity for customers to view manuals, maintenance plans, and open service requests. Figure 4 shows the different layers of the customer portal and also sheds more light on the IT backbone used to enable the different functions.

In summary, the customer portal is now an essential part of the interaction with existing customers and helped to secure the service business in difficult markets by strengthening the customer relationships with different digital self-services. In the future, the company wants to expand the customer portal functions by leveraging IoT technology and adding asset management features that allow for a better planning and execution of maintenance activities based on the actual condition of the asset.

2.6 Case Study 6: After-Sales Phase – Manufacturer of Offset Printing Presses

Situation faced: The German-based company is offering products and services along the entire value chain for printing products. One of the company's core

The different functions of the customer portal... **... are enabled by a strong IT backbone**

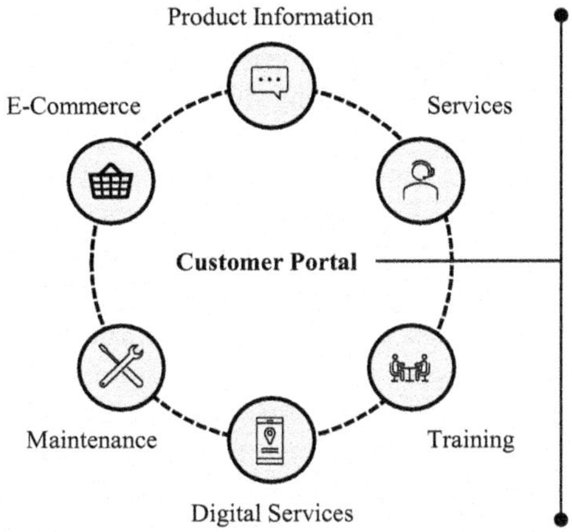

The customer portal contains bidirectional APIs to other important IT systems, such as

- **ERP-system**: Delivery settings, company master data, installed base, bill of materials, parts & product master data, machine specific documents, prices, reward information, quotations & orders
- **CRM-system**: Company master data, user data
- **CM-system**: Customer settings, user settings, search functions, e-mails, content pages
- **Photo Studio**: Parts images, renderings
- **PIM-system**: Machine images, machine documents, general machine data

Explanation:
ERP: Enterprise Resource Planning, CRM: Customer Relationship Management, CM: Content Management, PIM: Product Information Management

Fig. 4 Necessary IT backbone to enable the different functions of the customer portal

products is offset printing presses. Besides the leadership position in various product segments, the company developed a large portfolio of service offerings covering traditional repair or maintenance contracts as well as remote and digital services, such as predictive maintenance or workflow solutions. The high equipment costs and the complexity of the entire printing process necessitate a direct sales approach with field sales and key accounts serving small and large print shops, respectively. For a very long time, the order books were so filled that the company just had to distribute their printing products to fulfill the market demands. However, with the Internet becoming more popular and replacing print media, the market started to shrink continuously. In response to the changing market characteristics, the company decided to transform its business model into a more service- and solution-oriented approach. Due to massive investments in IoT technology, the case company was able to offer new sophisticated digital services to prevent unplanned downtime and improve the production performance of customers sustainably. While combing their hardware, service, and digital product portfolio, the company also started to sell subscription contracts that allow customers to only pay for the sheets produced. Although the new business model was accepted in the market, the case company realized that the fulfillment of promises made in such a subscription contract was extremely challenging. Every minute of downtime was costly for the case company and therefore put enormous pressure on corresponding service organizations to quickly resolve upcoming issues. As customer complaints about unplanned downtime increased, the service organizations all around the world were overloaded with tickets and thus struggled to deliver a quick solution, thereby threatening customer satisfaction and profitability. Consequently, the case company decided to revamp the entire after-sales phase by designing a new digital customer interface including several digital self-services.

Solution implemented: By following a design thinking approach, the case company started to develop a customer portal that enables customers to become more independent in resolving equipment-related issues during lifecycle operations. From the beginning, the customer portal was supposed to channel communications with existing customers by offering all necessary information about a print shop. Today customers can use a broad set of different functions to manage their daily printing operations. Further investments in IoT technology allowed to deliver digital self-services via the portal. In this context, customers today can use services, such as the prediction of failures or performance benchmarks, to increase the performance of their operations based on precise recommendations. Additionally, customers can access a smart web shop that – in case of a broken part – automatically suggests the corresponding spare part to repair and run the machine. The customer portal also offers functions to better plan maintenance tasks for the underlying assets and provides tutorials to execute these activities appropriately. Lastly, the data stemming from the customer portal is directly linked to the case company's CRM system and subsequently used for internal sales processes. This allows salespeople to obtain automatic reports showing current customer claims, or expiring contracts before a customer visit takes place. Therefore, the introduction of digital self-services based on the customer portal not only enables customers to operate their machines more independently and successfully but also salespeople to approach customers more efficiently and effectively.

3 Ten Success Factors for Implementing Digital Self-Services in Industrial Companies

Based on our research insights and project experiences in this field, the following sub-chapter puts forth ten success factors that help companies in the B2B industry to effectively develop and implement digital self-services in their organization.

1. Definition and alignment of strategic objectives
   Before venturing into project initiatives that involve the development of digital self-services, companies are well advised to first define and align strategic objectives. Given the multitude of opportunities arising from digital self-services across the entire customer journey, this can be a challenging endeavor. Therefore, important stakeholders from marketing, sales, and service should join corresponding discussions and agree on the strategic direction to be pursued with digital self-services. Based on the overall corporate strategy, three important aspects need to be considered when defining strategic objectives. First, everyone engaging in project initiatives that embrace the development of innovations should have a clear understanding of the underlying financial and non-financial goals. In this regard, it is not only important to communicate these

goals but also to develop a common understanding of how to achieve them. Many managers tend to overestimate especially the financial goals, such as revenue or profit inherent to digital self-services, and are thus surprised to see outcomes after the market introduction that perform far worse than anticipated. Instead of solely looking at financial KPIs, several examples highlight the role of digital self-services as an instrument to rather strengthen customer relationships with superior customer experience. Therefore, it is crucial to balance financial and non-financial goals carefully while not overestimating the financial results. Second, strategic objectives for digital self-services should always include both a short-term and a long-term perspective. Many companies start with various project initiatives without a long-term vision and thereby run the risk of creating isolated solutions that do not fit into a holistic picture after several years. In this context, there is a strong need to have a harmonized, long-term vision that lays the foundation for every single future activity around digital self-services. Third, strategic objectives should not only embrace customer needs but also focus on existing salespeople. Many companies underestimate the new level of transparency enabled by digital self-services. For example, salespeople that approach customers who have recently received important price changes via an online platform need to be updated about these changes before they do a customer visit. Otherwise, the online platform is likely to expose – and consequently – frustrate frontline salespeople. To ensure sales force buy-in for digital self-services, the new transparency needs to be shared with or communicated to salespeople. The idea that digital self-services will replace traditional salespeople also does not apply to many companies – especially those relying on products or solutions that require a considerable amount of consulting. Therefore, strategic objectives formulated for digital self-services should always consider the role of salespeople and their benefit, respectively.

2. Integration into the existing IT infrastructure
   The development of digital self-services is inextricably related to the existing IT infrastructure. Depending on the different functions of digital self-services, the integration into the current IT infrastructures might need a significant amount of work. In many cases, digital self-services require connections to other important legacy software, such as the ERP-system, CRM-system, Product Information Management (PIM)-system, CM-system, or CPQ (configure, price, quote) tools. Given the maturity of established software systems, the development of sophisticated digital self-services oftentimes entails large IT projects to first create the necessary IT backbone. Many companies recognize that these adjustments are far more costly and time-consuming than expected. For example, companies willing to introduce E-Commerce solutions frequently encounter major challenges regarding the quality and usability of their master data. To just establish the basis – which is often considered as the necessary "clean up job" – for web shops, several companies must invest several years of preparatory work. Therefore, it is helpful, to carefully examine the maturity of the existing

IT infrastructure when setting up a time frame for digital self-service projects as their progress hinges on the existing IT backbone.

3. Outside-in and customer-need-driven development
   Many established companies pretend to know their customers well when developing digital-self services, and therefore start project initiatives without even asking or involving relevant customer stakeholders. Not surprisingly, they often realize soon after the market launch that the solutions developed do not meet customer expectations. Consequently, the starting point for every innovation or idea should always be rooted in a customer problem or an unserved customer need. Choosing a digital technology due to its superiority and integrating it into the customer journey without considering the customers' perspective is likely to fail. New development methods, such as Design Thinking, can foster the development of suitable digital self-services and also help to create a more innovative culture in the entire organization. Therefore, the method puts customer centricity at the center of all activities and requires employees to think beyond their core processes and products. When evaluating customer problems, the examination of existing weaknesses should always begin with a comprehensive view of the customer journey and subsequently descend to single areas. Jumping right into specific issues of the customer journey can result in isolated solutions that are no longer consistent with each other and thereby degrade the customer experience. As a result, iterative processes are also necessary to validate findings on different levels of detail with both internal and external stakeholders. In summary, shifting the focus from a product-driven and inside-out-oriented way of thinking toward a customer-need-driven and outside-in-oriented way of thinking is key to developing and implementing digital self-services in the B2B industry.
4. Assembling the right project team
   Many companies see the roll-out of digital self-services as a temporary and short-term endeavor that is finished after the development. In doing so, they neglect necessary operations and maintenance efforts inherent to digital self-services. Consequently, companies need to assemble a project team of multiple business functions that can perform not only development tasks but also subsequent maintenance tasks. Depending on the functions, the core project team should therefore consist of representatives from marketing, sales, service, IT, legal, and logistics/supply chain management. The three different representatives from marketing, sales, and service seek to reflect the most important parts of the customer journey. Additionally, IT stakeholders need to be involved in corresponding project initiatives to ensure alignment with the existing IT infrastructure. Legal representatives are necessary to clarify all upcoming legal questions, e.g., arising from data protection issues or secure online payments. Finally, logistics or supply chain management stakeholders should be part of the project team when provided services touch upon their field of responsibility. This can, for example, include functions, such as indicating the product availability, delivery date, or delivery status. Most importantly, every project team should have a clear assignment of tasks that also covers necessary

customer support activities. When developing digital self-services, companies should also rethink established, inflexible project management approaches and move toward more agile and flexible ways of working, e.g., by following the SCRUM framework (cf. Gloger, 2010).

5. Selection of suitable implementation partners
   Project initiatives for digital self-services oftentimes vary regarding the scope and time frame. Many companies prefer to execute such projects mainly with internal resources. However, building up these capabilities in-house can be time-consuming and costly. Additionally, employees might be aware of relevant processes but are likely to have no prior experience in the development and implementation of digital self-services. Consequently, the progress and quality of the project fall short of initial expectations. In this context, companies should therefore carefully evaluate if it is helpful to rather involve implementation partners in the overall project which have already implemented similar solutions in other settings and know the circumstances well. The calculation of the business case at the beginning of the project should thus always include the option to – fully or partly – collaborate with external partners which may ensure more cost-effective and timely delivery of project results.
6. Sufficient resource allocation
   Given the necessary prerequisites of the current IT infrastructure, sufficient resource allocation for the development and deployment of digital self-services is of utmost importance. Many companies underestimate the actual efforts required to succeed in digital transformation initiatives and seek to delegate responsibilities to single workers in addition to their core business activities. While being caught in important tasks of the daily business, these employees can oftentimes pay only little attention to project initiatives addressing digital self-services. In many cases, it is, therefore, more appropriate to establish either a temporary or permanent project team that is taking care of all relevant project activities full time. This separation helps to draw attention to the project goals and ensures the necessary progress. In summary, companies should be aware that the digital transformation cannot be handled as a side business. To be successful, companies need to make targeted investments not only in digital technologies but also in human resources that can work with the new technologies and create business models around them. Companies should also be aware that software products are never finished as customers may propose new requirements continuously and expect their implementation soon. Allocating sufficient resources is thus necessary to meet the rising demands of customers and improve their satisfaction.
7. Extensive top management support
   Venturing into digital transformation initiatives is oftentimes associated with a company-wide transformation as both business models and underlying internal processes radically change. The magnitude of change pervading several business units, departments, and stakeholders can easily cause frustration and resistance of single employees. Consequently, managers need to ensure sufficient support throughout the entire transformation. Driving progress and

adoption of digital technologies requires the highest attention to both ends of transformational programs: the customers and existing salespeople or sales partners. Carving out a value proposition for both parties that outlines the rationale behind the chosen project initiatives is key to overcoming external and internal obstacles. Especially when facing high levels of internal resistance, managers need to embrace the advantages of digital interactions and communicate how salespeople can benefit from it as well. In summary, top management should make important digital transformation initiatives a top priority of their agenda to create the necessary internal and external visibility.

8. Marketing and communications of novel innovations
   When launching innovations, it is important to raise the awareness of internal and external stakeholders. In this regard, a deliberate marketing strategy is required to communicate the existence and benefits of novel innovations appropriately. Without sufficient communication, digital innovations are likely to get ignored or neglected by customers as they simply do not receive any information about novel offerings. Therefore, companies are well-advised to market innovations with an own brand or product name to trigger customers with advancements and additional benefits. This increases the likelihood that customers proactively request these offerings, thereby creating a pull effect that is further persuading internal sales stakeholders as well. Furthermore, choosing the right communication strategy is another important prerequisite to creating an innovative atmosphere within the own organization.
9. Appropriate performance management
   To measure the success of ongoing project initiatives, companies need to develop and apply the right KPIs that allow appropriate steering and performance management. For example, when introducing a marketing and sales platform, managers should at least observe the following KPIs:
   - Total sales generated through the platform, opportunity volume, and order entry [in €]
   - Digitization ratio [in %]
   - Adoption (average session time) [in h]
   - Adoption (monthly page views per user, customer, or country, self-service clicks, etc.) [in #]
   - SLAs (average ticket time for case- and inquiry management) [in h]
   - System performance (system downtime or average page load time) [in h]
10. Balance between individualization vs. standardization
    Soon after realizing the first steps in pilot projects, companies frequently start to recognize the required efforts to meet the demands of a sales network that serves different customer groups all around the world. Customers may have different preferences regarding functions, content, and language and thereby easily overstrain project teams by adding new requirements. Managers should therefore evaluate the need for tailoring functions to regional needs or rather sticking to a standardized approach. Balancing between both directions is important to not invest too many resources in unnecessary translations or costly adjustments that do not pay off in the later stages of the project.

4 Outlook: Where Are Marketing and Sales Organizations in the B2B Industry Heading?

The advancements in digital technologies will increasingly drive the digital transformation in marketing and sales. In search of future growth, differentiation, and enhanced customer experience, many companies look for new ways to exploit the different digital technologies available. One emerging avenue in this domain is the use of digital-self services that allow customers to find answers to their specific problems or questions on their own. Importantly, digital-self services are much more than web shops or purchasing platforms and offer new opportunities across the entire customer journey to acquire new and maintain existing customer relationships by enhancing customer experience. Venturing into the development of digital self-services can therefore involve new service-oriented business models and digital offerings with future monetization potential. Although the digital transformation is offering vast opportunities to shift customer touchpoints in the digital sphere, historically grown buyer-supplier relationships in the B2B industry require a careful consideration of existing sales structures. In this regard, neither all customer touchpoints will be digital in the future nor will digital technologies replace all salespersons. The challenge for many companies will rather concern the right integration of digital technologies and digital self-services into the customer journey of different customer groups. Therefore, future marketing and sales activities should not only seek to digitize every part of the sales process but rather establish sophisticated multichannel or omnichannel architectures where analog and digital touchpoints are merged to create a unique customer experience. Given the different drivers that accelerate the digital transformation in marketing and sales organizations, digital self-services will play an important role to cope with both the younger generations taking over influential positions in purchasing and the increasing cost pressure from the COVID-19 pandemic. Figure 5 depicts a possible scenario of what the integration of digital self-services in future marketing and sales organizations can potentially look like.

The figure illustrates the possible role of digital self-services in future sales coverage models of industrial companies. Even if digital technologies are very effective in terms of leveraging the interaction with smaller customers, physical relationships remain important for bigger key accounts. Consequently, companies need to evaluate both the need and potential of customers to appropriately respond with digital technologies and digital self-services respectively. In summary, the future success of marketing and sales organizations in the B2B industry will certainly hinge on the outcome of digital transformation initiatives and how well they embrace the customer experience. Aligning corresponding strategies and business models with rising and changing customer needs is key to succeeding in competitive markets and becoming a major differentiating factor for many companies. Since many companies are at the beginning of this transformation, it will still take a while until the B2B industry is catching up with the digital sales maturity known from the B2C industry.

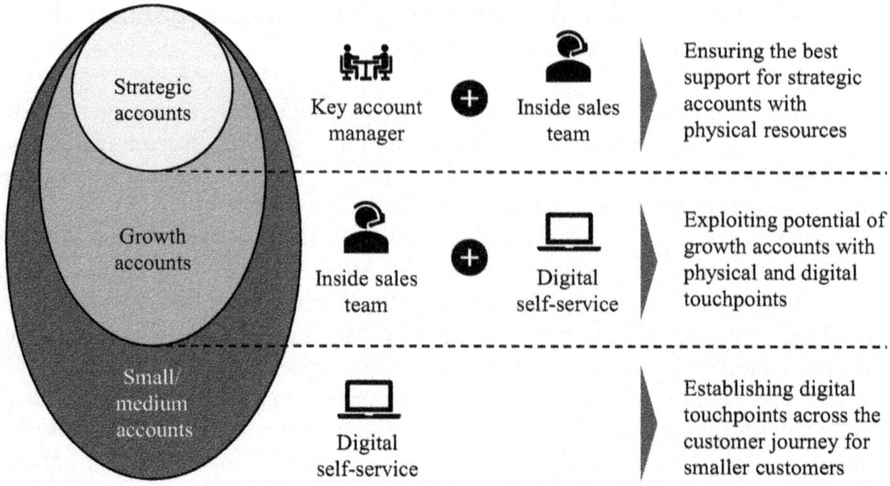

Fig. 5 A possible scenario for the future role of digital self-services in B2B sales coverage models

References

Andersen, P., Ward, M., Hede, K., Nekrasova, M., Mustaghni, B., Fabbri, F., & Merchant, J. (2021, June 17). There's no going back to the old B2B sales model. That's a good thing. *BCG Global*. https://www.bcg.com/publications/2021/hybrid-digital-sales-model

BCG Global. (2022, July 28). *Digital sales market insights*. https://www.bcg.com/publications/2021/sales-trends-digital-series

Binckebanck, L. (2015). Digital sales excellence—Systematischer Einsatz neuer Technologien im Vertrieb. *Marketing Review St. Gallen, 32*(6), 44–53. https://doi.org/10.1007/s11621-015-0580-y

Bloomberg, J. (2018, April 29). Digitization, digitalization, and digital transformation: Confuse them at your peril. *Forbes*. https://www.forbes.com/sites/jasonbloomberg/2018/04/29/digitization-digitalization-and-digital-transformation-confuse-them-at-your-peril/#78e677fd2f2c

Bulik, B. S. (2020). Grounded by the pandemic, pharma reps turn to digital tools to reach docs. https://www.fiercepharma.com/marketing/pharma-sales-reps-stay-home-minimize-face-time-physicians-as-covid-19-spread-continues

Forrester. (2021, March 3). *New research revealed at Forrester's SiriusDecisions summit 2020 shows coronavirus pandemic is accelerating modern b2b buying behavior*. https://www.forrester.com/press-newsroom/new-research-revealed-at-forresters-siriusdecisions-summit-2020-shows-coronavirus-pandemic-is-accelerating-modern-b2b-buying-behavior/

Gartner. (2019). *The buying experience: The most important thing in sales and marketing*. https://www.gartner.com/en/articles/the-buying-experience-the-most-important-thing-in-sales-and-mark

Gartner. (2022, July 28). The new b2b buying process | *Gartner*. https://www.gartner.ca/en/sales/insights/b2b-buying-journey

Gebauer, H., Arzt, A., Kohtamäki, M., Lamprecht, C., Parida, V., Witell, L., & Wortmann, F. (2020). How to convert digital offerings into revenue enhancement – Conceptualizing business model dynamics through explorative case studies. *Industrial Marketing Management, 91*, 429–441. https://doi.org/10.1016/j.indmarman.2020.10.006

Gloger, B. (2010). Scrum. *Informatik-Spektrum, 33*(2), 195–200. https://doi.org/10.1007/s00287-010-0426-6

Goonan, B. P. (2021, January 13). How to reoptimize sales channels for a post-pandemic world. *EY*. https://www.ey.com/en_us/consulting/how-to-reoptimize-sales-channels-for-a-post-pandemic-world

Guenzi, P., & Habel, J. (2020). Mastering the digital transformation of sales. *California Management Review, 62*(4), 57–85. https://doi.org/10.1177/0008125620931857

Hecker, D., Döbel, I., Rüping, S., & Schmitz, V. (2017). Künstliche Intelligenz und die Potenziale des maschinellen Lernens für die Industrie. *Wirtschaftsinformatik & Management, 9*(5), 26–35. https://doi.org/10.1007/s35764-017-0110-6

Hiemeyer, W.-D., & Stumpp, D. (2020). *Integration von Marketing und Vertrieb*. Springer Fachmedien Wiesbaden. https://doi.org/10.1007/978-3-658-27558-7

Huikkola, T., Kohtamäki, M., & Ylimäki, J. (2022). Becoming a smart solution provider: Reconfiguring a product manufacturer's strategic capabilities and processes to facilitate business model innovation. *Technovation, 118*, 102498. https://doi.org/10.1016/j.technovation.2022.102498

Ibáñez, P., Rugamas, R. G., Kohli, S., & Kuehl, E. (2022, January 13). *How to deal with price increases in this inflationary market*. McKinsey & Company. https://www.mckinsey.com/business-functions/operations/our-insights/how-to-deal-with-price-increases-in-this-inflationary-market

MIT Technology Review Insights. (2021, September 9). A customer-centric approach is key in a post-pandemic world. *MIT Technology Review*. https://www.technologyreview.com/2021/09/09/1035190/a-customer-centric-approach-is-key-in-a-post-pandemic-world/

Muro, M., Liu, S., Whiton, J., & Kulkarni, S. (2017, November 15). Digitalization and the American workforce. *Brookings*. https://www.brookings.edu/research/digitalization-and-the-american-workforce/

Ng, I. C., & Wakenshaw, S. Y. (2017). The internet-of-things: Review and research directions. *International Journal of Research in Marketing, 34*(1), 3–21. https://doi.org/10.1016/j.ijresmar.2016.11.003

Simon-Kucher. (2022, July 28). *B2B sales 2.0:* Remote selling in the midst of COVID-19. https://www.simon-kucher.com/de/blog/remote-selling-midst-covid-19

Verani, E. (2021, June 8). What is digital self-service? *Inbenta*. https://www.inbenta.com/en/blog/digital-self-service-definition/

The manufacturer's authorised representative in the EU is Springer Nature Customer Service Centre GmbH, Europaplatz 3, 69115 Heidelberg, Germany. If you have any concerns regarding our products, please contact ProductSafety@springernature.com

Printed and bound by CPI Group (UK) Ltd, Croydon, CR0 4YY
28/09/2026
02224085-0003